Puerto Rican Poverty
and Migration

Puerto Rican Poverty and Migration

We Just Had to Try Elsewhere

Julio Morales

PRAEGER

New York
Westport, Connecticut
London

Library of Congress Cataloging-in-Publication Data

Morales, Julio, 1942-
  Puerto Rican poverty and migration.

  Bibliography: p.
  Includes index.
  1. Puerto Rico—Emigration and immigration.
2. Migration, Internal—United States.   3. Puerto Rico—
Economic conditions—1952-   . I. Title.
JV7381.Z79U65   1986   325.7295   85-19439
ISBN 0-275-92020-8 (alk. paper)

Library of Congress Catalog Card Number: 85-19439
ISBN: 0-275-92020-8

First published in 1986

Praeger Publishers, One Madison Avenue, New York, NY 10010
An imprint of Greenwood Publishing Group, Inc.

Printed in the United States of America

∞

The paper used in this book complies with the Permanent
Paper Standard issued by the National Information Standards
Organization (Z39.48-1984).

10 9 8 7 6 5

For
María Ortiz Morales, my mother;
my sisters, Teresa and Ruth;
and my brother, Robinson;
and
Dedicated to the memory of
my father, Julio, Sr.,
who died without understanding our oppression;
and
to my son, David;
my daughter, Raquel;
my nieces, Yesemia and Yarima;
and nephew, Adam Julio.

May they understand what their grandfather could not.

Foreword

Pregunta:
>   Doña Lila (57 años de edad): ¿Porque dejó usted a Puerto Rico para vivir aquí en Waltham?

Respuesta:
>   Bueno, fíjate, en verdad no importaba tanto a donde fueramos - la cosa era salir de Puerto Rico y tratar otro sitio.

Question:
>   Doña Lila (57 years old): Why did you leave Puerto Rico to live in Waltham?

Answer:
>   Well, look, in reality it didn't really matter where we went—the thing was to leave Puerto Rico and try elsewhere.

Question:
>   José (25-year-old Puerto Rican): Why did you leave New York to live in Waltham?

Answer:
>   Julio, I just had to try elsewhere.

Acknowledgments

Much of this book was originally written as part of my doctoral dissertation, completed in September of 1979, at the Heller School for Advanced Studies in Social Welfare, Brandeis University. It has been edited and expanded upon, and an attempt has been made to update the information. The content of some chapters is based on interviews held during 1975 and 1976. That portion of the book is, therefore, locked in time . . . a time when Puerto Ricans were leaving New York and Puerto Rico for New England and elsewhere.

To a large extent this book is the effort of thousands of people. Hundreds of them were interviewed in Puerto Rico, New York, Massachusetts, and elsewhere. Their time, insight, and encouragement are appreciated. I am grateful to the 196 Hispanic families interviewed in Waltham and to the persons who helped me interview those families: Migdalia Bonilla, Osvaldo Burgos, Margarita Santiago Boudreau, Olga Diana, Maximino Jimenez, Roberto Jimenez, and Ana Viteri. Dr. Rocina Becerra and Dr. Fernando Torres-Gil helped me in the training of the interviewers, and I thank them for their aid.

To the Morales family in Orocovis, Puerto Rico; the clergy; Doña Ofelia and all other government officials of that town; and to the other individuals identified in this book, I wish to say "thank you."

I wish to thank and acknowledge the support and suggestions of Dr. Wyatt Jones, chairperson of my dissertation committee, and the other committee members, Dr. David Gil, Dr. Josephine Nieves, and Dr. Isaura Santiago Santiago. I also would like to thank the Ford Foundation for granting me the fellowship that made being a doctoral student possible and the University of Connecticut for granting me a semester's sabbatical to concentrate on completing this book.

I gratefully acknowledge the many students at the University of Connecticut School of Social Work who read the manuscript and offered suggestions. Special thanks to others who provided much assistance: Rebecca Lopez, William Breeding, Linda Tirado, Claudia Fedarko, Elisa Taylor, Louise Simmons, Grace Derrick, Judy Leve, and particularly Kanani Bell and Carolyn Longo.

Contents

List of Tables and Figures

Figures

Introduction

Historical records are only the residue of history, the scant outline of a succession of events. They are in themselves objects devoid of meaning and of little intrinsic value. It is in the relation between events that meaning resides and value accrues. History is, therefore, an interpretive discipline, with the historian's task being to sift through the records, interpret their relation to other documents and events, and provide a reconstruction of the past that helps to explain the present. Furthermore, history is, more often than not, an account of events from the perspective of those who emerge victorious in conflicts within and between human societies, as it is the victors who determine the rules and meanings by which both they and those conquered shall live and gauge the worth of their lives.

If history is to fulfill its obligation as a discipline that contributes to our understanding of the course of past events, the nature of present circumstances, and the possibilities for future development, then it cannot, and must not, be limited to any one perspective or single interpretation. It must instead view the historical records from a variety of vantage points and theoretical perspectives.

This book is an attempt to understand the forces that account for the humiliating conditions of poverty in which the overwhelming majority of Puerto Ricans live in the United States. Unlike most works that treat similar material, however, it is written from the perspective of Puerto Ricans, often the losers in conflicts between unequal powers. More orthodox accounts may ignore, willingly suppress, or be ignorant of sources and records that this work, by virtue of its viewpoint, finds important. Furthermore, what sources such "official" accounts do use are likely to be interpreted differently.

There are more subtle differences as well. This book seeks to give voice to the perceptions and understanding of the colonized Puerto Ricans and is typical of recent attempts made by social scientists to understand the nature of the relationship between political minorities caught in a web of powerlessness. This powerlessness is a function of what has been called neocolonialism, defined by Webster's dictionary as the economic and political policies by which a great power (in this case the United States) indirectly maintains its influence over other areas or people. This book explores the direct and indirect political, economic, and social forces that are responsible for Puerto Rican poverty, in Puerto Rico, New York, New England, and elsewhere.

Two other characteristics of neocolonialism are the tendencies to "blame the victim" and to see the conditions of the colonized as a "culture of poverty." Many of the features alleged to characterize this culture (including low income, poor education, high unemployment) are simply aspects of the definition of poverty itself. These conditions are an inevitable result of neocolonial oppression. The history of U.S. rule on the island outlined in this work confirms this oppression and explores Puerto Rican poverty after the takeover by U.S. forces in 1898. That the island continues to be a U.S. colony makes any attempt to "blame the victim" seem hollow.

This book is not, and was never intended to be, a polemic. On the contrary, conscious attempts have been made, through research and documentation, to arrive at some conclusions concerning the present circumstances of Puerto Ricans. Why are Puerto Ricans as a group at the bottom of the economic hierarchy?[1] Why do black U.S. citizens fare better? What has been, and is, U.S. interest in Puerto Rico? Why has this interest persisted? Why have Puerto Ricans failed to enter the U.S. mainstream when ethnic European immigrants have succeeded? What role has institutionalized racism played? What has been the role of the capitalist economic system?

This work attempts to provide answers to these and other questions by chronicling the military, political, economic, and social relations between the two countries. It also seeks answers in the history of the island prior to the involvement and takeover by the United States; in the history of European immigration to the United States; in the history of black migration to northern cities; in economic and social policy; and, finally, in the history of Puerto Rican migrations to New York, New England, and other parts of the country.

It is an assumption of this work that inequality in the United States is functional and systemic. This means that some people benefit from the exploitation of others and that present social arrangements perpetuate that inequality. In this process, society has condoned the exploitation of labor.

A group of poor people who are paid poorly (if at all) has been necessary to sustain the economic system. At times the groups have changed, but some groups must remain poor. Poverty is transmitted as an economic necessity.

Poor people are often poor, not because they do not work, but because they are paid poorly. In the United States, both whites and people of color have been exploited for their labor. Racism has made that exploitation even more raw and brutal and has led to the genocide of the Native Americans, the enslavement of black Africans, and the military takeover of much Indian and Mexican land, as well as the islands of Hawaii and Puerto Rico. The exploitation of Puerto Ricans, compared to that of other groups, and the usefulness to the system of such exploitation is explored in this book.

Whether and to what degree the scope of this effort contributes to history's obligations as a discipline I leave to the reader to decide. I do think that the perspective offered in this work contributes to an understanding of the United States that cannot be reached through any "victor's" history.

Finally, I think it important to point out that Puerto Ricans occupy a unique terrain among colonized peoples. In 1917, Puerto Ricans were "granted" U.S. citizenship though they had no real voice in the decision. Thus, the legal status of Puerto Ricans is that of any natural-born U.S. citizen, with the same rights, privileges, and responsibilities. The day-to-day reality of their lives, however, is that they too are treated as immigrants of color. The confusion inherent in this dual existence, when added to the already difficult conditions imposed by neocolonial oppression, makes the lives of Puerto Ricans that much more burdened.

NOTE

1. Nationwide only Native Americans rank lower. In New England and New York, however, Puerto Rican poverty is greater.

1

New York's History of Immigration, Migration, and Ethnic and Racial Competition

Once I thought to write a history of the immigrants in America. Then I discovered that the immigrants were American history.

> Oscar Handlin
> The Uprotted

Here, then was the way to produce a perfect slave: accustom him to rigid discipline, demand from him unconditional submission, impress upon him his innate inferiority, develop in him paralyzing fear of white men, train him to adopt the master's code of good behavior, and instill in him a sense of complete dependence.

> Kenneth Stampp
> The Peculiar Institution: Slavery
> in the Ante-Bellum South

We're a nation of professional, religious, ethnic, and racial tribes—who maintain a fragile truce, easily, and often broken.

> Paul Cowan
> The Tribes of America

In short, interest groups' liberalism is the implementation of an empty ideology rather than social justice.

> Robert H. Binstock
> "Interest Group Liberalism and
> the Politics of the Aging"

1

New York, the Statue of Liberty City, is a city of ironies, contrasts, and paradoxes. She is elegant and lovely, yet dirty and oppressive. She is the financial headquarters of the world but on the verge of bankruptcy. She enjoys tremendous wealth while suffering incredible poverty. Often referred to as the cultural capital of the world, New York is renowned for its theaters, museums, and galleries but feared for its high crime rate and drug abuse.[1]

New York is unique. Presently the largest city in the nation, it was, until recently, the largest in the world. It is a major world port and the largest of all ports in the United States. Its people make her at once unique and a microcosm of the nation as a whole. When the world's hungry and oppressed, and indeed the nation's own, seek to start a new life, it is often in New York that that new life begins. This fact has shaped and colored every aspect of life in the city.

> For in New York City ethnicity and class and religion are inevitably tied to each other. . . . To describe the economy of New York fully, one would have to point out that it is dominated at its peak (the banks, insurance companies, utilities, big corporate offices) by white Protestants, with Irish Catholics and Jews playing somewhat smaller roles. In wholesale and retail commerce Jews predominate. White collar workers are largely Irish and Italians if they work for big organizations, and Jewish if they work for smaller ones. The city's working class is, on its upper levels, Irish, Italian and Jewish; on its lower levels, Negro and Puerto Rican. Other ethnic groups are scattered everywhere, but concentrated generally in a few specialties.[2]

Ever since a great many white males began voting in the early nineteenth century, ethnic and religious differences have tended to be the most common source of political differences.[3] Even the working class finds solidarity only when "class," in economic terms, is combined with race, religion or ethnic origins, and locality.[4]

As early as 1660, 18 different languages could be heard on the streets of New York. At first, the majority of the newcomers were white, usually Anglo-Saxon and, more often than not, Protestant.[5] The group of English descent remained the largest in the city through the first half of the nineteenth century.[6] In the 1840s, large numbers of

Irish and Germans entered the city. By 1890, they and their descendants made up 52 percent of New York City's population.

During the 1880s, many Jews and Italians came to New York and continued doing so until the passage of the immigrant laws of 1921 and 1924.[7] Blacks began to enter the city in great numbers after World War I at the end of more than three centuries of voluntary white immigration. Puerto Ricans came to New York in significant numbers almost 30 years after the blacks. As Oscar Handlin so aptly put it, immigration is indeed the history of America.

The numbers certainly bear this out. According to the U.S. Immigration and Naturalization Service, 48,664,365 immigrants settled in the United States between 1820 and 1978 (see Table 1.1). The European immigrants coming after 1820 came primarily because poverty pushed them out of their own countries. Some went to the cities of Europe, providing labor for the factories of the Industrial Revolution. Others went from farm to farm looking for seasonal employment. Many heard of jobs, land, and opportunity in the United States. A sad but relieved Europe pushed her peasants toward the promised land.

The Irish left—4.5 million of them—because avaricious absentee landlords exploited them in that already too crowded island where English policy discouraged the growth of Irish industry. The potato famine of 1846 killed .5 million.[8] The United States pulled as Ireland pushed.

Four million left Great Britain. Farmers and artisans joined the landless peasants, exploited coal miners, and laborers on their voyage to the United States. Scots, Welsh, and English, as well as Irish who had previously gone to England, left as England too pushed many of her poor across the ocean.

From what later became the German Empire came 6 million dislocated artisans, ambitious industrial workers, emancipated peasants, and free husbandmen.[9] Two million Scandinavians also left their homeland as a result of crop failures, a decline in fisheries, and the growth of commercial agriculture.[10]

During the early decades of the nineteenth century, the United States was feeling the effects of the Industrial Revolution, and New York City even more than the rest of the country. By the middle of the nineteenth century, New York emerged as the nation's undisputed industrial leader, and her industry needed the work force that the peasants provided.[11] Thus, the Statue of Liberty City became the destination of nearly 40 percent of the United States' millions of immigrants.

TABLE 1.1   Immigration by Countries: 1820-1978

Countries	Total (1820-1978)	Countries	Total (1820-1978)
All Countries	48,664,965	Poland [4]	514,496
Europe	36,202,963	Portugal	445,354
Albania	2,256	Rumania	170,891
Austria [1]	4,315,692	Spain	259,551
Hungary [1]	--	Sweden [2]	1,271,925
Belgium	202,438	Switzerland	349,103
Bulgaria [3]	67,827	USSR	3,373,314
Czechoslovakia	137,029	Yugoslavia [3]	113,549
Denmark	364,160	Other Europe	55,605
Estonia	1,128	Asia	2,853,760
Finland	33,441	China	515,550
France	750,424	India	163,698
Germany [1]	6,977,743	Japan	406,438
Great Britain		Turkey in Asia	385,555
England	3,178,558	Other Asia	1,382,519
Scotland	820,063	America	9,050,711
Wales	95,127	Canada & Newfoundland	4,104,857
Not specified	804,822	Mexico	2,123,727
Greece	654,886	West Indies	1,686,801
Ireland	4,723,544	Central America	312,863
Italy	5,294,418	South America	713,024
Latvia	2,555	Other America	109,439
Lithuania	3,852	Africa	132,059
Luxembourg	2,867	Australia & New Zealand	118,508
Netherlands	352,594	Pacific Islands	24,571
Norway [2]	856,474	Not specified	282,393

[1] Data for Austria-Hungary not reported until 1861; Austria and Hungary recorded separately since 1905. From 1938 to 1945 inclusive, Austria was included with Germany.

[2] From 1820 to 1868, the figures for Norway and Sweden were combined.

[3] Bulgaria, Serbia, and Montenegro first reported in 1899. Bulgaria reported separately since 1920, while the Serb, Croat, and Slovene Kingdom has been recorded as Yugoslavia since 1922.

[4] Poland recorded as a separate country from 1820 to 1898 and again since 1920.

Source: U.S. Department of Justice. U.S. Immigration and Naturalization Service. 1979. The Statistical Yearbook of the U.S. Washington, DC: Government Printing Office.

The slums, an outgrowth of the Industrial Revolution, grew and spread to accommodate the swelling immigrant population. Social problems multiplied. According to a police report in 1852, 10,000 abandoned, orphaned, or runaway children were roaming the streets of New York.[12] In most cases, these were the children of the white immigrants. In 1859, only 23 percent of all persons arrested in New York City were native U.S. citizens, 55 percent were born in Ireland, 10 percent in Germany, 7 percent in England and Scotland, and 5 percent in other countries.[13]

The economic process that promised the immigrant freedom from poverty delivered instead a fierce competition for jobs. Traditional crafts and skills were of little value in an economy increasingly dominated by mechanization and the factory system. Such a system fostered competition between and within ethnic groups. Furthermore, men, women, and even children battled for the jobs that inevitably went to those who would sell their labor most cheaply.[14] All the advantages were with the employer whose position was further strengthened by governmental ideologies of laissez-faire economics and social Darwinism that had little concern for the welfare of individual workers.[15] The ethnic competition that still dominates New York's economic and political life was well underway.

The immigrants, by becoming a plentiful source of cheap labor, made possible the wealth of perhaps "the worst, the most unfit, the sharpest, and the basest elements of U.S. society."[16] Steamship lines, railroads, and the bigger industries seized the opportunity to set up recruiting offices in European towns and cities to attract and pull the people that Europe was pushing out. The exploitation of immigrants in New York City sweatshops became more the rule than the exception. Guilty consciences were soothed by individual acts of philanthropy.

In an 1888 message to Congress, President Grover Cleveland, surely no radical, stated:

We discover that fortunes realized by our manufacturers are no longer solely the reward of sturdy industry and enlightened foresight, but that they result from the discriminating favor of the government and are largely built upon exactions from the masses of our people. . . . [t]he communism of combined wealth and capital, the outgrowth of overweening cupidity and selfishness, which insidiously undermines the justice and integrity of free institutions, is not less dangerous than the communism of oppressed poverty and toil, which exasperated by injustice and discontent, attacks with wild disorder the citadel of rule.[17]

Still the immigrants came, raising on their shoulders as "they took over the dirty work, those who had the dirty work before them."[18] Thus did the southern and eastern Europeans who came at the turn of the century elevate the status of the Irish and German immigrants.

Five million came from Italy, their exodus accelerated by a cholera epidemic in 1883.[19] Eight million Poles, Jews, Hungarians, Bohemians, Slovaks, Ukranians, and Ruthenians left Eastern Europe after 1800 because of changes in the agricultural systems of the Russian and Austrian Empires.[20] Before the turn of the twentieth century, 3 million Greeks, Macedonians, Croatians, Albanians, Syrians, and Armenians were immigrating to the United States from the Balkans and Asia Minor.[21]

By the hundreds of thousands yearly, they came to New York City. For example, 60,000 Jews lived in New York City in 1870; by 1910, there were 1.1 million.[22] In 1890, less than 5 percent of New York City's population was Italian; by 1920, Italians comprised 14 percent of the city's population and by 1930 17 percent.[23] Former New York City Mayor John V. Lindsay stated that "New York City has been the nation's incubator for more than a century. Through its efforts, almost alone, a new middle class has time and again been raised . . . as wave upon wave of new immigration, always America's new poor, hit the Statue of Liberty city."[24]

These masses of people coming into New York City and the nation were regarded differently by different segments of the population. To second generation immigrants whose own forebears had been peasants, the immigrants were a reminder of their own history of poverty and "inferiority." It was "American" to see the new immigrants as well as blacks, as inherently dirty and ugly. The immigrants appropriated racism for their own benefit; seeing blacks as inferior helped even the latest European arrival feel more American. The blacks in turn looked upon the immigrants as "poor white folks" who would join all other whites in exploiting them.[25] To the businessmen, the immigrants were a ready supply of muscle necessary to keep wages down and profits up. The more immigrants, the more competition for jobs.

As immigration became more and more important to the industrial revolution, the locus of control for immigration changed. At first, the colonies and later the states assumed such control. The main concern was to prevent new arrivals from becoming economic burdens on the towns in which they settled.[26] As time went on, the federal government took greater responsibility for the immigrants, assuming complete control in 1882. In 1906, the Bureau of Immigration and Naturalization was established. Previously, the bureau had been part of the Treasury Department and later the Department of Commerce and Labor, reflecting the prevailing view of immigration as an economic concern.

As the ranks of the immigrant grew, so did the animosity felt toward them by native U.S. citizens. Nationalistic sentiments generated by World War I increased existing pressure to restrict immigration. Such organizations as the Immigration Restriction League often pointed to religious differences as reason enough for denying foreigners entry to the United States.[27] Racist fears were also strong.[28]

In his argument before Congress in 1896, in favor of a literacy test as a requirement for entry into the United States, Senator Henry Cabot Lodge voiced the prevalent feelings of Aryan superiority and immigrant inferiority: "In other words, there is a limit to the capacity of any race for assimilating and evaluating an inferior race. The lowering of a great race means not only its own decline but that of human civilization."[29]

In 1917, the Burnett Bill introduced a literacy test. In 1921, a quota system was established in which only 3 percent of each nationality's total population living in the United States as of the 1910 census was permitted to enter the United States.[30] Bowing to restrictionist sentiment, congress enacted even more stringent legislation with the Johnson-Reed Act of 1924. This act imposed a numerical limit (150,000 per year) on newcomers to the United States. The law grew out of the notion that immigration policy should be based on racial considerations. The 1924 statute attempted to stabilize the existing ethnic balance of the country by the assignment of a quota system that obviously favored northern Europeans.[31] Europe's declining birthrate, coupled with its own rapid industrialization and economic growth following the war, had already slowed down immigration, but the quota system and its complicated requirements for entry proved to be the greatest obstacle to new immigrants. Among Italians, for example, the whole 25-year period after 1925 produced fewer immigrants to the United States than did the single year 1907.[32]

The ethnic queuing process of newcomers arriving to take the dirty work at the bottom rung of the economic and social ladder was about to be halted. Immigrants, by taking over jobs with the lowest pay and worst working conditions did a service to those on the next rung of the social ladder.[33] By becoming members of an "industrial reserve army," the immigrants served the economic system too as they replaced the earlier immigrants who had left industrial employment when opportunities for becoming farmers, artisans, or stone masons had opened to them. Thus, immigration had facilitated the process of extensive and rapid capitalist development.[34]

Who would provide this service when European immigration declined? The Industrial Revolution had, to a certain extent, replaced labor with machines. New York City, on the cutting edge of this trend, had already lost most of its jobs in the primary industries, those that extract or produce raw materials, as in fishing, agriculture, lumbering, and mining. Even before the end of the white immigration, most of its workers had moved into such secondary industries as manufacturing and construction, making new materials into marketable products, such as tools and clothing.[35]

Blacks, and later Puerto Ricans, moved in to fill these low skill and poorly paid positions as the white population of New York City advanced into the tertiary or service industries (including public administration, real estate, retail, finance, insurance), which rely heavily on education and contact with the public, that is, customers, consumers, and clients.[36]

By 1950, the latter jobs accounted for almost half the labor force in the nation with a much higher percentage in New York City. The bottom rung on New York's socio-economic ladder became, and still remains, very crowded. Climbing up that ladder has become increasingly difficult. Blacks and Puerto Ricans were recruited for unskilled work as replacements for immigrants since, as U.S. citizens, they were not affected by the restrictive quota systems. However, in time, the unskilled work became harder to find. The competition that normally existed for such jobs became even tougher. Still they came to New York, these internal migrants. Why did they come? What did they find when they arrived?

Blacks came to New York City in large numbers only after the decline of European immigration, but, of course, they were part of the history of New York and the nation since the early part of the seventhteenth century.

Black African immigration to the United States was unlike that of any other racial or ethnic group. Initially, blacks came to the Americas in chains, transported as slaves by the Spanish, Dutch, and Portuguese to the Caribbean islands. By 1600, more than 1 million African slaves were in the western hemisphere.[37]

In August of 1619, the first group of blacks landed at Jamestown, Virginia, as indentured servants and were separated from the rest of the colonial American population by custom and by law. In 1661, Virginia passed the first law making blacks not servants but slaves. Other states soon followed. In the United States, the African slaves lost their tribal, regional, and family ties. They were not allowed to speak African languages or retain their cultures.

By the time of the American Revolution, more than 500,000 blacks were the possessions of white men. One-sixth of all people in the United States were slaves at a time when the newly written Declaration of Independence proclaimed that "all men are created equal."

The possibility of slave revolts obsessed slaveholders and other white Americans. As a result, inhumane laws against blacks were established and enforced. The Black Codes emerged all over the South and covered every aspect of the slave's life. Slaves were legally relegated to and treated as property. The purpose of the codes was to maintain discipline and insure that the slave's labor was exploited as much as possible. The codes were unapologetically oppressive. A slave had no standing in the courts, could make no contract, and was forbidden to own property. Killing a slave was rarely regarded as murder, and a slave could not hit a white person for any reason. The rape of a slave woman was usually regarded as a crime only because it was viewed as trespassing on or destroying another man's property. [38]

Other restrictions on slaves prevented them from assembling in groups, leaving plantations without permission, reading books, holding religious meetings without white witnesses, possessing firearms, and having friendships with free people. Slaves accused of wrongdoing were severely punished by their masters or overseeers. If they were brought into court at all, it was likely to have been an informal slave court. [39] Slavery was inherited; the child of a slave mother would be born into slavery.

In describing recommendations made by some slave owners to their peers, Kenneth Stampp writes, "Here, then was the way to produce a perfect slave: accustom him to rigid discipline, demand from him unconditioned submission, impress upon him his innate inferiority; develop in him paralyzing fear of white men; train him to adopt the master's code of good behavior, and instill in him a sense of complete dependence." [40]

In 1791, Eli Whitney invented the cotton gin, further spurring the expansion of cotton plantations and the demand for more African slave labor. By 1890, 4 million black slaves were in the United States. They ran away, sabotaged their owners, and staged uprisings. Gabriel Prosser's insurrection (1800) and Nat Turner's rebellion

(1831) are probably the best known revolts in the history of U.S. slavery. In both cases, the insurrections led to the adoption of even more rigid slave codes.

Freed black men and women were also victims in their competition with immigrant peasants for unskilled work. Violent rioting occurred in several northern cities during the Civil War. In New York in July of 1863, white workers, predominantly exploited Irish immigrants, went on a rampage that required federal troops to restore order. Frustration and the fear that cheap black labor would flood the North if slavery were abolished motivated the rioting that left 34 blacks and four whites dead and over 200 people injured. Similar riots took place in Cincinnati, Newark, Buffalo, and Troy, New York.[41]

After the Civil War, southern states were greatly concerned with controlling blacks. The laws enacted for this purpose resembled the old slave laws. Several limited the area of property that a black person could purchase or rent. Other laws, requiring blacks to work, included penalties for vagrancy and possible imprisonment for leaving a job. Laws limiting testimony in court to cases involving other blacks were also enacted. Fines for insulting gestures or acts, violating curfews, and possessing firearms were common. The Ku Klux Klan and other white terrorist organizations suppressed the thirteenth, fourteenth, and fifteenth amendments.[42]

Violence and intimidation confronted freed black men and women in the South. Approximately 100 lynchings took place every year in the 1880s and 1890s. In 1892 alone there were 161 lynchings.[43] Forty-six blacks were killed and 75 wounded in Memphis riots. One hundred were massacred in Colfax and Coushatta, Louisiana.[44]

In the Plessy versus Ferguson case of 1896, the Supreme Court established the separate but equal doctrine constitutional. Thus, the unofficial Jim Crow laws of the North became legally sanctioned by the nation's highest court and strictly enforced in the South. Separate Bibles for blacks and whites in courtrooms, separate cemeteries, separate seating in trains, separate schools, and separate toilet facilities became the law. Separate they were, but hardly equal.

This blatant racism, accompanied by the increasing mechanization of southern farms and plantations, began pushing black men and women to southern cities and northern slums. As blacks increasingly migrated north, race riots there became even more common.

The North, though less overt in its racism, treated blacks similarly to the manner in which they were treated in the South. In fact, as mentioned earlier, the infamous Jim Crow laws originated in the North as a specific mechanism for exploiting and segregating blacks in northern ghettos.[45] Large-scale, antiblack riots took place in 1900 in New York City; in 1904 in Springfield, Ohio; in 1906 in Greenburg, Indiana; and in 1908 in Springfield, Illinois. Thirty-nine blacks were killed in St. Louis in 1917. Throughout the North, homes of blacks were burned, blacks were lynched, and thousands were beaten. In Chester, Pennsylvania, whites rioted against blacks in 1917. In the same year, a similar riot took place in Philadelphia. Riots occurred in Washington, D.C.; Omaha; Charleston; Longview, Texas; Chicago; Knoxville in 1919; and in Tulsa in 1921. Fifty-eight black homes were bombed in four years (1917—21) in Chicago.[46]

Yet blacks continued to move north. Perhaps they mistakenly viewed it as a liberal area. Perhaps they felt anything had to be better than the South. For whatever reason, black migration more than tripled in the 1890s. Between 1880—90, 60,000 blacks left the South; 200,000 left between 1890 and 1900; from 1900—10, 207,000 southern blacks migrated north.[47]

As with previous white immigration from Europe and the Puerto Rican migration to come, one must look both at push and pull factors to understand the uprooting of black individuals and families. World War I created a demand for labor, which was no longer being adequately satisfied through European immigration. The war and restrictionist legislation created a gap that blacks from the South would fill. Industries recruited southern blacks the way they had Irish and Italian workers in the nineteenth century. The agents promised jobs and dispensed free railroad tickets.[48]

The draft of black men during World War I brought them to northern army bases and opened their eyes to another world. As black people were being wooed by northern industries, they were also being pushed from southern lands. The agrarian revolution was replacing them with mechanized farm equipment. Arizona and New Mexico were providing southern cotton growers with fierce competition. Such natural disasters as floods and the boll weevil infestation in the early 1900s further decimated the southern cotton crops and the ranks of black sharecroppers and tenant farmers who grew them.[49]

During the 1920s, 800,000 blacks left the southern states; 400,000 in the 1930s. The 1940 U.S. census revealed that the black population in the North had increased from 1.9 million in 1910 to 4 million. The shift continued through the 1940s, increasing dramatically during World War

II as blacks were once again recruited to fuel the war economy.

Meanwhile, in the South, sharecropping had almost disappeared. In the 1950s, 1.4 million whites left the South (often moving westward), while 2.6 million moved from rural areas into southern towns and cities. Blacks moving from the farms were more likely than whites to leave the South altogether; 2.75 million blacks left the South between 1940 and 1960.[50]

The U.S. Bureau of the Census reports that, in 1950, 68 percent of the black population lived in the South. In 1973, only 52 percent of the black population lived in southern states; 40 percent lived in the North.[51]

New York City's Harlem attracted many of these southern migrants and became a vital black community. in 1900, 16,000 blacks lived in New York City, thus accounting for 2 percent of the city's population. In 1910, the city's black population jumped to 92,000 but remained a steady 2 percent of the city's population. After 1920, New York City's black population increased at a greater rate than that of the city as a whole, probably because of the decline of European immigration. In 1920, 5,620,000 people lived in New York City; 3 percent of the city's population or 152,000 people were blacks. In 1930, the city's population had jumped to 6,930,000; 5 percent or 328,000 were black. Nine percent of the city's population were black in 1950 (748,000 out of 7,892,000). By 1960, the city's black population had reached 14 percent or 1,088,000 out of 7,782,000.[52] In 1970, according to the Bureau of the Census, blacks comprised 21 percent of the city's population, and in 1980 blacks accounted for 25.2 percent of New York City's total population.

In 1970, New York was one of two cities with more than 1 million black residents, Chicago being the other. However, Detroit, Philadelphia, Washington, D.C., and Newark, among other U.S. cities, had a higher percentage of blacks than did New York. New York City, however, with 1,784,337 blacks in 1980, has a larger black population than any other city in the United States or in the world.

The move from the South to New York City was in many ways as much of an uprooting as leaving Europe was for the famine-stricken peasants from Ireland, Italy, or Russia. One could view the black migration to New York City as a repetition of an old story were it not for several crucial differences. First, blacks have been in the country for centuries. They are migrants, not immigrants. Second, their language and culture is not as radically different as was that of the European immigrant. Third, blacks do not

look like the white majority. Their history of slavery can
be viewed as a function of color. Just as runaway slaves
could not easily hide, neither could black migrants bleach
their skin and melt into the city. Other groups faced
discrimination, but they could change their names or lose
their accents. Blacks confront both discrimination and
racism. Equally important, the country had become a
different place by the time of mass black migration. The
West had already been settled; the canals, railroads, highways, and subways had been built; the unions had become
powerful and their membership increasingly middle class.

At first, blacks in New York were predominantly domes-
tics, waiters, laborers, and unskilled workers. Poverty
was as common as racism for the black New Yorker.

During the 1930s, black workers earned three-fifths the
pay of white workers in New York City.[53] In the 1940s, as
many black women as men worked. More than three-fifths
of those women worked as private household workers.
Black families were often supported by female domestic
labor. One-third of the employed black males held service
jobs, such as bootblacks and watchmen. One-fourth worked
in semiskilled crafts and one-seventh as laborers. Professional, clerical, and sales workers comprised only a small
group; black businesses were almost nonexistent.[54]

Adverse conditions faced by black migrants in terms of
housing, employment, and education surpassed or equaled
those confronted by the white European peasants. Blacks,
however, were unlike the earlier immigrant group. Automation and new management techniques had reduced the
demand for unskilled labor. White collar occupations accounted for 97 percent of the total increase in employment
between 1946 and 1963. Furthermore, blacks arrived in
New York at a time when the majority of the nation's people
were not poor. Hence, blacks have become an economic, as
well as a racial, minority.[55] Puerto Ricans, the city's
newest arrivals, face these same obstacles, as well as the
language and cultural barriers confronted by the earlier
European immigrants.

Ethnic and racial competition, a historically perennial
reality in New York, has become increasingly fierce as
groups fight over an even smaller piece of the pie.

> [t]he ethnic and racial groups of the city are also
> interest groups, based on jobs and occupations and
> possessions. . . . [t]hey are also attached to
> symbols of their past. . . . [t]hey want to see
> members of their group raised to higher positions
> and respect. . . . [o]wing to the concrete nature

of their jobs (or lack of jobs), their business and their professions, they are also defined by interests.[56]

Because more than half of New York City's teachers were of Jewish heritage and a high percentage of students black, the school decentralization issue of the late 1960s and early 1970s was seen as a black–Jewish conflict.

Similarly, policies affecting the police affect New York's Irish population since there are more Irish on the police force than members of any other single ethnic group. Italians are overrepresented in the city's sanitation department, while blacks have increasingly moved into social service programs.

Recent demands for community control of the school system, especially on the part of blacks and Puerto Ricans, can be seen

not as new claims, but as an extension of those voiced by urban minorities in the past. . . . A lunch program on the lower East side with Kosher meals for Jewish children and Italian meals for Italian children . . . a governor who recommends that pupils be instructed by teachers speaking the same language . . . it is not a description of the community control movement in New York City in 1973. It is a description of an effort made 50 and 100 years ago to meet the needs of New York's immigrant school children . . . claims made by Irish Catholics in the 1840s; Jews in the period surrounding the turn of the century; Italians in the middle 1930s.[57]

As ethnic and racial groups established themselves in this country, they also created their own special institutions and organizations to insure their survival in a discriminatory and competitive society. Thus, by the 1930s, white ethnic groups, as well as U.S. blacks, had developed ethnic agencies and institutions. These ethnic, religious, and racial institutions were and continue to be used as tools for collective ethnic mobility. They have worked at obtaining allocations of power, prestige, and economic resources on the basis of ethnic, religious, or racial origins.

Most of the socially active ethnic institutions, while emphasizing ethnic, religious, or racial identity, have supported the existing system of competition. They have focused on eradicating discrimination in opportunities for members of their own backgrounds but have rarely directly challenged the system that creates the discrimination, exploitation, and inequity. Their aims have not contradicted the U.S. philosophy of competition, individualism, and the theoretical merit system. On the contrary, the hyphenated U.S. citizens, including, for examples, the Irish-Americans, Jewish-Americans, and Italian-Americans, have often taught and enforced the rituals necessary for a higher status in the present system, such as higher education, training, the acquiring of manners, learning English, and so forth.

A change in the competitive autonomy of these ethnic/racial institutions occurred with the depression. To a large extent, the economic disaster brought reliance on the state, especially for groups at society's lowest strata. The agencies and institutions already established became at least partially supported by the government. Most of these groups continue to be publicly financed in part. Nevertheless, control of the ethnic institutions still lies with the groups that founded them. Thus, it is not surprising that such institutions give preference to "their own kind" in terms of services and jobs.

Throughout the first half of this century, racial and ethnic groups used their collective force to right the wrongs felt by their members but too often ignored the injustices experienced by other groups. Individual or ethnic mobility often came at the expense of politically or economically weaker individuals or groups. United States history has produced, according to Theodore J. Lowi, "[a] mixture of capitalism, statism and pluralism."[58]

As the United States has moved more to conscious control of its political and economic policies, what self-regulating powers still exist have tended toward group rather than market competition.[59] Believers in a pluralistic system see this competition as leading toward an equilibrium and, therefore, as good.[60] Organized ethnic groups have historically competed for jobs, resources, and prestige. Some groups have more resources necessary to compete better than others; those who cannot compete are out. "Competition," says Lowi, "is imperfect."[61]

The issue becomes one of power, and power, like inequality, is a relative concept.[62] The competitive pluralistic system that the United States has become has given each new group a sense that, if it too organizes, it will also reap benefits. As new groups organize, older groups tend to feel threatened.[63]

The system often doles out the power to make public policy to private groups. When the legitimacy of government is challenged, new interest groups are brought into the process. "Interest group liberalism is the implementation of an empty ideology rather than social justice."[64]

"Citizen participation," "community control," "community involvement," "interest group representation," "cooperation," "partnership," "self-regulation," "delegation of power," "local option," "grassroots," "creative federalsim," "community action," "maximum feasible participation," and "participation democracy," are all slogans that eventually give way to whomever or whatever group is best organized and has the most resources at a specific time.[65] Too often such values as justice, equality, and liberty take a back seat to political, economic, and social pressures. Mobility in this manner does not guarantee humanism. At best, "there is only process."[66]

As interest groups vie for federal favor and dollars, we see the inevitable group conflicts that have characterized twentieth century ethnic mobility. Entrenchment of one ethnic or racial group in a certain market or service is one way of insuring ethnic access to money and mobility. Inevitably there is conflict when one interest group in an inferior position strives to move to a higher plane. Moynihan and Glazer document one such conflict between blacks and Jews:

> As Negroes move into governmental agencies, which are one of the most important areas of employment for the upwardly mobile, they come into contact with all the groups that got there before them. Jews in the 1930s entered government service in large numbers. This means that the Negro school teacher now often works under a Jewish principal, that the Negro social worker very often has a Jewish supervisor. . . . The relationship between inferior and superior in a hierarchy is inevitably tension producing, and the conflict between different people is always subject to interpretation in group terms. . . .
> Thus the dissatisfaction over social services for Negroes . . . often takes the form of complaints against Jews and Jewish agencies, an inevitable by-product of the distribution of wealth.[67]

The civil rights movement of the 1960s clarified for disenfranchised groups what they had long suspected—that organizing was the only way of gaining attention and money. Where the blacks once fought with the Jews for power, prestige, and resources, a plethora of other interest groups are now competing for a piece of the pie. Along with blacks, Chicanos, Puerto Ricans, and other Hispanics, we now add Asians, Indians, the disabled, the elderly, women, and other groups. As long as the resources available to these lower strata groups remain limited, the fighting between them will continue to be intense. As noted earlier with the Irish/black violence of the nineteenth century, black and white conflict is nowhere more visible than in this lower income sector of society. Among Jews, liberal racial attitudes prevail where blacks pose no economic threat. Where Jews are in competition with blacks, conflict emerges. Black and lower middle class Jews often share the same public schools, live in the same changing neighborhoods, and vie for the same marginal status jobs. These Jews occupy an only slightly higher rung on the economic ladder and in that position are often the easiest targets for black rage.[68]

At times, other working class groups use their ethnicity as a rallying cry in the competition with blacks for housing and jobs. According to Wilson, such has been the case with the Polish, Italian, and Irish in several Chicago communities when blacks have been felt as threats.[69]

Blacks themselves have become outraged by other minority groups jumping on the band wagon. Instead of forming a coalition of these minority interest groups, some black leaders have chosen to withhold support for their struggles. A classic example of this is the hostile attitude of some black leaders toward the women's movement.

Black men often see white women as being not only better organized, but as possessing more education, better living conditions, and more contacts in the corporate world. Women, on the other hand, feel that black men, just like white men, want to remain in a position superior to women.[70] The competition for scarce resources can lead to bitter disputes that gain no ground for either group.

In the struggle to assert who is more or less disadvantaged, more or less organized, the ethnic/racial/sex conflict continually emerges. The real problem of reorganizing our economic system to make resources more available to all these groups is too often ignored. The system reacts by accommodating, within limits, those groups who most threaten it. Struggles over economic concerns, even when bitter, generally lead to moderate reformist solutions rather than radical social change.[71]

Poverty, even if relative, has become institutionalized. The question remains who shall the poor be? Because group after group has become part of an accommodating system, the United States keeps missing the opportunity to become a truly egalitarian society. Thus everyone has lost. Nowhere is this struggle more intense than in the very lowest socioeconomic sector of our society. There the people with the least educational, social, and political resources are competing for scarce low-skill jobs, low-rent housing, and the dwindling supply of federal social assistance dollars.

After World War II, large numbers of Puerto Ricans migrated to New York City for the first time. They brought with them their own culture and language and a unique history of oppression at the hands of the U.S. government. As a multiracial Latino group with U.S. citizenship, they have entered a competitive system that pits them against the descendants of black slaves and European peasants who have, to various degrees, learned the meaning of ethnic and racial strife.

NOTES

1. For specifics on New York City's contrasts, especially as related to ethnicity and race, see Joseph P. Fitzpatrick, Puerto Rican-Americans: The Meaning of Migration to the Mainland (Englewood Cliffs, NJ: Prentice-Hall, 1971); Nathan Glazer and Daniel P. Moynihan, Beyond the Melting Pot (Cambridge, MA: M.I.T. Press, 1970); Oscar Handlin, The Newcomers, Negroes and Puerto Ricans in a Changing Metropolis (New York: Doubleday, 1973); Clarence Senior, The Puerto Ricans—Strangers—Then Neighbors (Chicago: Quadrangle Books, 1961); Harold L. Wilensky and Charles N. Lebeaux, Industrial Society and Social Welfare (New York: Free Press, 1965).

2. Glazer and Moynihan, Beyond the Melting Pot, p. 4.

3. Lee Benson, The Concept of Jacksonian Democracy (Princeton, NJ: Princeton University Press, 1961), p. 165.

4. Wilensky and Lebeaux, Industrial Society, p. 31.

5. Robert Ernst, Immigrant Life in New York City, 1825–1863 (New York: King's Crown Press, 1949).

6. Glazer and Moynihan, Beyond the Melting Pot, p. 7.

7. Ibid., pp. 7–9.

8. Oscar Handlin, The Uprooted, 2d ed. (Boston: Little, Brown, 1973), p. 32.

9. Ibid.

10. Handlin, Uprooted, p. 33.

11. David M. Schneider and M. Deutsch, The History of Public Welfare in New York State: 1867–1940, (Chicago:

University of Chicago Press, 1941). Also, David M. Schneider, The Road Upward (New York State Department of Welfare, 1938).

12. Robert H. Bremmer, From the Depths, the Discovery of Poverty in the United States (New York: New York University Press, 1964), p. 39.

13. Senior, Strangers—Then Neighbors, p. 21.

14. For example, "the 1900 census reported 800,000 workers aged 10 to 13—another million more were 14 and 15 years old." (p. 6, vol. 38, no. 6, Jan., 1980 Service Employees a monthly newspaper of Service Employees International Union, AFL-CIO, CLC.).

15. Bremmer, From the Depths, p. 21. Also see Richard Hofstader's Social Darwinism in American Thought, (Philadelphia: University of Pennsylvania Press, 1944).

16. Bremmer, From the Depths, p. 26.

17. Ibid., p. 23.

18. Glazer and Moynihan, Beyond the Melting Pot, p. 207.

19. Handlin, Uprooted, p. 33.

20. Ibid.

21. Ibid.

22. Irving Howe, "Immigrant Jewish Families in New York: The End of the World of Our Fathers," as adapted by New York Magazine, October 13, 1975, p. 51.

23. Glazer and Moynihan, Beyond the Melting Pot, p. 185.

24. Newsweek, October 27, 1975, p. 13.

25. See Handlin, Uprooted, pp. 245–48; also, Senior, Strangers—Then Neighbors; and Jacob A. Riis, How the Other Half Lives: Studies Among the Tenements of New York (New York: Hill and Wang, 1957); also, Charles E. Silberman, Crisis in Black and White (New York: Vintage Books, 1964), p. 104.

26. Schneider and Deutsch, Public Welfare in New York State; and Schneider, Road Upward.

27. Oscar Handlin, Immigration as a Factor in American History (Englewood Cliffs, NJ: Prentice-Hall, 1959), pp. 167–68.

28. Ibid., p. 168.

29. John J. Appel, ed., The New Immigration (New York: Pitman, 1971), p. 131.

30. Maldwyn Allen Jones, American Immigration (Chicago: University of Chicago Press, 1960), p. 276.

31. Ibid., pp. 276–77.

32. Handlin, Uprooted, p. 261.

33. Appel, New Immigration, pp. 177–78.

34. C. E. Rodriguez, "Economic Factors Affecting

Puerto Ricans in New York," in Centro Taller de Migración, April, 1974. ed. Centro de Estudios Puertoriqueños, Research Foundation of the City University of New York, 1975.

35. Willensky and Lebeaux, Industrial Society, pp. 90–114.

36. Ibid., p. 94.

37. National Commission on Civil Disorders, Report of the National Commission on Civil Disorders (New York: Bantam Books, March 1968), p. 207.

38. John Hope Franklin, From Slavery to Freedom (New York: Alfred A. Knopf, 1956), p. 188.

39. Andrew Billingsley, Black Families in White America (Englewood Cliffs, NJ: Prentice-Hall, 1968), p. 55.

40. Kenneth M. Stampp, The Peculiar Institution: Slavery in the Ante-Bellum South (New York: Vintage Books, 1956), p. 148.

41. National Commission on Civil Disorders, Report, pp. 212–13.

42. The thirteenth Amendment prohibits slavery, the fourteenth makes all persons born or naturalized in the United States citizens of the country, and the fifteenth gives black men the right to vote.

43. National Commission on Civil Disorders, Report, p. 21.

44. Ibid., p. 213.

45. For more on this subject, see C. Vann Woodward, The Strange Career of Jim Crow (London: Oxford University Press, 1955); and Harold Baron, The Demand of Black Labor (Somersville, MA: New England Press, 1971).

46. National Commission on Civil Disorders, Report, p. 219.

47. Silberman, Crisis, p. 25.

48. Ibid., p. 26.

49. Ibid., p. 28.

50. The statistics, according to Silberman, refer to net changes in population. Many rural southern blacks moved to southern cities, taking the place of blacks who had moved to the North. See Silberman, Crisis, p. 30.

51. U.S. Bureau of the Census, The Social and Economic Status of the Black Population in the United States, 1973, Current Population Reprints, Special Studies, Series P. 23, no. 48 (Washington, DC: Government Printing Office, 1974), p. 10.

52. Commission on Intergroup Relations, City of New York, Negroes in the City of New York: Their Number and Proportion in Relation to the Total Population, 1950–1960, prepared by Florence M. Cromien, 1961.

53. Glazer and Moynihan, Beyond the Melting Pot, p. 29.

54. Ibid.

55. Silberman, Crisis, p. 33.

56. Glazer and Moynihan, Beyond the Melting Pot, p. 84.

57. Nicolaus Mills, "Community Schools. Irish, Italian, and Jews," Society 11 (March/April 1974):76.

58. Theodore J. Lowi, The End of Liberalism (New York: W. W. Norton, 1969), p. 29.

59. Ibid.

60. Ibid., p. 47.

61. Ibid., p. 295.

62. See Edward W. Lehman, "Toward a Macro-Sociology of Power," American Sociological Review 34 (August 1969):453–65.

63. Lowi, End of Liberalism, p. 90.

64. Robert H. Binstock, "Interest Group Liberalism and the Politics of the Aging," The Gerontologist 12 (August 1972):265–66.

65. Lowi, End of Liberalism, p. 95.

66. Ibid., p. 97.

67. Glazer and Moynihan, Beyond the Melting Pot, p. 73.

68. William Julius Wilson, The Declining Significance of Race (Chicago: University of Chicago Press, 1978), p. 118.

69. Ibid., p. 117.

70. Steven V. Roberts, "Blacks and Women Clash on Access to Jobs and Aid," New York Times, February 20, 1979, p. 10.

71. André Gorz, Strategy for Labor: A Radical Proposal (Boston: Beacon Press, 1967), p. 21.

2

Puerto Rico and the Migration to New York City

Puerto Ricans, unlike other groups, are a people coming from a land that has never been liberated.
Julio Morales

. . . the greatest concentration of human misery in this trouble-beset metropolis is among the million-member Puerto Rican community. They represent only about one-eighth of the total population, yet they constitute between a third and a half of New York City's welfare recipients. Thirty percent live below the poverty line in terms of family income.
New York Times, January 30, 1976

Although most history books credit Christopher Columbus with discovering Puerto Rico on November 19, 1493, he obviously did not since the Island was inhabited by Taino Indians, who called their home Borinquen. In 1508, within 15 years of Columbus' "discovery," Juan Ponce de Leon disembarked on the Island and the Spanish colonization of Borinquen began. Ponce de Leon's charge was to mine any gold that might exist on the Island, send it back to Spain, and bring Christianity to Puerto Rico.[1] When the Spanish governor enslaved the Tainos in order to mine the gold, the Indians rebelled, and, in 1511, war broke out between the Taino Indians and the Spaniards.[2] Because of their superior weapons, the Spaniards quickly defeated the resisting warriors.

22

In 1520, the Spanish crown ordered that the Indians be given freedom and congregated in pueblos.[3] These orders did not preserve the island's indigenous population as a separate ethnic entity since what remained of the Taino "was gradually assimilated into a heterogeneous community to which the African was being added.[4] Nevertheless, "a 1787 census revealed that there still remained more than 2,000 pure-blooded Indians in Puerto Rico and that thousands of other Puerto Ricans were of partial Indian origin."[5] The Taino nation, despite this seemingly small number, remains an important element in Puerto Rican history, culture, language, and physical appearance.[6]

A few domestic slaves were brought to Puerto Rico in 1507 by Spanish settlers. Although evidence indicates that slaves were not brought in large numbers, they were frequently requested.[7] Initially, mining in Puerto Rico was considered good. After 1540, however, production declined and the island's economy shifted from mining to agriculture.[8] This shift further increased the demand for slaves. In 1582, blacks were officially requested, by Puerto Rico's royal inspector general, as a replacement for Indian workers.[9]

Perhaps because of a lack of economic resources in comparison to the other Spanish territories in the Americas, few slaves were ever brought to Puerto Rico. However, as early as 1664, Puerto Rico became a haven for those escaping from neighboring slave islands.[10] In his History of Black Slavery in Puerto Rico, Luiz Diaz Soler explains how, during the eighteenth century, Puerto Rico became more recognized as a slave refuge.[11] If they accepted Catholicism and loyalty to Spain, slaves were accepted as freed persons on the island. Diaz Soler estimates 7,487 slaves lived in Puerto Rico in 1775; 41,758 in 1860; and in 1873, when slavery was abolished in the island, 32,000 out of 617,383 inhabitants were slaves.[12] Despite the inherent evil of slavery, one can argue that as an institution it did not take on in Puerto Rico some of the more negative characteristics that it did in North America.[13]

Because of Spain's own early history of ethnic blood mixing (Celts, Iberians, Phoenicians, Greeks, Carthaginians, Romans, Visigoths, Moors) the attitude of the people toward different races, and perhaps blood mixing in general, was more accepting than that of other European nations. Spain's closeness to Africa had exposed many of her people to blacks; to the Spaniards, blacks were not considered subhuman, as they were in the United States. The Catholic church insisted that slaves were to be baptized and seen as equal to all other people under the eyes of God. In addition, because the overwhelming numbers of people on the island were poor, blacks and whites frequently worked together. These facts may explain why slaves were allowed to buy their freedom and why laws prohibited selling members of a slave family to different owners.

According to Morales Carrion, "the Spanish settler in Puerto Rico did not come primarily as a tiller of the soil . . . he was a crown officer, a trader, a founder of towns . . . impatient, restless, eager for fame and wealth."[14] Perhaps, as a result, the Spanish crews initially sailed from Spain without Spanish women, which provided further encouragement to racial intermixing. Whether through rape, concubinage, commonlaw marriage, or marriage, the mixing of the Puerto Rican bloodline took place early in the island's post-Columbian history.[15]

The intermixing, which led to Puerto Rico becoming a multiracial society, may also have been a function of Spain's initial inability to maintain a large Spanish population in Puerto Rico. Spanish settlers often preferred the vastness of Peru, Mexico, and other conquered Spanish territories. They were also fearful of the perennial attempts, by pirates and Spain's international rivals, to conquer the island, which was the key point in the route to the Indies. Its geographic location at the entrance of the Caribbean Sea, coupled with its excellent ports, brought to Puerto Rico a constant flow of men and supplies and a reputation as a trading center. "Puerto Rico was an alluring hunting ground for successive generations of French, English and Dutch corsairs . . . and the sea captains of the Western Kings."[16] Spain chose to protect its "Caribbean Gibraltar" and to attempt to limit its trade with foreigners. The result was clandestine trade with the non-Hispanic Caribbean and more attacks on the island, which further "hindered the colonization process."[17] Accepting, protecting, and freeing runaway slaves made it possible to populate the island, while economically hurting the rivals of the Spanish empire. Spanish policy favored white colonizers by granting them 170 acres of land, twice what was offered mulattos and escaping slaves.[18]

Obviously, Puerto Rico was not able to completely escape the effects of European racism, but it has been and continues to be unique in racial relations, providing a climate that permitted the mixing of races into a fairly united society. This uniqueness explains Puerto Rican leadership in the movement to abolish slavery in the Spanish-speaking world.

Spanish neglect in developing Puerto Rico into a tropical colony of exploitation, as the French and English had done in their Caribbean islands, contributed to the evolution of a society with less racial tensions and a more homogeneous population than the neighboring establishments. The leveling force of poverty has given rise to a rustic equality unmatched by the sugar colonies of the capitalistic empires. This legacy persisted.[19]

Tumin and Feldman's studies conclude that in Puerto Rico "the majority feel that people of dark color are not blocked from major opportunities by their color."[20] Charles Rogler in 1946 found that "whether the children were either 'bastards,' or legitimate did not operate seriously to prejudice the persons involved."[21] Renzo Serrano notes that "in Puerto Rico the relationships between Negroes and non-Negroes were considered the best in the West Indies."[22] Gruber and others also comment on the mixture of the Indians, mestizos, mulattos, Africans, Spaniards, and other Europeans into one people. She writes, "He is not a Negro. . . . He is not an Indian. . . . He is not a Spaniard. . . . The blood stream of all these soon fused to make the Puerto Rican."[23]

During the 19th century the white community of Spanish settlers was augmented by continued migration from Spain. Many Spanish loyalists came to Puerto Rico from Central and South America in the wake of a series of pro-independence revolutions. Frenchmen came from Louisiana when it was purchased by the United States and from Haiti when the slaves revolted. In the 1840's labor shortages brought Chinese workers to Puerto Rico. Italians, Corsicans, Lebanese, Germans, Scots and Irish also spiced the melting pot. . . . [t]he racial composition of Puerto Rican's society covered the spectrum from whites (blancos) to blacks (prietos or negros), with a large in-between category known as the trigueños (tan, "olive-skinned," . . .) and very fuzzy lines dividing the groups because of racial intermarriage.[24]

The mixture was not only physical; it was cultural, linguistic, spiritual, and religious. By the end of the eighteenth century, the Puerto Rican, with a personality and culture distinct from the Taino, African, or Spaniard, had emerged. Puerto Rico's geography helped to mold this culture, which, according to social scientists, was conceived in the humid, green mountains of the island and is exemplified by the jibaro. Jibaro is an old Spanish word meaning wild, untamed, or uncultured. The word was initially applied pejoratively to the farmers and the peons; however, jibaro music, poetry, wit, and beliefs cemented the Puerto Rican culture and society.

Puerto Rico's racial composition and location were key elements in the U.S. takeover of Borinquen and decision to maintain possession of the island. The islander's distinct multiracial character have made Puerto Ricans different from both the white immigrants and the black migrants discussed in the previous chapter.

TOWARD INDEPENDENCE

On a Mercator projection of the world, the island of Puerto Rico appears as an outpost of the Americas. It is the most easterly of the Greater Antilles and is 100 miles long varying in width from 35 to 40 miles. Because of its location at the entrance to the Caribbean Sea, it is a geographic gem, and Spain and the United States have always considered it of great strategic value.

Puerto Rico was one of Spain's longest held possessions, although the independence movement in Puerto Rico spans centuries. That movement was necessarily an underground operation because the least suspicion of participation in such a movement resulted in a trip to the dungeons and torture chambers. Hanging or exile was the usual punishment.

The Lares revolt of 1869, the most serious of several uprisings during the nineteenth century, constituted the successful part of an ultimately abortive attempt at insurrection. Political repression continued for the rest of the century and worsened in 1887 with the reign of terror instituted by Governor Palacios. Nevertheless, Puerto Ricans in 1897 had secured from Spain a significant amount of independence and reform through a charter of autonomy.

> The autonomous Charter constituted a significant improvement in the state of things. . . . Puerto Rico could elect delegates with votes to the "cortes" (Spanish Congress) . . . a Chamber of Representatives of the island . . . and an Administrative Council of fifteen members, of which Puerto Rico elected eight. . . . The Puerto Rican legislature

was given power to handle every important island
issue such as taxes and budget. All trade agreements made by Spain that affected Puerto Rico had
to be approved by the Puerto Rican Legislature.[25]

Shortly after the Autonomist Charter was put into
effect, it was invalidated by the U.S. invasion of July 25,
1898. The incident that led to the celebrated battle cry of
"Remember the Maine" and the subsequent war that resulted
in the annexation of Puerto Rico were not unplanned,
"fortuitous" events. Manuel Maldonado Denis argues that
the United States had long eyed Puerto Rico as a stra-
tegically valuable colony. The United States actively
thwarted any move of South American revolutionaries to
liberate Puerto Rico from the hands of Spain, knowing that
it would be more difficult to annex an independent island
than to acquire a colony from the slowly disintegrating
Spanish empire.[26]
Maldonado Denis demonstrates that, as far back as
President Adams, U.S. politicians expressed intentions of
acquiring Puerto Rico. He further documents that,
throughout the nineteenth century, the United States
supported Spanish colonization in Puerto Rico and Cuba.
He quotes Secretary William H. Seward as having said in
1867, "The United States has constantly cherished the belief
that someday she can acquire these islands by just and
legal means with the consent of Spain."[27] Maldonado adds
that, in 1876, James G. Blaine, Speaker of the House for
the forty-first, forty-second, and forty-third Congresses,
more explicit even than Seward, said, "I believe there are
three non-continental places of enough value to be taken by
the United States. One is Hawaii, the others are Cuba and
Puerto Rico."[28] In an outstanding account of that takeover
process referred to as the United States' "new manifest
destiny," historian Julius Pratt meticulously documents U.S.
expansion into Hawaii, the Caribbean, and the Philippines.
The ideology of the time, the religious and business attitudes, as well as the military support for U.S. impe-
rialism, are carefully and judiciously examined by Mr.
Pratt. His historical analysis, first published in 1936,
supports Maldonado Denis' interpretations. Professor Pratt
concludes as follows:

In response to the urgings of destiny, duty,
religion, commercial interests, and naval strategy,
the United States had utilized the war with Spain to
acquire an island empire in the Caribbean and the
Pacific. It was now free . . . to use its new

power in whatever way would best promote the
interest of the citizens of the United States and the
inhabitants of said islands—and it is to be noted
that the interests of the citizens of the United
States were placed first.[29]

POLITICAL, ECONOMIC, AND MILITARY
EXPLOITATION: A NEW BEGINNING

One must see U.S. expansion into Puerto Rico in 1889 in its
proper perspective. The United States had already purchased the Louisiana Territory, acquired Florida from
Spain, appropriated by declaration land from Native Americans, bought the Oregon territory from England, and
gotten into a war with Mexico thus acquiring California,
New Mexico, and other Mexican land. By 1898, the
philosophy of manifest destiny had been incorporated into
U.S. institutions, values, traditions, culture, and
language. Capitalism and racism went hand in hand with
the country's calculated westward expansion. By 1898, the
policy of expansion and violence that manifest destiny
symbolized was a reality. It "was a movement destined to
gain commercial, industrial, and financial hegemony in the
Western Hemisphere, and, as a necessary corollary to that,
naval and military bases indispensable to maintaining this
hegemony. Nor can this expansionist movement to the
south be seen apart from U.S. expansion toward the
Orient—in search of new markets in the Philippines, Hawaii,
China, and other countries for its surplus products."[30]

ENTER AMERICA

General Miles and his troops invaded Puerto Rico on July
25, 1898, and took over the island.[31] The country that
espoused democratic ideals had come to "liberate" Puerto
Rico from centuries of Spanish rule. General Miles, in his
first speech to the Puerto Rican people, revealed the "white
man's burden" attitude that the United States felt toward
the island. Full of democratic promises, the United States
with its "enlightened civilization" would watch over its
benighted neighbor.

The people of the United States in the cause of
liberty, justice and humanity, come bearing the
banner of freedom, inspired by a noble purpose,
that is, to bring you the fostering arm of a nation

of free people, whose greatest power is in justice and humanity to all those living within its fold. We came here not to make war upon the people of a country that for centuries has been oppressed but, on the contrary, to bring you protection, not only to yourselves, but to your property, to promote your prosperity, and to bestow upon you the immunities and blessings of the liberal institutions of our government and to give to all within the control of its military and naval forces the advantages and blessings of enlightened civilization.[32]

The immunities and blessings of the liberal institutions of (U.S.) government that Miles praises euphorically took the form of the Foraker Act of 1900. This act provided the first civil government for Puerto Rico, but in reality it reflected U.S. insistence on maintaining total control of the island. The rationale that was given for holding a tight rein on Puerto Rico, compared to the granting of semi-autonomy to the other spoils of the war, underscores the predominant racist attitudes of the era. The Puerto Rican people were more "white" than the Philippinos or Guamanians and, therefore, more receptive to U.S. ways. Of course, there was no denying that the island was a strategic gem. In his speech to the House in support of the Foraker Act, Representative Thomas Spight (Dem., Mississippi) reiterates these arguments: "Its people are, in the main, of Caucasian blood knowing and appreciating the benefits of civilization, and are desirous of casting their lot with us. . . . Its proximity to our mainland, the character of its inhabitants, together with the advantages—commercial, sanitary and strategic—all unite to enable us to make her an integral part of our domain."[33]

According to the provisions of the Foraker Act, the governor of the island and the ten-member upper chamber of the legislature were to be appointed by the president, pending approval of the U.S. Senate. The lower chamber of the legislature, 35 members strong, would be publicly elected. All laws had to be approved by both chambers of the legislature; the governor had the power to veto any law, while the U.S. Congress had the ultimate veto power.[34] In short, the government was not by the consent of the governed, but by the consent of the United States.

The superimposition of an administrative structure responsible only to the U.S. government unloaded on Puerto Rico an avalanche of administrators who were often incompetent or immoral. With few exceptions, the criterion used by the president of the United States for choosing a colonial governor and his cabinet was one of compensation for political favors. Many of the men who came to "govern" did not know the language nor, in many cases, even the location of the island. "The same can be said of many of the bureaucrats sent to Puerto Rico in the colonial free-for-all. They were ignorant and prejudiced, with the feeling of superiority common to all colonizers."[35] "The colonial governors who filed through Puerto Rico during the first four decades of this century were with very few exceptions a living illustration of ineptitude, insolence, and lack of respect for the Puerto Rican people."[36] In colonial relationships, the primary interest of the colonizer is to exploit the colony for its own benefit, and what benefited U.S. industries most was to turn Puerto Rico into a one crop society. The crop selected proved to be highly profitable for the new owners of Puerto Rico but devastating for the island's population.

It is no wonder that the Puerto Rico of 1940, as described by John Gunther in Inside Latin America, was indeed "the poorhouse of the Caribbean." After 42 years of U.S. administration, Puerto Rico had one of the highest infant mortality rates in the world and one of the lowest rates of average income per worker (less than 40 cents a day.[37] In enumerating the reasons for Puerto Rican poverty, Gunther emphatically describes the forces deriving from the colonial relationship that adversely affects the Puerto Rican worker. Specifically, he identifies the U.S. controlled sugar economy and the high profits generated by four large absentee-owned sugar companies. "These profits leave Puerto Rico."[38] Gunther underscores that "the grinding season for sugar is very brief; thousands of itinerant workers can count on only a few months work a year."[39] Secondly, Gunther explains that the U.S. tariff, meant to protect U.S. goods, forces Puerto Ricans to pay outrageous prices. He adds that overwhelmingly Puerto Ricans are "miserably poor, yet, pay precisely what we pay, though our standard of living is enormously higher."[40] Gunther further notes that the concentration of land ownership in big estates keeps Puerto Ricans out of the economy. Finally, he adds that "[t]he United States coast-wise shipping laws . . . and . . . the unreasonable cost of shipping, which is a United States monopoly" translates into even greater exploitation of the colonial relationship.[41] As a final example of Puerto Rican poverty, Gunther observes that "the daily per capita consumption of milk in the United States is three quarters of a pint. In Puerto Rico it is exactly one teaspoonful."[42]

Maldonado further explains Puerto Rican poverty of the

1940s:

> At the moment preceding American occupation of
> Puerto Rico, our island's economy centered around
> three basic commodities: coffee, tobacco, and
> sugar. Most of the land belonged to the peasants
> that cultivated it. According to the study made by
> the Diffies, Puerto Ricans were owners of 93 per-
> cent of the farms that existed in Puerto Rico in
> 1899, so that a great number of persons belonging
> to the rural population were homeowners and per-
> manent residents of the Island. . . . Out of the
> Island's 3,535 square miles 41 percent was devoted
> to coffee, 15 percent to sugar cane, 32 percent to
> foodstuffs, and 1 percent to tobacco. But by 1930
> the sugar industry raised its area of cultivation
> . . . [A]t that juncture 60 percent of all sugar
> production was monopolized by four great absentee
> corporations, and the same held true for tobacco
> (80 percent), public services and banks (60 per-
> cent), and maritime lines (100 percent).
>   The move toward the concentration of property
> in the hands of a few absentee corporations went
> hand-in-hand with the creation of a cash-crop,
> monoculture, plantation type of economy. The
> demise of the coffee plantations, the closing of the
> traditional European markets . . . the devaluation
> of the Puerto Rican peso led to the unfolding of a
> process in which the campesinos of the coffee
> plantation sub-culture were forced to seek jobs on
> the great plantations and centrales. This led to
> the creation of a rural proletariat whose life
> chances were geared to the sugar factories, and by
> the conclusion of the first three decades of Amer-
> ican rule Puerto Rico had become—within the in-
> ternational division of labor—an economy basically
> dependent upon the price of sugar in the world
> market.[43]

In addition to enumerating the economic exploitation of
the island up to 1941, Gunther describes Puerto Rico as the
Caribbean's Gibraltar and Puerto Rico's attendant military
exploitation:

> Puerto Rico is a vital pivot in United States defense
> . . . not only because Puerto Rico straddles the
> Antilles and thus helps to block off the eastern
> approaches to the Panama Canal . . . it is an

outright possession of the United States. It is the only site in the Caribbean (except the canal itself) where we can go as far as we want in any way we please, since it does belong to us.

Our defense efforts in Puerto Rico have been prodigious since the summer of 1939. San Juan is like an anthill bursting with military activity. To mention only one detail: the garrison of the island was increased from 800 men to 16,000 in the eleven months from March 1940 to February 1941.

Such a vast augmentation brings vexing problems—social, economic, administrative—problems of health control, labor, military and naval priorities, local education, food reserves, air-raid defense, and the like.[44]

OPERATION BOOTSTRAP

The descriptions of Puerto Rico, as presented by John Gunther have been repeated in much of the literature on Puerto Rico: "[M]isery, disease, squalor, filth . . . make the hovels of Calcutta look healthy by comparison . . . shocking enough in the remote uplands of Peru . . . but to see it on American territory. . . ."[45] Under American colonization Puerto Rico had become the "poor house of the Caribbean." Industrial development of the island was seen as the answer to its misery. Attempts to continue land reform in Puerto Rico were dropped and U.S. industries and capital were to be wooed in order to industrialize the island and promote jobs.

The Puerto Rican Development Corporation was established in 1942. This governmental agency started as an obscure bureaucratic dependency, which grew to huge proportions after World War II. Puerto Ricans called it "Fomento." Initially, taxes on rum financed Fomento. During the war, the alcohol that had formerly gone into whiskey was needed for the war effort. Puerto Rican rum was available to the United States and was sold in greater quantities as whiskey became more scarce. Between 1941 and 1942, federal excise taxes collected on the sale of Puerto Rican rum in the United States and remitted to the Puerto Rican treasury amounted to more than 160,000,000 dollars above normal revenue.[46]

The administrators of the island used the rum revenue to create public corporations that would give the island the basic services (electricity, water, roads, and sewage systems) necessary for the establishment of industries.

Several government-owned industries were started, but, in spite of heavy capital investment (20,000,000 dollars), only 2,000 jobs were created. Nevertheless, since agrarian reform was abandoned and a program directing available capital toward industrialization had been initiated, there was no turning back. The solution supported by Washington and Puerto Rico was "Bootstrap," that is, Americanization of the industrial process.

The guarantee of seven years of tax exceptions, a cheap labor force, and political stability as a result of the ever-present police and military installations attracted U.S. businessmen. Overnight, Puerto Rico went from an agrarian society to an industrial one.

San Juan had been a popular tourist attraction since 1948 when airplane traffic from New York to San Juan became more commercial. La Havana, being "foreign" but closer, bigger, and more developed in tourism, had often been preferred by U.S. tourists. However, in 1959, with the closing of Cuba to the United States, Puerto Rico became the tourist attraction of the Caribbean.

By 1965, tourism was earning 100,000,000 dollars a year. Near the hotels where tourists stayed, Puerto Rico had undoubtedly changed. Industrialization and tourism, business and tourist ads boasted, had transformed Puerto Rico from the "poorhouse of the Caribbean" to a "showcase of democracy," from an "orphaned island" to the "miracle of the century."

The growth of capital investment, industrial jobs, and net income has certainly been enormous. The per-capita income in 1949 was 121.00 dollars. It was 571.00 dollars in 1960 and 1,124.00 dollars in 1970. The net national income has gone from 225 million dollars in 1949 to 1.5 billion dollars in 1960, to 3.74 billion dollars in 1970. There were 28 factories on the island in 1949, 660 in 1960, and 2,500 in 1970.[47]

Gunther highlighted that, in addition to its economic exploitation, Puerto Rico has been exploited militarily as well. Thirteen percent of Puerto Rican land is used for military purposes. Large numbers of U.S. National Guard, the Air National Guard, Reserve Corps, the Marines, and other armed forces personnel are stationed, are trained, and "practice" war maneuvers in Puerto Rico. The island municipality of Vieques, for example, is used for target practice, for the storage of war machinery and weapons, and for the training of armed forces personnel through simulated land, sea, and air invasion maneuvers that have killed or injured Vieques' people. The military use of Vieques began during World War II; however, World War II

has yet to end there. With the intensified rivalry of the
United States and the Soviet Union, the Cuban missile
crisis, the invasion of Granada, and the perceived com-
munist threat in the Caribbean and Central America, Puerto
Rico has become more and more necessary to U.S. commercial and military hegemony. Three-fourths of the land in
Vieques is under the jurisdiction of the Marines, and the
people who continue living on the island are quarantined in
one section of this Puerto Rican municipality.

If one combines the armed forces personnel and the
National and Air Guard personnel, with that of the F.B.I.,
C.I.A., and the ·police force of the island in 1970, one
would find one policeperson for every 28 residents of
Puerto Rico.[48] Obviously, the bases and the police force
remain for the protection of U.S. business and military
interests in Borinquen, as well as for the policing of the
Caribbean.

Evidence seems to indicate that with U.S. industrialization, tourism, and military expansion has come U.S.
racism. United States businessmen seem to be altering
Puerto Rico's unusually easy race relations by hiring
light-skinned Puerto Ricans as first priorities.[49]

Supporters of U.S. colonization in Puerto Rico argue
that Operation Bootstrap and military activity in Puerto Rico
have led to greater per capita income, greater net national
income, more factories, and greater well-being for the
Puerto Rican population. While these claims can be sub-
stantiated, one can also substantiate the continuation of
ubiquitous poverty and despair in the Gibraltar of the
Caribbean. Like the United States, Puerto Rico offers a
series of major contradictions. In 1960, 25 percent of
Puerto Rican families received 3 percent of the total family
income, while 9 percent of the families received 40 percent
of the island's family income. In 1969, 20 percent of the
population received emergency food.[50] In 1980, according
to the U.S. Census, 62 percent of Puerto Rico's population
had incomes below the poverty level. In January of 1984,
the official unemployment rate in Puerto Rico was 23 percent.[51] In her 1971 article, "Needs and Aspirations of the
Puerto Rican People," Ligia Vazquez de Rodriguez concludes:

In sum, 5.4 percent of the total population has the
richness of the country, 45 percent has malnutrition
and for every working person, there are 4.5 persons depending upon him, who are unemployed.
Thirteen percent of the population is unemployed,
which includes one of every four persons between

the ages of 18 and 24 who are actively seeking
work. Many more are underemployed or do not
continue to look for a job after having lost all hope
of finding one.[52]

One can also conclude that industrialization in Puerto Rico
has been responsible for forcing Puerto Ricans to migrate to
agricultural areas of the U.S. Northeast (the South uses
blacks, the West Chicanos) and to industrial sectors where
dirty work may be available for very low wages. During
the industrialization of the island, almost one third of the
population left Borinquen for the urban slums of New York
City. What forces compelled Puerto Ricans to leave the
tourist attraction that had been heralded as an island
paradise and the showcase of democracy? What combination
of factors explain a migration unprecedented in U.S. history?

Puerto Rico's economic problems, caused or complicated
by U.S. policy on the island, acted as the push factor. As
were Handlin's European peasants, Puerto Ricans were
pushed from their native land. Unlike the immigrants,
however, Puerto Ricans were U.S. citizens. The Jones Act
of 1917 had forced citizenship on the island's population.
Puerto Ricans, like black U.S. citizens moving to the
industrial North from southern farms, were migrants.
Unlike the black southerners, however, Puerto Ricans were
pushed out of the farms not by the boll weevil epidemics or
the rise of commercial farming, but by an economic system
that had abandoned a one-cash-crop agrarian society in
favor of the industrial society and profits that Operation
Bootstrap promised. Thus, thousands upon thousands of
Puerto Ricans left the rural areas of Borinquen for the
island's cities, searching for work in the factories. In this
process, slums in Puerto Rican cities were created or made
worse. Yet, unfortunately, the cities did not provide
enough work for these internal migrants.

The Puerto Rican government (that is, the U.S. government) clearly failed to reduce unemployment on the island
despite Operation Bootstrap and other development programs. This failure best explains the movement of hundreds of thousands of people from Borinquen to the United
States. Even though the Puerto Rican population increase
has been offset by the migration of its peoples, the unemployment rate on the island has officially remained at
about the 12 percent level for the last 30 years. According
to the Bureau of Labor Statistics, Puerto Rico Department
of Labor, the unemployment rates were 11.8 percent in
1947; 14.7 in 1950; 14.3 percent in 1955; 12.0 percent in

1960; and 11.3 percent in 1965. Nieves Falcon arrives at a 30 percent unofficial rate for 1969.[53] In 1984 unemployment was officially recorded at 23 percent.[54]

Unofficially, the figure is nearer 35 percent, as many of the jobless simply have given up trying and thus have ceased being unemployment statistics. Food stamps alone keep the wolves from the door. Some 15 percent of the entire U.S. supply of food stamps finds its way to Puerto Rico.[55] In 1984, approximately 60 percent of Puerto Rico's population qualified for food stamps.

Although poverty and unemployment are and have been painfully present in Puerto Rico, it is imperative to stress that migrations cannot be explained solely by push factors. Most economists consider the pull factors to be equally important. Economist Michael Piore argues that the pull, especially the employer recruitment, is more important.

> Thus it is the employers, not the workers . . . that are strategic. . . . It is difficult to distinguish recruitment efforts from the voluminous information that flows back and forth. . . . But when the origin can be identified, it is invariably the employer who is the active agent. . . . Employers, acting on their own or through steamship companies, were active in the recruitment of European immigrants to the United States prior to World War I. The black migration from the rural South to Northern industry by similar recruitment activities on the part of employers and railroads, begins with the war itself and continues in the twenties.[56]

Piore adds that his studies on Puerto Rican migration to the Boston area tend to confirm the pattern of employer recruitment. He suggests that employer recruitment activities also "appear to underlie the migration of undocumented workers."[57]

Without a doubt, Puerto Ricans were recruited to the United States. In Chapter 4, I shall describe how governmental agencies helped employers recruit Puerto Ricans. Handlin notes that in times of prosperity migrants increased and during depression they decreased. "This has been particularly the case among the Puerto Ricans."[58]

> The opportunity to come to the mainland was enlarged by the postwar immigration laws which virtually put an end to the admission of Europeans. That left vacant a complex of jobs for unskilled

workers partly being filled by Negroes but for
which Puerto Ricans could also compete. . . . The
shipping lines which tied the island to the mainland
had their terminus in New York, so that the bulk
of the newcomers landed in the city and stayed
there.[59]

The Puerto Rican migrants initially settled in Brooklyn,
East Harlem, and the lower East Side, paving the way for
the later arrivals.[60]

Undoubtedly, citizenship explains why Puerto Ricans
and not other people from the Caribbean were consistently
recruited to fill poorly paid jobs in New York City and
elsewhere. The increased commercial use of the airplane
after 1948 also facilitated the recruitment process. This
type of transportation was relatively inexpensive, safe, and
quick. One could borrow the 50.00 dollar plane fare and
be in New York City in eight hours. Furthermore, the
island's need to rid itself of unemployed, discontented
people who could kindle a social revolution led to the
government's encouragement of the emigration process and
the Puerto Rican exodus to New York. It is important to
add that a great number of Puerto Ricans were drafted
during World War II and the Korean War. Many of them
settled in New York after completing their obligatory
service, thereby becoming members of the growing Puerto
Rican communities in that city and luring their families to
join them.

Historically, wars have stimulated the economy by
requiring the manufacture of uniforms, tanks, guns, canned
goods, parachutes, airplanes, and so forth for the U.S.
effort and the efforts of the allies. Simultaneously, wars
have removed men from the labor force. Additional workers
are required for both the expanding economy and as replacements for the men who must enter the armed forces.
Women and minorities are then recruited into the labor force
during these times. The traditional male native workers
often have the opportunity to move to the better paying,
more stable, preferred jobs. The recruitment of women and
minorities is for the jobs that are less desirable. There are
jobs that neither white women nor other minorities will take,
and it is for these jobs that Puerto Ricans are recruited.
Because of differences in language and culture, and because of the dark color of many Puerto Ricans, these
migrants confront the ethnic, the cultural, and linguistic
discrimination felt by the European immigrants, as well as
the racism felt by the black migrants. This combination of
factors, coupled with lack of Puerto Rican political clout,

begins to explain Puerto Rican poverty in New York City
and elsewhere in the United States.

Puerto Ricans are the first major group of U.S.
citizens, living outside the United States, to migrate and
settle in New York City and elsewhere in the continental
United States. In 1940, 61,463 or 87.8 percent of Puerto
Ricans residing in the Untied States lived in New York
City. In 1970, 30 years later, the number of Puerto Ricans
in New York had increased to 887,119 but represented only
56.8 percent of Puerto Ricans residing in the continental
United States.[61] The 1980 census data indicate that,
although the percentage of Puerto Ricans in New York City
has increased, their absolute number has not changed
significantly. Furthermore, although the number of Puerto
Ricans in the United States increased by 40 percent, or
approximately 600,000 more persons than in 1970, the
proportion of Puerto Ricans living in the city of New York
dropped to 46 percent.[62] Obviously, Puerto Ricans are
migrating elsewhere.

Unfortunately, regardless of where they reside, evidence reveals that, as a community, Puerto Ricans, even
more so than blacks or other Hispanics, are suffering from
unbelievable poverty.

> The median income for Puerto Rican families in May
> of 1979 was $8,282, lower than that of all other
> minority groups. For all U.S. families in May of
> 1979, the median income was $17,640. For Black
> families the median income was $12,566; Mexi-
> can-American families, $12,835; Cuban families,
> $15,376; and for other Spanish-origin families,
> $14,272. . . .
>   They live in the ruins of inner cities . . .
> forced to raise their children in housing that is
> mostly uninhabitable, attempting to raise their
> young in school systems that reject them, working
> at jobs that lead nowhere.[63]

Puerto Rican poverty is indisputable, as are the myriad
problems that daily confront Puerto Ricans and define that
poverty. Poor housing, high levels of unemployment, low
levels of formal education, increased incidence of mental
illness, resentment of the justice·system, and crime all too
often characterize Puerto Rican communities. New York
City's Puerto Rican community is the largest, oldest, most
organized, and most politically aware in the United States,
and yet even there we clearly see that Puerto Ricans are at
the drowning point as judged by most economic indicators.
A Time Magazine article of October 1978 compares Puerto

Ricans with blacks, showing that, although both groups are minorities, there is considerable inequality among the have-nots.

> Puerto Ricans are even more hard pressed than New York's ghetto blacks. Forty eight percent earn less than $7,000 a year compared with 42 percent among blacks. The proportion of Puerto Ricans on welfare is 34 percent vs. 32 percent for blacks. Among Puerto Ricans over 16 years old, only 6 percent have completed any job training. The rate for blacks is twice as high. . . . Puerto Ricans hold only 3.1 percent of police department jobs and 1.3 percent of those in the fire department.[64]

Unlike the European immigrants, Puerto Ricans, for reasons beyond their control, keep losing ground in their economic struggle. Puerto Ricans were recruited for jobs in the 1940s and 1950s. Unfortunately, many of those jobs have disappeared or been lost to suburbia. "New York City has lost thousands of jobs in both the private sector and in the civil service. Almost 50 percent of the Puerto Ricans who held civil service jobs lost them in recent cutbacks. In earlier years immigrant groups often moved upward into such jobs, and kept them."[65]

In 1979, according to the U.S. census, 95.8 percent of Puerto Ricans in the United States lived in metropolitan areas, and an outstanding 79.2 percent live in central cities. This compares with 45.6 percent for persons of Mexican origin, 33.7 percent for persons of Cuban origin, and 25.8 percent for persons not of Spanish origin.[66]

Puerto Ricans then are living in the nation's cities at a time when those cities do not have the economic possibilities for adequately supporting a new group. The declining number of entry level, low skill jobs in cities has made the employment picture particularly bleak for Puerto Ricans. "In 1959, Puerto Rican family earnings were 71 percent of the national average, but by 1974, Puerto Rican family earnings dropped to only 59 percent of the national average, and continued to drop. By 1979, Puerto Rican family earnings were 49 percent of the national average. . . . Generally, Puerto Rican families were worse off in 1979 than twenty years earlier."[67]

Data on income have been presented as indicators of poverty. But one must keep in mind that poverty affects all aspects of living, including housing, education, nutrition, clothing, medical care, and recreation.

From 1969 to 1971 the average annual mortality rates from accidents, homicides, bronchitis, influenza, and pneumonia, were higher for Puerto Ricans under 15 years old than for the total population under 15. The average annual mortality rates from homicide, drug dependence, and accidents, were higher for Puerto Ricans in the age group 15 to 44 than for the total New York City population, and equal for cirrhosis of the liver.

The rates per 100,000 population of admissions to community mental retardation facilities for all psychiatric diagnoses were 2,270.5 for Puerto Ricans, 2,113.1 for blacks, and 1,067.9 for whites. . . . Rates for mental retardation were 85.7 for Puerto Ricans, 53.5 for blacks, and 21.4 for whites.[68]

Obviously, such data are incomprehensible unless one explains these startling statistics as functions of poverty, class, language, and cultural and racial differences that too often lead to inaccurate diagnoses.[69]

Poverty also has psychological ramifications that have been widely documented: "feelings of powerlessness, deprivation, insecurity, and a relative simplification of the experienced world. The individual under constant siege may well experience estrangement and become alienated. This alienation has the components of anomie, isolation, powerlessness and meaninglessness."[70]

In a study of residential succession patterns in New York City, Terry Rosenberg and Robert Lake analyzed various types of neighborhoods from "stable mixed" (high status) to "high turnover" (low status) areas. Their research shows that black migration to "stable mixed" census tracts increased by 91.3 percent from 1960, showing increasing mobility for urban blacks. At the same time, Puerto Rican migration to "stable mixed" tracts declined by 17.7 percent over the decade.[71] They also found that regardless of the neighborhood type, blacks outdistance Puerto Ricans in median family income.

According to Moynihan and Glazer, "The 1960's may go down as the worst decade for the Puerto Rican in New York. . . . The long-range economic and political changes in city and country may record the continual agony of the Puerto Rican in the city."[72] Statistics indicate that the 1970s and 1980s were no better.

Puerto Ricans are the latest arrivals in New York City. They have come after the blacks. The past patterns seem to persist; the bottom is relegated to the latest arrivals. Blacks seem to have prospered in the 1960s and 1970s. Not only have Puerto Ricans remained without gains, but evidence indicates that relative to other communities, Puerto Ricans have moved backward.

NOTES

1. For more detail, see Luis Antonio Cardona, hijo, The Coming of the Puerto Ricans (Washington, DC: Unidos Publications, 1974).
2. Centro Social Juan XXIII, Puerto Rico: Showcase of Oppression, Book I, (San Juan, 1970), p. 3.
3. Arturo Morales Carrion, Puerto Rico and the Non Hispanic Caribbean (Barcelona: Artez Graficas Medinaceli, 1974), p. 4.
4. Ibid.
5. U.S. Commission on Civil Rights, Puerto Ricans in the Continental United States: An Uncertain Future (Washington, DC: October, 1976), p. 11.
6. María Teresa Babin, Panorama de la Cultura Puertorriqueña (New York: Las Americas, 1958) and The Puerto Rican's Spirit: Their History, Life and Culture (New York: Macmillan, 1971).
7. Morales Carrion, Puerto Rico, p. 5.
8. Ibid.
9. Centro Social Juan XXIII, Puerto Rico, p. 3.
10. Morales Carrion, Puerto Rico, p. 63.
11. Luis Diaz Soler, Historia de La Esclavitud Negra en Puerto Rico (1493–1890) (Madrid: Imprenta Viuda de Galo Saez, 1956). See also Morales Carrion, Puerto Rico, p. 67.
12. Morales Carrion, Puerto Rico, p. 63.
13. Luis Díaz Soler, La Esclavitud Negra en Puero Rico (San Juan: Instituto de Cultura Puertorriqueña, 1969).
14. Morales Carrion, Puerto Rico, p. 4.
15. William G. Baggs, Puerto Rico Showcase of Development, reprint from the 1962 Britannica Book of the Year. (New York: Encyclopedia Britannica, Inc., 1962).
16. Morales Carrion, Puerto Rico, p. 13.
17. Ibid.
18. Ibid., p. 142.
19. Ibid., p. 143.
20. Melvin M. Tumin and Arnold Feldman, Social Class and Social Change in Puerto Rico (Princeton, NJ: Princeton University Press, 1961), p. 239.
21. Charles C. Rogler, "The Morality of Race Mixing in Puerto Rico," Social Forces 25 (October 1946):77–81.

22. Renzo Sereno, "Cryptomelanism, A Study of Color Relations and Personal Insecurity in Puerto Rico," Psychiatry 10 (August 1947):263.

23. Ruth Gruber, Puerto Rico: Island of Promise (New York: Hill and Wang, 1960), p. 84.

24. U.S. Commission on Civil Rights, Puerto Ricans in the Continental United States, p. 11.

25. Puerto Rico Commission on the Status of Puerto Rico, Hearings Before the United States, Vol. 1: Legal Constitutional Factors in Relation to the Status of Puerto Rico, San Juan, Puerto Rico, May 14–18, 1965, pp. 215–16.

26. Manuel Maldonado Denis, Puerto Rico: A Socio-Historic Interpretaton (New York: Random House, 1972), p. 55.

27. Ibid.

28. Ibid.

29. Julius W. Pratt, Expansionists of 1878: The Acquisition of Hawaii and the Spanish Islands (Baltimore: John Hopkins Press, 1936), p. 360.

30. Maldonado Denis, Puerto Rico, p. 67.

31. Cardona, The Coming of the Puerto Ricans, p. 21.

32. Gamaliel Perez, "A New Approach to the Puerto Rican in his Society," in A New Look at the Puerto Ricans and Their Society, ed. The Institute of Puerto Rican Studies, Brooklyn College. (New York: Brooklyn College, 1972), p. 16.

33. José A. Cabranes, "Puerto Rico: Out of the Colonial Closet," Foreign Policy 33 (Winter 1978–79):74.

34. Perez, "A New Approach," p. 17.

35. Maldonado Denis, Puerto Rico, p. 67.

36. Roberto H. Todd, Desfile de Gobernadores de Puerto Rico, 2d ed. (Madrid: Ediciones Iberoamericanas, 1966).

37. John Gunther, Inside Latin America (New York: Harper and Brothers, 1941), p. 424.

38. Ibid., p. 426.

39. Ibid.

40. Ibid.

41. Ibid.

42. Ibid.

43. Maldonado Denis, Puerto Rico, p. 307.

44. Gunther, Inside Latin America, p. 433.

45. Ibid., p. 424.

46. Baggs, Puerto Rico Showcase, p. 20.

47. The figures on this page have all been extracted from Ligia Vazquez de Rodriguez, "Needs and Aspirations of the Puerto Rican People," reprint from Social Welfare Forum (New York: Columbia University Press, 1971) and Luis

Nieves Falcon, "Social Class and Power Structure in Puerto Rican Society," in A New Look at the Puerto Ricans and Their Society, ed. The Institute of Puerto Rican Studies, Brooklyn College. (New York: Brooklyn College, 1972).

48. Centro Social Juan XXIII, Puerto Rico.

49. See Juan Rodriguez Cruz, "Las Relaciones Raciales en Puerto Rico," Revistas de Ciencias Sociales (November 1971).

50. Nieves Falcon, "Social Class and Power Structure."

51. Norma Boujouen and James Newton, The Puerto Rican Experience in Willimantic (Williamantic, CT: Windham Regional Community Council, 1984), p. 2.

52. Vazquez de Rodriguez, "Needs and Aspirations."

53. Nieves Falcon, "Social Class and Power Structure," p. 115.

54. Boujouen and Newton, "The Puerto Rican Experience."

55. Daily News, January 4, 1976, p. 67.

56. Michael J. Piore, Birds of Passage (Cambridge: Cambridge University Press, 1979), pp. 19, 23, 24.

57. Ibid., p. 24.

58. Oscar Handlin, The Newcomers, Negroes and Puerto Ricans in a Changing Metropolis (New York: Doubleday, 1959), p. 57.

59. Handlin, The Newcomers, p. 51.

60. For a discussion of Puerto Rican settlement areas, see Joseph P. Fitzpatrick, Puerto Rican-Americans: The Meaning of Migration to the Mainland (Englewood Cliffs, NJ: Prentice-Hall, 1971), pp. 53–57.

61. Please note that Puerto Ricans have traditionally been undercounted by the census. Language, as well as color, culture, and class issues contribute to the under count.

62. U.S. Department of Commerce, Bureau of the Census, Supplementary Report—Persons of Spanish Origin by State, 1980, p. 2.

63. "Puerto Ricans Seen as Deprived," The Hartford Courant, October 6, 1980, p. A4.

64. "It's Your Place in the Sun," Time, October 11, 1978, p. 48.

65. Milton Leebaw, "Puerto Ricans and Economics," New York Times, October 17, 1976, IV, p. 5.

66. U.S. Department of Commerce, Bureau of the Census, Persons of Spanish Origin in the United States, 1979, p. 13.

67. The Next Step Toward Equality, National Puerto Rican Forum, New York, 1980, p. 5.

68. Ibid., p. 13.

69. Ibid., p. 5.

70. Emelizia Mizio, "The Conceptual Framework," in Training for Service Delivery to Minority Clients, ed. Emelizia Mizio and Anita J. Delaney (New York: Family Service Association, 1981), p. 98.

71. Terry Rosenberg and Robert Lake, "Toward a Revised Model of Residential Segregation and Succession: Puerto Ricans in New York, 1960–1970," American Journal of Sociology 81 (March 1976):1148.

72. Nathan Glazer and Daniel P. Moynihan, Beyond the Melting Pot (Cambridge, MA: M.I.T. Press, 1970), p. 70.

3

Black–Puerto Rican Competition in New York City: The Inevitable Systemic Outcome

Either all are free and equal, brothers and sisters in a universal process towards social development, or none will gain freedom and fulfillment.

> David Gil
> "Social Policies and
> Social Development"

The first chapter of this book documents ethnic rivalry and competition between the various groups of European immigrants in the United States. It further presents racial competition and, at times, violence between black U.S. citizens and the Irish, Italian, Poles, and other white ethnics. To a large extent, that competition and strife is systemic, a function of built-in labor market economics.

In what is recognized as one of the first accounts of the Puerto Rican migration to the United States, Lawrence R. Chenault's 1938 book, The Puerto Rican Migration in New York City, discusses the competition of black U.S. citizens with black West Indians. "The American Negro is inclined to resent all people from the West Indies because of their competition in the labor market. In the past years there has been a definite conflict between the colored workers from the West Indies and the colored group here. The American Negro especially resents the worker from British West Indies."[1] Chenault also introduces the black–Puerto Rican conflict. He adds that "the Puerto Rican is apt to encounter the same resentment."[2] Chenault further notes stressful competition between the people of the Spanish-speaking Caribbean—Puerto Ricans, Cubans, and Dominicans, and between the Spanish speaking and the Orientals.[3]

In the summary of his pioneer effort, Chenault identifies some similarities between Puerto Ricans and the European group whom the Puerto Ricans, as a result of restricted immigration, have replaced. Because of their environmental similarities with black U.S. citizens, Chenault prophetically warns that for the Puerto Rican a longer period of residence in this country cannot help but bring out more forcibly the social consequences of such an environment.[4] He speculates that the Puerto Rican, having "negro blood" will face "discrimination and prejudice" and like the black U.S. citizen must deal with "a color line."

To Chenault, there is "little doubt that the poverty suffered by the Puerto Rican in his native island is even greater than that of the Negro in the South."[5] The Puerto Rican worker is not as familiar with U.S. customs as is the U.S. black and does not have the black's ability to speak English.[6] As will be further detailed, during the next decades, the poverty suffered by the Puerto Rican in the North will be greater than that of the black in the North.

Chenault implies that Puerto Rican migrants, particularly an overwhelming number of them in the 1930s, settled in New York City, partially because they were recruited there, perhaps because of their color and minority status. "[T]he Cubans as well as native colored labor in Florida, Texas and California were already supplied with Mexican labor. . . . California also had its Oriental workers and people from the Philippine Islands employed at relatively low wages."[7]

In New York City, relations between blacks and Puerto Ricans have been adversely influenced by U.S. racism and oppression of immigrant/migrant labor. Chenault observes that in the 1930s Puerto Ricans often shared neighborhoods with black U.S. citizens. "[F]inding the American-born Negro confronted with serious disadvantages in this country, the Puerto Ricans want to maintain their own group and to distinguish themselves from him because they believe that through this means they will avoid this social position."[8] To a large extent, .this was true of all arrivals to the city. Unlike Europeans, however, Puerto Ricans, especially dark-skinned Puerto Ricans, also face the color barrier. According to Chenault, the darker skinned the Spanish-speaking West Indians are, the louder they will speak Spanish so as to disassociate themselves from the U.S. black population.[9] Chenault states that the black

U.S. citizen "does not appear to be particularly anxious to fraternize with the Puerto Rican. This is often shown by his criticism of the Puerto Rican's manner of living. Since Puerto Ricans speak Spanish they are even more likely to be resented than the English-speaking migrants from the Caribbean.[10]

In 1930, the Puerto Rican population in New York state, according to the U.S. census, was 45,973. In 1980, the Puerto Rican population in that state numbered about 1 million. As the Puerto Rican population grew, it became more of a competitor for the city's black population.

Inevitably, the battles of various ethnic groups for inclusion and dominance in the U.S. system take place on all fronts, including employment, politics, housing, education, and health care. Such conflicts have often intensified the tendency of each group to look out for its own interests even at the expense of other groups.[11] My discussion of black-Puerto Rican competition will center on the educational arena and on the "Great Society" programs of the 1960s as illustrative of New York City's more recent ethnic combat zones.

Excluded from the U.S. political process for more than 200 years, blacks in the 1960s were nationally propelled into it perhaps "by fiat but by a fiat with force, accompanied by an intricate and authoritative process of administration."[12] The civil rights movement demonstrated that black U.S. citizens had entered the U.S. interest-group battle. They had seized enough clout to bargain—bargain for themselves. In fact, blacks reaped most of the benefits from the Kennedy-Johnson antipoverty programs, because the programs were designed specifically for them rather than for all minorities, and whites fueled the conflict by setting up the boards that became responsible for OEO's (Office of Economic Opportunity) black bias. Commenting on this bias, Sar Levitan, author of The Great Society's Poor Laws, says, "It was possible to view the early OEO as a potential institutional base for the second phase of the civil rights movement."[13] Since antipoverty programs were often funded through (and at times became part of) traditional social service agencies, school programs, and health facilities, these programs offered the possibility of jobs and job training, advocacy, community outreach, and the potential structures for challenging stereotypes, myths, and staffing patterns of the institutions that administered the programs. Furthermore, the creation of such antipoverty agencies as Mobilization For Youth, HARYOU (Harlem Youth), and Bedford Stuyvesant Youth In Action enhanced the concept of community involvement and citizen participation, thus helping to develop and foster articulate and knowledgeable grass-root leadership.

During the 1960s, in order to build a stronger case for their disadvantaged status, blacks would often combine black and Puerto Rican statistics of poverty under the rubric of "minorities." Puerto Rican poverty, being greater, added a stronger sense of urgency to proposals aimed at ameliorating the needs of both groups. However, as projects and programs were funded and developed, Puerto Ricans proportionately obtained less than their relative need warranted. The phrase "blacks and Puerto Ricans" often resulted in minimal rewards for Puerto Ricans as well as a submergence of Puerto Rican identity and distinct problems. By 1964, it was obvious to most politicians, service providers, and community leaders in minority communities that the legislative antipoverty package was primarily aimed at relieving the growing tensions in U.S. black communities. "Blacks would not only do battle with Puerto Ricans, Chicanos, and Native Americans for program resources, but would also compete with whites for control of the programs."[14]

Puerto Ricans argue that in New York City blacks have been prepared to manipulate the system through social services, programs initiated by the War on Poverty, and black-oriented institutions. Blacks, they add, have moved into and are exercising control in the school system by using the skills and techniques they have acquired. In neighborhoods where Puerto Ricans are the majority, blacks are often in possession of more than their proportional share of jobs and influence. Because blacks have greater numerical strength in New York City as a whole and a broader political bloc, Puerto Ricans are often less influential even in areas in which they dominate numerically.

The relative success of the community control movement for blacks as compared to that for Puerto Ricans seems to be analogous to the previous systemic cycles of past newcomers to the city; in other words, white Anglo-Saxon Protestants replaced by large numbers of poor Irish, replaced by the Italian poor, replaced by poor Jews, replaced by poor blacks. As other groups move on and out, the more organized and more powerful of the newcomers step in. Viewed in this manner, the immediate problem for Puerto Ricans is that they are the last group of newcomers who are poor and who, as citizens, enter the country without legal restrictions.[15]

Will there be other massive legal arrivals of poor people into the city? Because of the immigration laws, the most probable answer is "no." Even if the answer were "yes,"

the next question would be "when?" How long does the
Puerto Rican wait? Statistics quoted earlier clearly indicate
that there has been no significant change for New York
City's Puerto Rican population since statistics on Puerto
Ricans have been kept. The problems that Puerto Ricans
face in terms of housing, education, and unemployment
today are as great as they were in 1950. However, the
larger question is: Can Puerto Ricans use the same vehicles
for upward mobility that past groups have used? Are those
vehicles available in today's world? The Irish used the
political clubs and the police department of the City of New
York; the Italians used the city's sanitation department and
the image of the Mafia; the Jews have used the educational
system; and the blacks have used and are now using the
social services. The white ethnics have used the union
movement, and both whites and blacks have created their
own ethnic institutions.

Traditional avenues for mobility indeed may be closed
today. United States' racist history further blocks the
mobility of peoples who are not white. Compared to whites,
blacks have still not "made it," and, compared to blacks or
to whites, Puerto Ricans have not "made it." Puerto Ricans
and blacks seem to be forced into competing against each
other and all others at the bottom. Blacks have been at
the lowest stratum of the socioeconomic political ladder for
centuries and are not about to countenance one more group
moving ahead of them in the present system.

The competition for services and for the jobs that such
services create has led to visible systemic conflict, and,
unless steps by responsible leadership from both groups
attempt to prevent it, this conflict will increase between the
two groups.

When discussing the Black Power movement, Luther
Gerlach and Virginia Hine point out that money, power, and
prestige became available in sizeable amounts as a result of
this movement. Some of the money came from the white
establishment. Blacks have been skillful in perceiving the
motives behind white contributions and in exploiting white
remorse, guilt, or fear.[16]

Having greater economic, social, and political need,
many Puerto Ricans often resent the fact that none of the
guilt, fear, or remorse money is directed to them. They
feel that the organizational and political clout that blacks
have acquired is often used to give blacks greater advantages in the struggle for survival. Black institutions are
seen at times as using their influence to support blacks at
the expense of Puerto Ricans.

The competition of the 1960s and 1970s in the school

system between blacks and Puerto Ricans documents this struggle for power. When speaking of the discriminatory educational system, black leaders argue that the concessions they have obtained are not enough. A frequently offered example is that the number and percentage of black personnel in the New York City school system does not reflect the numbers and percentage of black children attending public schools. Puerto Rican leaders have been arguing that the same inequity not only holds true for them, but is even worse.

Using the variable of ethnicity of New York City's student population and school personnel, one can easily conclude that what both black and Puerto Rican leaders have been saying is true.[17] As we will see in Chapter 8, conditions in 1984 had not changed significantly.

In his study on New York City's Board of Education, called Race, Resources and Achievement, Paul Ritterband emphasizes the inequities of an educational system that favors one disadvantaged group (blacks) over another (Puerto Ricans) because of political pressure. The Board of Education's policy has been to spend more money per pupil in schools that have lower levels of achievement. This policy should favor Puerto Ricans, because Puerto Ricans' achievement is lower than that of blacks. Ritterband documents that in fact such is not the case. He notes that pupil–teacher ratio is lower for blacks than for Puerto Ricans while the mean teacher salary is higher. Obviously the Board of Education is not responding to failure but to ethnicity, a political rather than an educational response.[18]

Apparently, the Board of Education is more responsive to black parents than to Puerto Rican parents. Puerto Rican leaders point out that basic elementary books in New York City's schools have been moving away from the Fun With Dick and Jane types to more city-oriented books. Many of the white children in the books have been colored black. Until very recently, few, if any, have been identified as Puerto Rican. Groups of parents of Puerto Rican background also stress that black parents usually head and run parent's associations in predominantly Puerto Rican schools. The percentage of Puerto Rican paraprofessional staff in Puerto Rican schools is still minimal when compared to the percentage of black or white paraprofessional staff. At this level, formal educational requirements are minimal and, in most cases, would not rule out Puerto Rican parents.

The changing racial population of the schools has also provided another mobility route for black teachers and other staff. Jack Douglas in <u>Youth in Turmoil</u> states that the suburbs will have the "jobs, the land, the industries, the tax base to support the schools and other services, the wealth and the whites; the central cities will have the blacks, the browns, and the broke."[19] Geographic trends indicate that white families with children continue moving to the suburbs so the school system continues losing substantial numbers of white students.[20] Among staff, the loss has been less than expected, since most teachers and administrators commute to New York to continue working there. Nonetheless, where the number of white staff members has decreased, the trend has been to replace whites with blacks, since the black community can articulate its needs better, has more political clout, and can influence more institutions than does the Puerto Rican community. As blacks vacate positions (by promotions or for other reasons), they often consciously assure that the positions go to other blacks and Puerto Ricans are locked out. In many cases, Puerto Rican leaders argue that "it is easier to get what they want from white administrators than from black administrators."[21]

Historically, Puerto Ricans have claimed that blacks block bilingual programs benefiting Puerto Rican youngsters, many of whom speak little or no English and who are therefore doomed to failure. In most cases, whites do not attend the schools that non-English-speaking Puerto Rican children do. Blacks view bilingual education programs as strictly for Puerto Ricans and feel that funds and staff will be diverted from other programs that will benefit blacks.

In March 1972, two Puerto Rican social workers, Maria Cuadrado and Carmen Hernandez, analyzed the status of Puerto Ricans in the City University of New York. They assert that "a comparison of the growth of Puerto Rican students, in the City University of New York, with other groups in the University indicates where the University has placed the Puerto Rican population in its scale of priorities."[22]

In the four year span from 1967 to 1971 the Puerto Rican student population increased by only 2.6 percent in the senior colleges. In comparison, the black population increased by 9 percent in the senior colleges and 8.1 percent in the community colleges. In the same time span, the white population decreased by 9.8 percent in the senior colleges and by 9.4 percent in the community colleges. It appears that from 1967 to 1971 the black student population increased at approximately the same rate at which the white population decreased, while the Puerto Rican population showed a slight change.[23]

In terms of staffing patterns of special programs within the City University of New York, Cuadrado and Hernandez observe that blacks tend to be appointed directors of programs aimed specifically at supporting minority and poor students. The authors add that, as black directors resign, the Puerto Rican assistants are kept as assistants or forced to leave and new black directors are hired; thus, blacks continue to occupy the top positions in university programs for the poor.[24]

Ms. Cuadrado and Ms. Hernandez also note that, in two programs that serve the special needs of Puerto Ricans (the College Discovery Program and SEEK [Search for Excellence, Education and Knowledge]), there was not one Puerto Rican counselor although there were many Puerto Rican students. "Obviously, special programs are not relating to Puerto Ricans as a group with specific needs."[25]

In social services, too, there is a scarcity of resources. Those who need or want them must scramble to obtain them. The fight over programs and jobs ostensibly designed to alleviate the misery of poverty often results in one-winner-takes-all sweepstakes. "Winner takes all means not only lack of jobs for the loser but lack of services as well."[26]

The civil rights movement of the 1960s gave blacks "an organizational base which was lacking among whites who were poor."[27] It should be added that it was lacking as well among Puerto Ricans who are often forgotten in a world accustomed to dealing with people as either black or white. The civil rights experience provided blacks with the sophistication and clout necessary to obtain the programs of the Great Society. Liberals in New York City and perhaps throughout the nation focused on black-white coalitions. For whatever reasons, the Puerto Ricans, the Chicanos, and the Native Americans were given little attention by government officials and white liberal reformers. Initially, they were left out of the War on Poverty.

Looking at New York City's antipoverty community corporations of the 1960s, one quickly realizes that, of 26 established, most were controlled and administered by blacks. When funds were distributed to the poor, blacks were well enough organized to move in and demand them. Some Puerto Rican leaders suspect that blacks, in general, believe that they are responsible for legislation that brought money to the poor and that they, therefore, should keep the money and control the programs. This same feeling seems to permeate the school system's programs and reforms made possible as the result of the movement for community control.

Although Puerto Ricans often understand the situation, their understanding does little to alleviate the problems that confront them as a community. Blacks, especially black administrators and politicians, tend to "take care of their own," even if it means adding to the problems confronting Puerto Ricans. Puerto Ricans in the fend-for-yourself society cannot get the funds, services, or sympathy from the black power structure any more than they can from the white one. Puerto Rican understanding has slowly turned to disappointment, bitterness, and perhaps hostility.

The 1960s and early 1970s may have been the worst decade for Puerto Ricans in New York City. This decade, however, may have been the best for black mobility in New York and nationally. In New York City, such mobility may have come at the expense of Puerto Rican progress. The continuation and worsening of Puerto Rican poverty in the 1960s may have been a function of black bias on the part of black and white administrators as well as the inability of the Puerto Ricans to successfully compete in the political arena for jobs and services.

The widely heralded success of the civil rights movement did not bring about a change in the competitive nature of the present system. The Puerto Ricans still struggle at the bottom. Lowi reluctantly concludes that:

> It is one of the tragedies of our time that so many Negro leaders themselves took the War on Poverty as their own. . . . [T]hey should have known that discomfort and immobility for them were mere symptoms that would pass away for most of them in a just society. [28]

Other minority groups have experienced black rivalry. For example blacks and Chicanos have long been competing for housing, jobs, and resources in the southwest. According to an article in the New York Times, some Mexican U.S. citizens feel that in the 1960s it was fashionable to hire blacks and reject Chicanos. [29] In August of 1965, Isaias Aguilera, head of the San Jose Chapter of MAPA (Mexican-American Political Association), wrote an angry letter that he sent to the regional Office of Economic Opportunity (OEO), the head of the OEO, and the press, charging that Chicanos were "purposely ignored" and the benefits of the War on Poverty were going to blacks. [30]

As mentioned in the previous chapter, blacks have become outraged by other minority groups, including women, jumping on the bandwagon. During an April 1979 conference at the National Association of Black Social Workers, the association agreed to reject the use of the term "minority" for themselves because, as the organization's Executive Director, Cenie J. Williams, said:

> The term minority has been bastardized to the extend that it has caused black people to receive less than an equitable share of available resources. . . . We share the concerns of others classified as minorities, however, we cannot at this time support additional black expenditures allocations based on minority needs. . . .
> Other ethnic and religious groups have piggybacked on our real and conceptual thrusts and like parasites have walked away with resources authorized by Congress and allocated by the President intentionally to benefit black people.[31]

Leonard Fein's analysis of community control as a social and political theory highlights a growing hostility and competition between blacks and Jews within New York City's school system.[32] He views the hostility between blacks and Jews as unavoidable under the present U.S. socioeconomic order, since Jews are often in the position of defending a bureaucracy of which they as teachers and administrators are an integral part.[33] Furthermore, the teachers' union, with a clear Jewish majority among its membership, often clashes with blacks in community control issues. In the black–Jewish conflict for jobs in the social services and educational arenas, Puerto Ricans are often the losers since the gains of either blacks or Jews mean that there will be fewer resources from which Puerto Ricans may benefit.

It is important to underscore that some black scholars call attention to class issues as they relate to the U.S. black community and the civil rights movement. William Wilson sees the civil rights movement as having made greater gains for the black middle class than for lower class blacks. This movement, declares Wilson, "did not sufficiently address the unique problems of class subordination and de facto segregation in the black ghetto. Indeed ghetto blacks had little direct involvement in the civil rights protests."[34] Wilson suggests that the civil rights movement offered the black middle class a mechanism for political participation and pressure from outside the system. Blacks have historically been denied access to the traditional political machines and have often been legally blocked from the political process. Wilson observes that, on the other hand, the European immigrants, earlier in the century, had built up political clout that was used to better the occupational and status mobility of the lower class ethnic—at times at the expense of blacks. Centuries of exploitations and racism had robbed the black middle class of political clout, and they had reached the 1960s with minimal political participation.[35] Perhaps, for this reason, black leadership in the civil rights and community control movements was viewed as crucial.

Unfortunately, the upward mobility of one sector of black society has not necessarily led to a better existence for the entire race. While more blacks continued to prosper even in the recession of the 1970s, poorer blacks have experienced greater unemployment, a greater reliance on welfare to survive, and considerably less opportunity to rise above the poverty level. "The net effect has been a deepening economic schism in the black community that could very easily widen and solidify."[36]

From the foregoing presentation, one may conclude that, as long as the U.S. values of competition—"fend for yourself" and "let others take care of their own"—prevail in this society, environmental change, benefiting specific segments of the population, will be possible only through a struggle that uses organizational tools and pressure tactics familiar to interest U.S. interest groups. Is this competition not what many blacks have been forced to accept and perhaps even assimilate into their life style?

Change did result from the community control of the school system in New York City and can be measured by the achievement of the short-run goals of specific interest groups. However, while achievement of these goals meets some important spiritual and developmental needs of the groups involved, it can at best only pave the way for more fundamental change.[37] Cooperation and mutual support among those at the bottom of society must be a basic part of this change. Recent conservative politics may force blacks and other oppressed populations to enter into a new era of increased coalition building.

The stresses and the strains created by the movement for community control of the school system in New York City created counterpressures along vested interest lines. Such long-range goals as equality for all children and parents in the system became harder to obtain. In this case, the results of the changes benefited the group most articulate, most organized, and most threatening to the established order—New York City's black community. The greater the gains, the better the position of blacks to achieve more of the same in the short run; those who have will be given more, or will at least be in a better position to get more.[38]

In terms of black mobility, recent findings suggest that progress has been made.

> In 1973, the U.S. Census Bureau reported one of the most significant statistics in American history. For the first time, the percentage of black Americans of college age entering an institution of higher education was identical with the proportion of comparably aged white youth. . . . Clearly, of course, . . . many blacks . . . are attending the more inferior segments of higher education: junior colleges, . . . less prestigious state colleges, etc. . . . Yet the statistic is very important, for college attendance has a major credential function. To obtain a job in the better paid sector of the American economy, one has to go to some sort of college.[39]

As the black middle class grows, so do the avenues that maintain and foster mobility. Recruitment visits to black or predominantly black colleges and universities from corporate representatives have consistently grown.

> The figures reported are indeed striking, indicating that the average number of recruitment visits of representatives of corporations to predominantly black colleges increased from 4 in 1960 to 50 in 1965 and then jumped to 297 in 1970. And schools, such as Atlanta University and Southern University, to which no visits were made in 1960, received respectively 510 and 600 corporate representatives in 1970.[40]

In striking contrast, in 1970 there were no Puerto Rican colleges or universities on the mainland that could foment mobility in the same way.

Unfortunately, in many New York City communities, resentment toward blacks has developed on the part of Puerto Ricans who are less able to attain needed gains. Many Puerto Ricans have concluded that within the present system they, as a people, must resort to their own pressure techniques. Some of those techniques may have to take the form of confrontation and conflicts with blacks. Puerto Rican parents in the school system have said that blacks, wishing to "hang on" to what they have and need-ing to get more, find it easier to control Puerto Ricans than to continue to attack the system exploiting them both.

> When the stratum is escapable, individuals will escape. When the stratum becomes to them unjust, they revolt, even if escape is made easier. Negroes had their Black Revolution. The only question was what they would do with it. Brought to leadership in an age of interest-group liberalism, they could not have chosen worse.[41]

Did those in power know that this would happen? Is this systematic? Are those united in a common struggle to be pitted against each other after the slightest of victories? "At the moment minority movements remain separate, often competing with each other . . . struggles of survival of the disunited poor."[42] In U.S. society, the gains of one minority group appear to almost equal another's losses. Competition for scarce resources may lead Puerto Ricans, blacks, Chicanos, women, Native Americans, poor whites, and the elderly poor to perceive each other as enemies. Unfortunately, in the struggle for sharing in the "American dream" of affluence, it seems to matter little who gets sacrificed in the process.

Certainly, no real change will be possible unless the issue of relativity of power is considered by policy makers advocating greater equality. Affirmative action and social program efforts should not be based on what ethnic group is best organized but rather on which groups of persons are most in need. Logic calls for the transformation of U.S. society from a system in which individuals and groups continuously attempt to increase their share of wealth and resources to one in which people base values less on profit and more on mutual aid, cooperation, and institutionalized responsibility for all.[43] The rainbow coalition, which the Reverend Jesse Jackson began to develop during his presi-dential campaign, certainly is encouraging.

As David Gil concludes in his essay, "Social Policies and Social Development," "social development, like human freedom and dignity, is indivisible. It simply cannot be secured for segments of a population at the price of ex-ploiting and oppressing other segments."[44] That each ethnic group has been exploited is no justification for the continuance of exploitation. "Either all are free and equal, brothers and sisters in a universal process towards social development, or none will gain freedom and fulfillment."[45]

Puerto Rican poverty in New York City is undisputed. At a recent conference of social workers, New York City officials and educators produced convincing evidence of increased Puerto Rican despair. Among the evidence cited are the following statements: "The percentage of Puerto Rican children in New York below the poverty level increased five times, more than for any other group of children, and is now up to 52 percent. . . . Only 57 percent of the heads of Puerto Rican families in New York are working and only one of three of these heads of families graduated from high school. . . . The income of Puerto Rican families in New York has plummeted from 71 percent of the national average in 1959 to 47 percent in 1979".[46]

Conference participants acknowledged that some Puerto Ricans have made it in the big city, but they pointed out that their number is small compared to all those who have been unable to break away from poverty's vicious circle even after 30 or 40 years in New York.[47] Chenault's prophecy of the 1930s has been validated. The Puerto Ricans who remain in New York and continue occupying that city's crowded lowest stratum have several options. They can continue to hope that past patterns will prevail and that some remarkable expansion in the economy will allow for a new legally sanctioned group of poor people on whose back they could raise their own standards of living. They can further the brewing conflict with blacks for assistance dollars, perhaps gaining their fair share from their fellow sufferers. Or they can ally themselves with other groups working to break the cycle of ruthless competition that allows for one group to triumph over another. To some extent, Puerto Ricans will be reacting to the larger society, to general policy, to the priorities of their leaders, and to the actions of other minority groups.

Many Puerto Ricans have abandoned New York City, looking elsewhere in the United States for economic and social betterment. Hundreds of thousands have moved to smaller U.S. cities and towns. The growing Puerto Rican communities throughout the country, especially in the Northeast, further confirm the Puerto Rican diffusion.[48]

Note also that a smaller number of Puerto Ricans abandoning New York City are returning to Puerto Rico. However, a greater number continue migrating from Puerto Rico—some to New York City, but now also to elsewhere.[49] Massachusetts, Connecticut, and the New England region are examples of that elsewhere.[50] When that elsewhere changes, will the patterns of inequality also change?

NOTES

1. Lawrence R. Chenault, The Puerto Rican Migration in New York City (New York: Columbia University Press, 1938), p. 82. Please note that Chenault recommends W. A. Deming, "The Tropics in New York," Survey 3 (March 1, 1925):650, for further discussion on this labor market competion.

2. Chenault, Puerto Rican Migration.

3. Ibid., pp. 82, 83.

4. Ibid., p. 157.

5. Ibid., p. 156.

6. Ibid., p. 158.

7. Ibid., p. 55.

8. Ibid., p. 150.

9. Ibid.

10. Ibid., p. 151.

11. Fred Barbaro, "Ethnic Resentment," Society 11 (March/April, 1974):67–68.

12. Theodore J. Lowi, The End of Liberalism (New York: W. W. Norton, 1969), p. 51.

13. Barbaro, "Ethnic Resentment," p. 70. For more information, see Sar Levitan, The Great Society's Poor Laws (Baltimore: Johns Hopkins Press, 1969), and Frances Fox Piven and Richard A. Cloward, Regulating the Poor (New York: Pantheon, 1971).

14. Barbaro, "Ethnic Resentment," pp. 69–70.

15. The issue of the undocumented worker will be addressed in Chapter 8.

16. Luther P. Gerlach and Virginia H. Hine, People, Power, Change: Movements of Social Transformation (New York: Bobbs-Merrill, 1970), p. 49.

17. PARE (People Against Racism in Education), September/October, 1973, p. 6.

18. Paul Ritterband, "Race, Resources and Achievement," Sociology of Education 46 (Spring 1973):167.

19. Jack Douglas, Youth in Turmoil (Washington, DC: HEW Publication No. 2058, 1970), p. vii.

20. A more recent trend, gentrification, is that of white, middle-class professionals returning to the city. More often than not, however, they tend to be childless. See "Why More and More People Are Coming Back to Cities," US News & World Report, August 8, 1977, pp. 69–71; and "Flight from Inner Cities Goes On," US News & World Report, September 11, 1978, p. 49. Note also that white affluent families in the cities tend to send their children to private schools.

21. Fred Barbaro and Carol Peacock, "Anti-Black Sentiments By Other Minorities," mimeographed, January 1972, p. 16.

22. Maria Cuadrado and Carmen D. Hernandez, "Status of Puerto Ricans In the City University of New York," mimeographed, March 30, 1972, p. 2.

23. Ibid., p. 4.

24. Ibid.

25. Ibid., p. 8.

26. Barbaro and Peacock, "Anti-Black Sentiments," p. 15.

27. Ibid., p. 25.

28. Lowi, End of Liberalism, p. 248.

29. New York Times, October 17, 1965, p. 82.

30. Barbaro and Peacock, "Anti-Black Sentiments," p. 24.

31. Thomas A. Johnson, "Term Minority, Shunned by Black Social Workers," New York Times, April 22, 1979.

32. Leonard J. Fein, The Ecology of the Public Schools: An Inquiry Into Community Control (New York: Pegasus, 1971), Chapters 1-3.

33. Ibid.

34. William Julius Wilson, The Declining Significance of Race (Chicago: University of Chicago Press, 1978), p. 142.

35. Ibid., pp. 81-82.

36. Ibid.

37. Roger McNeely, "In Public Education: Is Community Participation the Answer?" (Paper presented at the Florence Heller Graduate School for Advanced Studies in Social Welfare, Brandeis University, Fall 1973).

38. Fein, Ecology of Public Schools.

39. Seymour Martin Lipset, "Education and Equality: Israel and the United States Compared," Society 11 (March/April, 1974):59-60.

40. Wilson, Declining Significance of Race, pp. 100-1.

41. Lowi, End of Liberalism, p. 249.

42. Barbaro and Peacock, "Anti-Black Sentiments," p. 42.

43. See David Gil, "Resolving Issues of Social Provision in Our Society: The Role of Social Work Education," (Paper presented at the 1976 Annual Program Meeting of the Council on Social Work Education, Philadelphia, PA, March 3, 1976).

44. David Gil, "Social Policies and Social Development," mimeographed, June 25, 1975, p. 30.

45. Ibid.

46. "Puerto Ricans in New York: It's Still Despair," The Evening Bulletin—The Providence Journal, December

14, 1983, p. A17.

47. Ibid.

48. See José Alvarez-Hernandez, "The Post-Development Crossroads of Puerto Rican Migration" in A New Look At Puerto Ricans and Their Society (New York: Brooklyn College, 1972), pp. 71–85. See also Karl Wagenheim, A Survey of Puerto Ricans in the United States Mainland in the 1970s (New York: Praeger Publishers, 1975); U.S. Department of Commerce, Bureau of the Census, Current Population Survey: Persons of Spanish Origin in the United States, March, 1974 (Washington, DC: Government Printing Office, 1975); Centro Taller de Migracion, Conferencia de Historiographia: April, 1974. Center for Puerto Rican Studies, Research Foundation of the City of New York, 1975; and U.S. Department of Commerce, Bureau of the Census, Persons of Spanish Origin By State: 1980 (Washington, DC: Government Printing Office, 1982).

49. See José Alvarez-Hernandez, Return Migration to Puerto Rico (Berkeley: Berkeley Institute of International Studies—Regents of the University of California, 1967). See also New York Daily News, Sunday, January 4, 1976, pp. 3 and 66–67; New York Daily News, Monday, January 5, 1976; "Returning Migrants Find Puerto Rico Inhospitable," New York Times, Friday, October 3, 1975, pp. 1 and 20–22; William Stockton, "Going Home: The Puerto Ricans' New Migration," New York Times Magazine, November 12, 1978, pp. 20–22 and 88–93.

50. According to the 1980 census, the Puerto Rican population in Massachusetts increased by 227 percent between 1970 and 1980. In Connecticut, the percentage of Puerto Rican population increased by 135 percent in that same ten-year period.

4

The Ethnic Queue and the Dual Market: Further Clarification on Today's Mobility

[There is] . . . not a whole population competing indiscriminately for all occupations, but a series of industrial layers . . . within each of which the various candidates for employment possess . . . power of selections while those occupying the several strata, for all purposes of effective competition, are practically isolated from each other.

> J. E. Cairnes
> Political Economy, 1874

In New Bedford during the 60's, Negroes became black men and women . . . but the Puerto Ricans became the Niggers.

> A black antipoverty worker
> in New Bedford, Massachusetts

In his Ph.D. thesis, Robert N. Horn posits that the dual labor market theory had its "pre origins in the writings of several economists of the classical school."[1] For example, John Stuart Mill, nineteenth century British economist and philosopher, saw the possibility of interclass mobility as remote and recognizes that "the range of occupations available to a worker depends upon the socio-economic status of his father."[2] In 1874, U.S. economist J. E. Cairnes noted that the existence of noncompeting industrial groups is a feature of all society.[3] Mill and Cairnes observe that the classes do not necessarily compete with each other. The competition exists within the classes. There are jobs for the wealthy and their sons and different jobs for the poor and their children. The dual market theory more clearly explains that there is no single "the market" but at least two distinct labor markets—primary and secondary.

While the primary market will not guarantee wealth, it does offer high wages, job security, and possible promotions, vacation, sick leave, health insurance, other benefits, and decent working conditions compared to the secondary market. The secondary labor market, on the other hand, contains jobs that pay low wages and provide little if any security, few benefits, and poor working conditions—in short, dirty work. Poor people will then remain poor, not necessarily because they do not work, but because their jobs are in the secondary labor market. To a large extent, the children and grandchildren of the European immigrants, as explained earlier, had been able to move into the primary market as that market expanded.

European peasants had provided a continual flow of low wage labor at a time that northern industry had demanded it. Blacks were initially a source of slave labor and later cheap wage labor for the southern secondary labor market economy. After the end of European immigration, blacks were recruited to the North. In the late 1920s and early 1930s the United States entered a depression, thereby curtailing the demand for workers. However, after the depression, large numbers of low-wage workers were needed to replace the European peasants, so more blacks were recruited from the South and Puerto Ricans from Borinquen.

The South had used Jim Crow laws to maintain the majority of black U.S. citizens in secondary labor market jobs. A byproduct of the Jim Crow laws was the creation of a black middle class in the South. Segregated schools, colleges, hospitals, stores, beauty salons, funeral parlors, and social services generated black teachers, professors, nurses, doctors, clerks, beauticians, insurance personnel, and other primary market type jobs. Discrimination in the North often led to de facto segregation in housing, education, employment, and other areas within a white administered and often staffed system. Thus, the North did not have to produce black professionals. Nevertheless, a more liberal North in which the NAACP, the Urban League, and other civil rights organizations became increasingly stronger could not use the law to promote Jim Crowism. The civil rights movement of the 1950s and 1960s concentrated on ending Jim Crow laws in the South, while in the North its accompanying black pride and resistance provided an impetus and climate for moving blacks away from secondary to primary market employment. It could not, however, eliminate the forces generating the need for dirty work.

Black leaders used the War on Poverty for mobilizing and creating an organizational base to enter the U.S. interest group battle. Second generation black northerners often refused to do dirty work and insisted that other avenues be opened. Given the present system, another group of first generation poor had to replace them in New York City's ethnic queue. In New York, in Massachusetts, in Connecticut, and in various New England towns and cities, Puerto Ricans did just that. Cities that may have previously encouraged black migration for secondary work in the labor market recruited Puerto Ricans instead. Black militancy, according to some factory foremen, frightened some potential secondary market employers. The non-English-speaking, poorer, first generation rural Puerto Rican worker was seen as less threatening and therefore more acceptable. "The occupational distribution of both groups shows that with respect to white collar, blue collar, and service jobs, the Puerto Rican workers are today where blacks were 10 years ago."[4] A black antipoverty worker in New Bedford, Massachusetts, stated that, "in New Bedford during the 60's, Negroes became black men and women . . . but the Puerto Ricans became the Niggers."[5]

Between the 1960 and the 1970 U.S. census, the Puerto Rican population in Massachusetts grew from 5,217 to 23,332. By 1980, 76,450 Puerto Ricans lived in Massachusetts, representing a 227 percent increase in ten years, by far the highest growth of any group in the state. The main thrust of the growth occurred during the early 1960s, but in some communities the Puerto Rican migration began as recently as the mid-1970s. In Connecticut, the growth has been almost as dramatic. Puerto Ricans totaled 15,247 in 1960; 37,603 in 1970; and 88,361 in 1980, representing a 135 percent increase between the 1970 and 1980 census.

Why has Puerto Rican migration to New England increased so dramatically over the past 20 years? What processes are involved in the migration? Has that migration improved the lives and opportunities of Puerto Ricans? Stymied in New York City, will Puerto Ricans find upward mobility in Massachusetts, Connecticut, or elsewhere in New England?

I have made the following guiding assumptions in attempting to answer these questions:

The diffusion of Puerto Rican individuals and families into New England cities initially began as Puerto Rican workers were recruited for seasonal employment on farms, orchards, and nurseries throughout New England.

• Eventually such workers stopped going back to Puerto Rico after seasonal employment ended and began moving to areas that had available housing and year-round employment providing low-skill manufacturing jobs associated with the secondary labor market.

• Relatives and neighbors of the migrating Puerto Rican workers followed them to the new communities to also avail themselves of job opportunities. Kin and friends thus facilitated the acclimation process.

• These relatives and neighbors came directly from Puerto Rico (often rural areas with very high rates of unemployment) and in some cases from New York City, the latter also looking to escape poverty.

• The areas to which Puerto Rican populations migrated have similar characteristics: available low income housing, a need for an impoverished group at the bottom of the socioeconomic structure, and availability (at least initially) of facilities that would provide low skill jobs, and social service networks willing to provide assistance.

• The conditions of Puerto Rican communities in Connecticut and Massachusetts are the results of a long history of Puerto Rican exploitation and that group's inability to break the cycle of poverty and oppression.

• The oppression and poverty that Puerto Ricans face are caused by the colonial relationship that the United States maintains with Puerto Rico, by a competitive economic system that often pits one ethnic or racial group against another, and by a pervading racist ideology.

• Historically, the last group with large numbers of poor persons entering the economic competition has been relegated to a position at the bottom of the economic ladder.

• The issues and problems that Puerto Ricans found in New York City often repeat themselves in other communities.

I chose to study Waltham, Massachusetts, a town of approximately 75,000 people, 2,000 of whom are Puerto Rican, because I am familiar with its Hispanic population and because Waltham reflects basic patterns of migration to small metropolitan areas in New England. In general, Waltham also meets the criteria of this study in that the proportion of Puerto Ricans to other Hispanic groups is similar to that of the two groups in Connecticut and Massachusetts.

Several economic theories offer additional insight into explaining the Puerto Rican migration to New England. Puerto Rican economist, Rita Maldonado, sees the classical and neoclassical migration theories as partially describing the migration patterns of Puerto Ricans to and from and within the United States.[6] She maintains that economic variables are only one aspect of the push and pull causes of migration. Michael Joseph Piore, professor of economics at the Massachusetts Institute of Technology (MIT) views the dual-market character of the labor force as being helpful in explaining Puerto Rican migration to New England.[7] Perhaps a more extensive discussion of these theories is warranted at this time.

Maldonado, in an article entitled "Why Puerto Ricans Migrated to the United States in 1947–73," explores the complex network of economic and noneconomic variables that have confused the reasons for Puerto Rican migration.[8] The problem arises because our economic system is not as simple as it was in the nineteenth century or the first decade of this century. "In the classical sense, economic opportunity for migrants has meant employment opportunities or higher wages, or both. Today, it involves other dimensions as well: better employment compensation, higher welfare payments, more generous disability benefits, and a package of related social assistance considerations."[9]

Before detailing noneconomic factors, Rita Maldonado reviews the classical-neoclassical theories of migration. She notes that, according to traditional economic theory, migrants move from areas where there is an abundance (surplus) of workers and where the wages are low to areas where there is a need for workers and where the wages are higher. As this process takes place, all else being equal, wages fall in the areas that have attracted the workers and rise in the areas from which the workers have moved. When the differences in wages between the two areas are eliminated or greatly reduced, the migration of workers stops. Maldonado stresses that this classical theory "takes into account only free market sources such as wage rates, per capita income, labor force changes and the like."[10]

This traditional explanation helps us understand why Puerto Ricans began leaving the farms of Puerto Rico and moving to work in farms and nurseries in the New England area from the 1940s to the 1960s. It does not explain subsequent migration since farm wages in the New England states continued to increase. The classical theories fail to take into account governmental intervention. In the case of

Puerto Rican migration to New England farms, the government of Puerto Rico and the Department of Employment Services attempted to incorporate wage increases into contracts for Puerto Rican migrant workers.[11] Perhaps this explains the ability of New England farmers to continue attracting Puerto Rican workers, thus avoiding the need for legally restricted, undocumented workers, which many Texas and California farmers experienced. The slight wage increase and improving working conditions may have been enough to maintain a "legal" work force. Contracts called for government inspections, which took place sporadically, making it difficult for farmers to hire cheap undocumented Hispanics on their New England farms. This in turn created a greater need for additional Puerto Rican workers.

Another category of traditional economic theory does take into account government programs as well as private free market forces. This category, for example, acknowledges that the differences in such government transfer payments as unemployment compensation, welfare benefits, and public services are important to consider when attempting to determine factors influencing migration patterns. "The same equilibrating tendency occurs, only here more factors form the basis of the migration decision."[12]

It was not until recently that comparable transfer payments and public resources have become available in Puerto Rico. The introduction of food stamps in Puerto Rico, for example, may have curbed migration from Orocovis, Puerto Rico, to Waltham, Massachusetts, and other cities in the United States.[13]

> The third category of classical–neoclassical theory—and the most encompassing of all migration theories—takes into account the variables mentioned above, but in addition holds that migration will be affected by such factors as climate, landscape, recreational and educational facilities, racial composition of the population, and the chain effects of cumulative migrations. Thus, for example, as more persons migrate to a region, it becomes easier for future migrants to adjust to the new region because they have more information about it and might receive help from previous migrants in adapting to their new surroundings.[14]

This broader theory forms the foundation for Maldonado's study. She concludes, after collecting and analyzing data for a 27-year period, that unemployment rates and average yearly earnings were the most important

variables in determining the Puerto Rican migration from
1947 to 1967 and that the welfare variable appeared to be
insignificant. These findings, however, do not hold true
for the years 1968 to 1973. After 1968, wages became more
important than unemployment. In other words, initially (as
a result of the economic factors discussed in Chapter 2) a
very large proportion of Puerto Ricans on the island had no
jobs and no benefits. The decline in agriculture and the
attempt to industrialize the island left hundreds of thousands of Puerto Ricans with no jobs as opposed to very
poorly paying jobs. Unemployed Puerto Ricans wanted to
work at even very poorly paid jobs in the United States.
When all was taken into consideration, secondary-market
employment anywhere was seen as attractive. However, as
wages rose in Puerto Rico, Puerto Rican migrants became
interested in migrating if wages in the United States were
significantly higher than those in Puerto Rico. Furthermore, as benefits were added, Puerto Ricans were less
likely to migrate just because they were unemployed.
However, if the migrants after arriving in the United States
could not secure a higher wage or unemployment benefits,
they could fall back on welfare benefits, hopefully just
temporarily. To a certain extent, for many secondary-
market workers in the United States, welfare acts as
insurance against the unavailability of jobs with significantly higher wages than unemployment benefits or welfare
payments.[15] Puerto Rican migrants, as U.S. citizens, can
decide where they have the best chances for survival. It
is important to keep in mind that I will be looking at Puerto
Rican migrations to Massachusetts that have taken place
after the 1960s. Thus, factors beyond the traditional
supply-and-demand market theory analysis are important.

     In discussing the Puerto Rican migration to Waltham,
Massachusetts, and to other elsewheres in New England, the
more encompassing neoclassical theory may be most significant. I believe that the receiving communities do have
certain characteristics (low income housing, social services,
and other economic and noneconomic variables) that make
those sites more accessible for Puerto Rican migrants.
Maldonado discusses and dismisses human capital theory,
which she describes as essentially a "cost/benefit model in
which migration is determined by the present value of
future net earnings the individual can receive from migrating."[16] She sees as its problem an inability to quantify
effectively the "present value of net future earnings from
migration" and the exclusion of such factors as unemployment rates, welfare payments, unemployment compensation,
public and private schools, police protection, and racial

composition of the population even though these explanatory variables may be implicit.[17]

Maldonado is quite critical of migration theory in general due to its dependence on economic variables and notes that several noneconomic variables have been left out of the "economic" perspectives on the Puerto Rican migration. For example, in 1965, Congress created a seven-category preference system giving immigration priority to relatives of U.S. residents, immigrants with needed talents or skills and their immediate families, and refugees.[18] Large numbers of Dominicans have entered Puerto Rico following the Dominican Civil War of 1965. Many of these entered legally as refugees, but many entered illegally and subsequently moved to the United States, at times passing as Puerto Ricans in an effort to escape immigration problems. The same can be said of Cubans. Immigration studies have not attempted to differentiate Puerto Ricans from the non-Puerto Ricans leaving the island for the United States or entering the island from the United States.

Most migration studies on Puerto Ricans have not sufficiently looked at just who is returning to Puerto Rico. Many Puerto Ricans are not returning for purely economic reasons. Maldonado refers to a study that shows that as many as 70 percent of Puerto Ricans returning to the island cite personal reasons for doing so. Health reasons, familial problems, deaths in families, homesickness, and an inability to adapt to the violence that too often characterizes U.S. schools and life in general are often as important as the economic reasons in explaining a return migration. Some of these very reasons are given by people who return to Puerto Rico but later migrate again to the United States.

Some of the return migration is permanent, but much is migration out of desperation. Unemployment, personal stress, and other economic and noneconomic issues force Puerto Ricans to try to live in Puerto Rico again after having lived in the United States. Many such migrants will return to the United States for a second or third time, perhaps migrating to a different U.S. city the second or third time that they leave the island. Each time they expect better results than the previous attempt. School systems in Puerto Rico and the United States have continuously noted this pattern among some Puerto Rican families.[19] It is also true that some of those returning to Puerto Rico, like this author's parents, went home to retire and die in their beloved Borinquen. As previously mentioned, however, some of those going to the island are non-Puerto Rican Hispanics who prefer the Hispanic culture of Puerto Rico to the Anglo American culture in the United

States. Maldonado notes, for example, that in Puerto Rico the identified foreign-born population increased by 43,000 between 1960 and 1970.

Michael J. Piore also observes that noneconomic factors in the job market play a significant part in understanding Puerto Rican migration. His work on the dual-market theory focuses on the psychosocial nature of work as well as on the traditional economic variables.

Piore's work on the dual-market theory, in conjunction with the ethnic queuing process analyzed earlier, helps to elucidate why Puerto Ricans have been used to replace black workers. This theory clarifies the reasons for Puerto Rican entrapment in the lowest level of the U.S. ethnic strata. According to Piore, the dual-labor-market hypothesis was popularized in the 1960s in an effort to explain simultaneous labor shortages and high unemployment, as well as high job turnover rates among ghetto dwellers. Furthermore, the hypothesis addresses urban dissatisfaction, which tends to increase with greater educational attainment.[20] Eliminating poverty entails moving workers from the secondary to the primary labor market.

In further defining the characteristics of the dual markets, Piore emphasizes that the distinction between primary and secondary jobs cannot be ascribed merely to a lack of technological skill nor to specific enterprises. "A substantial portion of the work in the economy can be organized for either stable or unstable workers . . . through subcontracting, temporary help services, recycling of new employees through probationary periods and the like."[21] Primary and secondary employers may thus generate either secondary or primary jobs. At times, Puerto Ricans hold secondary-market jobs while employed by firms that offer most of their workers primary-market employment.

Most often, however, secondary jobs are found in such industries operating on a slim profit margin as "textiles, apparel and related products, cigar manufacturing, fertilizer manufacture, agriculture, and the retail and service trades."[22] These industries tend to be competitive and labor intensive. Demands for their commodities are quite elastic so that a small increase in price reduces the demand for the product. In order to stay in business, the firms in these industries depend on cheap labor. "The choice of workers in this industry is not low wages or higher wages, but low wages or no wages."[23] When firms in traditional secondary-market industries become highly unionized or mechanized and survive the transition, the workers often become members of the primary sector and second generation migrants compete for the jobs. At times, even small changes in industries, especially when there is high unemployment, will make jobs more attractive to natives. For example, as farming became more automated and minimum wages increased, Puerto Ricans were at times pushed out of farms and nurseries in favor of homemakers, part-time and summer high school students, and other natives who had difficulty finding part-time employment. Some jobs that initially are physically exhausting, considered demeaning, very low paying, and provide little, if any, benefits become less strenuous as a result of automation or the invention of some tool that facilitates the job. For instance, floor scrubbing and polishing machines replaced the scrub brush and mop. If the workers organize, demand and win more such machines, as well as greater pay and benefits, those jobs become more attractive to a wider range of potential workers. In this process, school janitors become custodians and garbage collectors become sanitation engineers. As such, the jobs move from the secondary labor market to the primary labor market, and whites often push people of color out of the positions.

Generally, however, marginal low-wage industries have become a failing economic breed. As wages in other manufacturing sectors increase to meet the high cost of living, the low-wage industries have been slow to follow suit.

> Rather than closing, the earnings gap between low-wage industries and most high-wage industries appears to be growing. Relative to the average worker in society, the working poor wage-earner is more poor today than he was 20 years ago, and although some workers in low-wage industries have escaped absolute poverty . . . their income position, relatively speaking, has deteriorated.[24]

Barry Bluestone notes in his article, "The Characteristics of Marginal Industries," that "[t]he working poor are being exploited by the economy as a whole rather than by the individual firms employing them."[25] He concludes that "precisely where the market approaches its theoretical best—in the firms furthest from monopoly and closest to laissez faire—the market cannot supply jobs adequate enough to feed a man's family satisfactorily."[26]

Moving from the secondary sector to the primary sector is not a common or easily accomplished occurrence. Piore observes that workers are often excluded from the primary sector through discrimination based on race, ethnicity, or sex, and statistical discrimination, a process that discriminates based on predetermined expectations for job performance.[27] Both forms of discrimination enlarge the captive force in the secondary sector, thereby lowering the wages for secondary workers.

An example of the low-wage worker's inability to move beyond that sphere of poverty can be seen in Robert Horn's careful documentation of marginal industries in Manchester, New Hampshire.[28] In his extensive interviews with management in the footwear industry, one personnel manager described his labor force as "the low end of the labor market."[29] On-the-job training was neither a requirement nor a possibility in the footwear factories. The management attitude toward training is a reflection of their feelings about upgrading low-level workers:

> [P]ersonnel directors indicated there were no formal job ladders for production workers . . . in their organizations . . . most workers were hired into entry level positions and were said to receive periodic pay increases . . . [but] remained at the job they were initially hired to perform. . . . The impression was given that "insiders" were simply not managerial or supervisory material. One company reported to have tried an in-house pre-supervisory training program, but found internal production to be ineffective: "Standards were below par." The company concluded that in order to maintain an acceptable rate of growth, hiring at mid-level positions and above must be done externally. In all cases, upper level positions were said to require academic training. Obviously, this tends to limit that range of opportunities available to production workers.[30]

It is no surprise that Horn documents the turnover rate "in excess of 100 percent per year in all firms visited."[31]

Piore points out that, indeed, the possibilities for upward mobility in the secondary sector are limited. In fact, continued employment in the low-wage jobs is a tenuous prospect, due to the economic nature of these marginal industries. He further concludes that employment in the secondary sector is compatible with public assistance and illegitimate activities, such as illegal gambling, and that workers move from one job to another as jobs become more or less rewarding.

Marginal-industry employers whom Piore interviewed do not necessarily condemn welfare and welfare benefits. Very often the employers felt that their workers wanted to work but had to be laid off. Because they can obtain welfare benefits, the workers see unemployment as less of a threat and this "welfare back-up system" is a major reason for the continued success of marginal industries in employing Puerto Ricans.

Second generation blacks and Puerto Ricans may prefer unemployment to demeaning, degrading, poorly paid, physically demanding, dead-end jobs that fail to offer even an illusion of mobility. This interpretation also begins to address the issue of high unemployment among the poor while employers complain about jobs going begging.

Jobs in the secondary market are often jobs that machines cannot yet do and that are "leftovers," unwanted by yesterday's white immigrants. Today's migrants often associate these jobs with the exploitation of their parents. Many of these menial, degrading, "service" positions will continue far into the foreseeable future. The European immigrants had done jobs of this nature. They had competed for this dirty work. However, they looked for advancement and encouraged their children to aspire to better work. In general, the European peasants moved on to jobs in the primary sector.

Traditionally, second generation immigrants have refused the dirty work of their parents. With the end of the European immigration, new first generations have been sought and found in the South and in Puerto Rico. Puerto Rican migrants, like their European counterparts, foresaw a better future for themselves and for their children. Unlike the Europeans, however, they were already U.S. citizens and were people of color.

In the liberal and hopeful 1960s, younger people of color, born and raised in New York and other northern cities, usually having more formal education than their black and Puerto Rican parents, refused to accept dirty work that could only offer poverty wages and the label of inferiority. Yet, these dirty, unpleasant tasks still needed to be done in hotels and restaurants, on farms, orchards, and nurseries.

Evidence indicates that the migration of blacks to northern cities has stopped.[32] After the militant 1960s, more and more second generation blacks may have ruled out secondary jobs as options. Piore suggests that Puerto Ricans in Massachusetts were the ethnic group that filled the vacuum.[33] For many first generation Puerto Ricans, such jobs were not ruled out since they offered employment or better pay than those held in Puerto Rico.

As we shall see in the next chapters, Puerto Ricans migrating to New England are still predominantly of the

first generation. They thus replace second generation
disgruntled workers, thereby offering another supply of
"dirty workers" for this portion of the liberal North.

First and second generation Puerto Ricans in New York
City are also leaving New York, looking for employment or
higher wage jobs in either of the labor markets. The 1980
census notes that the Puerto Rican population in New York
City, for the first time in its history, has stopped growing.
Are second generation Puerto Ricans going to the same
place as their first generation compatriots? Furthermore, if
Puerto Ricans are leaving, who is doing the dirty work in
the Statue of Liberty City?

NOTES

1. Robert N. Horn, "Labor Market Segmentation and
the Political Economy of Manpower and Job Creation Programs," (thesis, Whittemore School of Business and Economics, University of New Hampshire, 1978).

2. Ibid.

3. Ibid.

4. C. E. Rodriguez, "Economic Factors Affecting
Puerto Ricans in New York," in Centro Taller de Migracion,
Research Foundation of the City University of New York,
1975, p. 162.

5. New Bedford, MA, October 1977, interview.

6. Rita M. Maldonado, "Why Puerto Ricans Migrated to
the United States in 1947–73," Monthly Labor Review,
September, 1976.

7. Michael J. Piore, Birds of Passage (Cambridge, MA:
Cambridge University Press, 1979). Also see Michael J.
Piore, "The Dual Labor Market: Theory and Implications,"
in Problems in Political Economy, ed. David Gordon (Lexington, MA: D. C. Health & Company, 1971).

8. Maldonado, "Why Puerto Ricans Migrated."

9. Ibid., p. 7.

10. Ibid., p. 8.

11. The "contract" and the rules governing it will be
discussed in the following chapters.

12. Maldonado, "Why Puerto Ricans Migrated," p. 8.

13. See Chapter 7, especially interviews with various
persons from Orocovis, Puerto Rico.

14. Maldonado, "Why Puerto Ricans Migrated," p. 9.

15. Ibid., p. 11. See also City University of New York
History Task Force/Centro de Estudios Puertorriquenos,
Labor Migration Under Capitalism, 1979, p. 215–17.

16. Ibid., p. 8.

17.   Ibid., p. 16.

18.   U. S. Commission on Civil Rights, The Tarnished Door, Civil Rights Issues in Immigration (Washington, DC: Government Printing Office, September 1980), p. 11.

19.   U. S. Commission on Civil Rights, Puerto Ricans in the Continental United States, An Uncertain Future (Washington, DC: Government Printing Office, 1976), p. 97.   Nat Quinones, Chancellor of the Public School System of New York City, mentioned this mobility pattern in an interview (February 25, 1985).

20.   Michael Joseph Piore, "The Role of Immigration in Industrial Growth: A Case of Economics" (working paper, 112, Department of Economics, Massachusetts Institute of Technology, May 1973), pp. 1–2.

21.   Michael Joseph Piore, "The Dual Labor Market: Theory and Implications," in Problems in Political Economy, ed. David Gordon (Lexington: D. C. Heath and Company, 1971), p. 92.

22.   Barry Bluestone, "The Characteristics of Marginal Industries," in Problems in Political Economy, ed. David Gordon (Lexington: D. C. Heath and Company, 1971).

23.   Ibid., p. 105.

24.   Ibid., p. 102.

25.   Ibid., p. 103.

26.   Ibid., p. 107.

27.   Correlation of such workers' traits as color, race, test scores, accent, dress, age, and job performance are used to select workers.   Puerto Ricans may be confined to secondary jobs because they are stereotyped.   Often possible job applicants are very qualified for primary sector employment but excluded because they possess or do not possess specific traits.   This process has been identified as statistical discrimination.

28.   Horn, "Labor Market Segmentation."

29.   Ibid., p. 91.

30.   Ibid., p. 92–93.

31.   Ibid., p. 93.

32.   "Study Shows Black Migration to Cities Has Ended," Hartford Courant, December 1, 1978, p. 6.   According to this article, a new study from the U. S. Census Bureau shows that the trend of blacks moving into the large cities has ended.   "The number of black city residents has fallen by 275,000 since 1974 . . . blacks moving to suburbs accounted for 14% of the net increase in the overall suburban population attributable to migration . . . black migration to suburbs appeared to be accelerating . . ." the study said.

33.   Piore, Role of Immigration.   See also Piore, Birds

of Passage; and Centro de Estudios Puertorriqueños, Labor Migration Under Capitalism (New York: Research Foundation of the City University of New York, 1979).

5

The Migration of the Puerto Rican Agricultural Worker to New England

. . . and the men told me that they used to roll their clothing around their work boots and used these as pillows . . . and then there is the tragedy of a small farm that used four Puerto Rican migrant workers. The owner housed his horses on the first floor. One night the barn caught fire and everyone rushed out to rescue those horses. But, you know, nobody thought of rescuing the Puerto Ricans.

> Antonio Del Rios
> Framingham, Massachusetts
> Interview, June 20, 1977

The peasant who comes to the States to pick crops for other people's families while his own family is often hungry, and who, upon completion of his work, returns to the same cyclic conditions of poverty, is a most obvious victim of American infiltration in the island.

> Enid J. Cruz
> "The Puerto Rican Seasonal
> Farm Laborer: A Victim"

Between 1940 and 1974, Puerto Rico's agricultural labor force decreased by 78 percent.[1] Average employment on tobacco farms declined from 19,000 in 1950 to 10,000 in 1962. In the same 12-year period, the number of jobs in the production of sugar cane fell from 84,000 to 48,000. Employment on other farms, including pineapple, vegetable,

77

and dairy, also fell from 84,000 in 1959 to 54,000 in 1962.[2] The farm workers, however, were not absorbed by Puerto Rico's industrialization process. Operation Bootstrap, as explained in Chapter 2, did not provide sufficient unskilled work for the island's displaced farmers. The massive unemployment of Puerto Rican farmers provided a pool of secondary labor workers easily recruited to the eastern cities of the United States and to the farms of New England, as well.

Since 1948, the Commonwealth of Puerto Rico has negotiated contracts (agreements) between Massachusetts farmers, Puerto Rican agricultural workers, and the Department of Employment Services of the Commonwealth of Massachusetts, although Puerto Rican migrant workers had already been recruited to Massachusetts and elsewhere in New England before then. For example, Mr. D., a farmer in Massachusetts, reported that he started hiring Puerto Rican workers (without contracts) from Borinquen in 1943. In 1948, 4,906 Puerto Ricans were covered by official government agreements, and the number continued to increase. In 1968, 22,902 came to work in as many as 14 states. By 1973, the number of migrant farm workers coming to the United States from Puerto Rico under contract had decreased to slightly over 14,000,[3] while the number of noncontract workers, which has usually been three to four times greater than those with contracts, was "approximately 60,000, and some officials with the Commonwealth of Puerto Rico suspect that the figure may be as high as 200,000 (if the winter migrations to the Florida farms are counted)."[4] Many of these Puerto Rican noncontract workers had previously worked on farms and preferred to have the option of leaving them if other employment opportunities became available.

Mr. B., an administrator for the Farm Placement Division of the Department of Employment Services (DES), suspects that the first migrations of Puerto Ricans to Massachusetts were into the Connecticut River Valley for work on tobacco farms. First brought into the Hartford, Connecticut, area, the use of these workers spread up the Connecticut River Valley into Massachusetts.[5]

In discussing the history of the migration of Puerto Ricans into Massachusetts and the use of contract labor in the state, Mr. B. feels that migrants from Puerto Rico were brought in during the 1940s to fill the needs created by the war. At that time, farmers were given permission to recruit workers from the island if they could prove to the DES and the attorney general that they could not find domestic labor even after extensive advertising. The actual recruitment was carried out by the Department of Labor in Puerto Rico, which negotiated and enforced the contract in conjunction with DES and the farmers.[6] Puerto Rican workers were an available, experienced, inexpensive, interstate labor force in contrast to foreign labor pools that required visas and alien registrations.

Annual DES reports, dating from the early 1950s, stress the intent to aid the farmers in their search for workers. The expansion of the better-paying industrial sector had created severe labor shortages in the agricultural industry. The DES recruitment offices were established throughout Massachusetts to attract farm workers. In 1951, 909 Puerto Rican farm workers were recruited to Massachusetts from the island or New York City through the formal arrangement of DES and the Department of Labor in Puerto Rico.[7]

Throughout this decade of increasing industrial expansion, Puerto Rican workers were sought to meet the labor needs of the state's farms. The controversy over hiring island versus hiring New York Puerto Ricans pervades the DES reports of this era. Farmers deemed New York's Puerto Ricans as "unreliable, with a constant turnover rate."[8] The 1953 report ends with this statement: "Many farm employers who used Puerto Ricans from New York during 1953 have expressed a desire to change over to those directly from the Island."[9] That New York's Puerto Ricans were not as compliant as Islanders supports certain aspects of the dual-labor-market theory. The more sophisticated New York Puerto Ricans rejected as demeaning and "dead-end" the migrant farm labor that more recent migrants readily accepted. New Yorkers were more likely to leave a Massachusetts farm for a better paying job in the burgeoning factories, although they might initially accept farm work until they could secure such employment.

Many of the reports of the 1960s mention the competition between farmers and local industry, restaurants, and hotels for Puerto Rican labor. The greater availability of such work and the growth of Puerto Rican communities accounts for the increasing number of noncontract workers, an issue highlighted in this decade's DES reports. The larger numbers of noncontract workers may have been a result of Puerto Ricans, from both the island and nearby communities, wanting the opportunity to leave the farms if factory and other unskilled employment became available. Some may initially have come as contract workers but then became attracted to noncontract arrangements as they became more familiar with other avenues of employment.

The direct recruitment of Puerto Ricans by the farmers

visiting the island also led to an increase in the number of noncontract workers. Enid Cruz writes: "Don J. knew very well that the success of his farm depended very heavily upon the seasonal labor of these men. In fact, in December of 1971 he went to visit Serafin in Arroyo, Puerto Rico. Although this visit was allegedly social, I am sure that his motivation was to assure that the men come again to work for him."[10]

The Immigration and Naturalization Act (Bracero Act) of 1964, restricting the use of foreign nationals for temporary farm work gave further impetus to the flow of Puerto Ricans from the island to various towns in Massachusetts. The number of Puerto Rican contract workers jumped dramatically from 1964 to 1965.[11] Many Puerto Rican communities started taking hold in towns near sizeable agricultural areas during the 1960s. Coming first to work on the farms, the island men and women moved on to better working conditions. Enid Cruz, in her detailed analysis of migrant life, emphasizes the "dirty work" that Puerto Rican farm workers endured and sought to leave: "Picking tomatoes is back-breaking work. In order to make decent wages one has to be fast, consistent and physically strong. The sun beats down on your head, the tomatoes stink of worms and rot, and the mosquitoes swarm around your head, arms, and back."[12] Interestingly enough, she observes the competition which was encouraged among the men:

> The men constantly compete with each other. The system allegedly has devised a plan to encourage competition in the following manner: the morning count of bushels is left in the van where all have public access to it—therefore they seek out how much each other picked that morning. In the late afternoon, the count is brought to the camp and posted in the kitchen where all seek it out immediately. Also posted above the refrigerator is the weekly record of each man's wages. These public records act as competition orientators for the men, as they are constantly aware of the earnings of each other . . . they push each other to work.[13]

Given the long hours, low wages, humiliating work inducements, and at times unbearable conditions, who would not look for an opportunity to go elsewhere if this were possible?

The beginning of the 1970s marked a reduction in farm acreage, as well as an increase in mechanization, thus signaling a decline in DES recruitment efforts.

In terms of Puerto Rican agricultural workers, the DES reports, as a whole, provide the following:

- Specifics on the number of Puerto Rican workers brought to Massachusetts and the Northeast from Puerto Rico, as well as from New York City;
- A sense of the effects of weather, strikes, economic and employment trends, and mechanization on the use of migrant labor. Fluctuations in the use of Puerto Rican contract workers is explained by: mechanical development, the availability of higher paying industrial jobs, reduced acreages, airline strikes, delays in negotiating work agreements between farmers and the Puerto Rican Department of Labor, weather (hurricanes, droughts), improvements in recruiting local labor (such as using day haul programs for youths, V.A. patients, servicemen, and the unemployed), the growth and development of industries and housing developments in previously "rural" areas, and laws affecting the use of foreigners.
- The slow growth of benefits and protection for contract workers;
- Some evidence that migrant workers did, in fact, stay in the Northeast as more "permanent" residents. It was often mentioned in some of the reports that "skips"[14] seemed to be related to industrial job opportunities. Reports state that, in fact, some Puerto Rican farm workers did shift to industrial and service jobs, that some of the workers did stay locally, and that these trends were increasing.

What is clear from the reports is that there was a tremendous influx of Puerto Rican workers to the Northeast from 1950–70 and that the high number of walk-ins and noncontract workers throughout meant that many stayed and began a flexible migratory process that was responsive to economic opportunities. The reports document that, at least initially, approximately 25 percent of the Puerto Rican contract workers were from New York. It is particularly noteworthy that the number of noncontract workers, both from the island and New York, remained very high in spite of the substantially higher benefits and wages earned by contract laborers. Contract workers were required, however, to stay for extended periods due to the financial penalties that resulted from broken contracts. Walk-ins were another indication that many of these individuals were already living in areas adjacent to the farming operations. The high return rate to visit relatives and home is not surprising after a grueling work period, but it certainly does not preclude return trips to take advantage of economic opportunities opening up in the Northeast.

Table 5.1 shows the numbers of various categories of Puerto Rican migrant workers from Puerto Rico and New York City known to the DES. These statistics were extrapolated from the annual reports and attempt to break down the numbers of contract, noncontract, and walk-in Puerto Rican workers used by farmers from 1951 to 1971. Unfortunately, the statistics are not complete. They do not reflect the number of Puerto Ricans who were recruited from places other than New York City or the island. For example, hundreds of Puerto Rican workers were recruited from Connecticut, New Jersey, Pennsylvania, or Massachusetts itself.

On June 20, 1977, Mr. Antonio Del Rio, the first person to serve as director of the Massachusetts Migration Division Office of the Commonwealth of Puerto Rico, was interviewed in response to a request that he discuss the Puerto Rican migration into Massachusetts. Mr. Del Rio began by tracing the history of his own career as a representative of the Farm Division of DES and as the head of the Massachusetts Migration Division Office of the Commonwealth of Puerto Rico. He confirmed that, even before 1948, farmers from Massachusetts and other New England states had brought Puerto Rican migrant workers to the United States through DES. Specifically, DES had arranged and assisted in the contracting between the farmers and the Puerto Rican Department of Labor. "Apparently," Mr. Rios stated, "the migration began after farmers, facing severe labor shortages following the war, placed sufficient pressure on DES to initiate the recruitment and transportation of Puerto Rican farm workers." Table 5.2 gives us an idea of the number of Puerto Rican men brought to the United States.

In 1954, Mr. Del Rio was hired by DES in Massachusetts as an interpreter for the farm program. He became the main link between the Puerto Rican workers, DES, and the farmers. Mr. Del Rio served as an ally and advocate of the Puerto Rican workers in seeking to improve such working and living conditions as housing, health, and safety. Mr. Del Rio approximated that 1,800 Puerto Rican farm workers were recruited to Massachusetts (22,500 in New England as a whole) in 1954.

In 1956, Mr. Del Rio was hired by the Commonwealth of Puerto Rico to establish a migration division office in Massachusetts. The New York office was founded in 1948. As at DES, Del Rio was responsible for overseeing farm

TABLE 5.1   Number of Puerto Rican Workers: 1951-71

	1951	1952	1953	1954	1955	1956	1957
Contract							
from island	568	819	1,403	583	569	755	831
from New York	28	100		284	340	244	174
Noncontract							
from island			195	466	507	598	696
from New York			543				
walk-ins			175	220		519	212
TOTALS	596	919	2,316	1,553	1,416	2,116	1,913

	1958	1959	1960	1961	1962	1963	1964
Contract							
from island	518	652	1,261	1,237	1,097	983	969
from New York	80	24	37		23		
Noncontract							
from island	1,018	728	685		627	684	589
from New York							
walk-ins		616	378		55	1,030	750
TOTALS	1,616	2,020	2,361	1,237	1,802	2,697	2,308

	1965	1966	1967	1968	1969	1970	1971
Contract							
from island	1,446	1,890	1,655	1,913	2,028	2,173	1,302
from New York							
Noncontract							
from island	651	571	465	485	438	300	421
from New York		221					
walk-ins	228						
TOTALS	2,325	2,682	2,120	2,398	2,466	2,473	1,723

Source: Department of Employment Services, Annual Agricultural and Food Processing Reports, Boston: Department of Employment Services, years 1951-1971.

83

TABLE 5.2 Total Number of Puerto Rican Agricultural Workers Referred to U.S. Mainland: 1948-73

Year	Number	Year	Number
1948	4,906	1961	13,765
1949	4,598	1962	13,526
1950	7,602	1963	13,116
1951	11,747	1964	14,628
1952	12,277	1965	17,385
1953	14,930	1966	19,537
1954	10,637	1967	21,654
1955	10,876	1968	22,902
1956	14,969	1969	21,864
1957	13,214	1970	18,884
1958	13,067	1971	14,119
1959	10,012	1972	11,900
1960	12,986	1973	14,641

Source: National Migrant and Information Clearinghouse, Migrant Programs in the Northeastern States, Austin, TX: Juarez Lincoln Center, 1974, p. 198.

labor contractors and conditions; the difference was that he was now able to negotiate with farmers and DES as the representative of the Commonwealth of Puerto Rico. In addition to providing a program of support for the farm workers, Mr. Del Rio and the Migration Division were concerned with the problems of adjustment encountered by Puerto Rican communities developing in Massachusetts. Mr. Del Rio's involvement in these communities was apparent in his numerous accounts of the difficulties faced by newly arriving Puerto Ricans and his response to those problems. He described educational barriers, such as Puerto Rican students being labeled "culturally deprived" by school systems that made no meaningful effort to provide relevant, helpful services, and the economic struggles of Puerto Ricans seeking work, yet having to compete with other low income groups for the available jobs. As a representative of the Puerto Rican government, Mr. Del Rio often served as a spokesperson for Puerto Rican communities in attempting to mediate discrimination disputes in towns and cities where the influx of Puerto Rican workers threatened the economic base of other groups in the community. He actively sought housing, jobs, and educational programs for

Puerto Rican communities and individuals. An important
function of the Puerto Rican Office of Migration was the
development and organization of community centers that
provided meeting places for the social and cultural events
that fostered greater cohesiveness within the nascent Puerto
Rican communities.

According to Mr. Del Rio, the Catholic Church was a
major ally of the Puerto Rican communities in these endeav-
ors. In addition to providing many of the buildings that
housed the community centers, it also assigned Spanish-
speaking priests to the Puerto Rican neighborhoods.
Perhaps the best known collaboration between the Puerto
Rican Commonwealth Office and the Catholic Church was the
founding of the Cardinal Cushing Hispanic Center in the
south end of Boston.

The breadth of the activities of the Migration Division
is evident in the categories of services listed in their
annual reports to the Puerto Rican government. The
categories are (1) farm programs; (2) social services; (3)
employment; (4) education; (5) community organization; and
(6) documentation.

The year 1959 is significant, according to Mr. Del Rio,
because it marks success in obtaining a comprehensive
health insurance plan as well as other benefits for the farm
workers, which increased through the years. These benefits included higher wages, workmen's compensation, and
better working conditions. The need for such protection
was tragically illustrated by several fatal accidents involving migrant workers during the 1950s. The efforts for
insurance benefits were further strengthened by the establishment of a migrants' committee in the Massachusetts
Office of the Governor. The collaboration between the
Governor's Office, the Puerto Rican Migration Division
Office, and the Catholic Church increased awareness about
the plight of the migrant workers over the years and
helped bring about the upgrading of contract stipulations
by the Commonwealth of Puerto Rico.

Mr. Del Rio stated that, in his experience, the majority
of Puerto Ricans came to the United States seeking a better
life for which they were willing to work very hard. While
Mr. Del Rio felt that some might have migrated to take
advantage of welfare benefits, they clearly were in the
minority. He praised the high quality of Puerto Rican labor
in both factory and farm work as well as the perseverance
of the workers in making sacrifices to find better opportunities for their families and for themselves.

According to Mr. Del Rio, many of the migrant farm
workers did in fact stay on in surrounding towns to work if

jobs were available. He gave several examples of towns in which migrant farm workers took over local factory jobs and of his role in helping to alleviate some of the resultant local resistance. For instance, his experience in Framingham, Massachusetts, was that the first Puerto Rican migrants were farm workers who subsequently found housing and other jobs.

Once these migrants had been able to secure employment and housing, they sent for their families. Mr. Del Rio describes this as a gradual process that occurred over several years and involved various trips between the island and New England. Mobility reinforced the pull of the United States; workers returning to the island were faced with the reality that they could earn a substantially higher income for comparable, or perhaps less, work in New England.

According to Mr. Del Rio, even in the larger metropolitan cities such as Boston, Springfield, and Hartford, the first Puerto Rican residents came as migrant farm workers, (in Springfield-Hartford into the tobacco farms). He gave examples of many leading Puerto Rican citizens in Boston and Framingham who first came to the mainland as migrant farm workers.

Mr. Del Rio added that some of the migration into Massachusetts was from the Puerto Rican communities of larger metropolitan areas such as Hartford and New York City. He cited the problems of urban decay, particularly in New York, and the search for better job opportunities as the impetus behind these migrations. He noted that this group has several advantages over other Puerto Rican migrants in obtaining jobs, such as better language skills, "know how," and assertiveness.

Jobs in the agricultural sector were seen as desirable by the older Puerto Ricans. However, as the farms became more automated, as wages rose, and as more local labor replaced the older men, fewer Puerto Ricans were hired. Puerto Rican migrants, still needing employment in the United States and seeing the possibility of factory work in Massachusetts' older cities, began moving to such cities as Waltham, Massachusetts. In essence, Puerto Ricans initially began leaving farms as they were lured by manufacturing jobs in the decaying cities near the farms. Later, they continued going to those cities because the farms stopped recruiting Puerto Ricans in large numbers, preferring to hire local teenagers or homemakers. In both cases, having the nucleus of a Puerto Rican community in New England's older cities facilitates Puerto Rican migration to various elsewheres in New England.

Like others, Del Rio noted the drastic reduction in the use of Puerto Rican contract workers by Massachusetts farmers. He attributed this decline to the following factors:

- Increased benefits and wages mandated for the farm workers had made the costs of hiring, transporting, and housing migrant workers higher than in the past. For this reason, farmers preferred using local laborers part time. Wages for farm labor had risen to the point that farmers could attract a sufficient labor pool from local communities.

- Many farmers felt that the lack of quality and intractability of the Puerto Rican workers (that is, problems with no shows, contract violations, poor performance) did not justify the expense and complications of bringing them to the United States. Mr. Del Rio attributed this intractability and lack of "quality" to diminished enthusiasm and dedication on the part of the younger workers, many of whom are high school educated and have had little farming experience or training. In contrast, he noted, the older, less formally educated, more experienced farm workers who were first brought into Massachusetts and the New England area were excellent workers and greatly valued by their employers.

- The young Puerto Ricans were being wooed by factory work. This account correlates with previous discussions: Older and younger generation migrants have different views of the jobs and the economic structure. Older workers see the available jobs as a profitable opportunity to better their standard of living. Younger workers perceive those same jobs as undesirable positions with no future. They accurately perceive that the available "secondary" jobs are at the bottom of the socioeconomic ladder and are unattractive, occupational cul-de-sacs. Younger Puerto Rican workers share the same goals as the rest of the society in which they live.

Low income Puerto Rican workers are in economic limbo. Even those wanting to return to Borinquen find no work on the island. Its agrarian economic structure has been dismantled and replaced by an industrial system, which is even less able than the economy of the United States to provide dependable, meaningful jobs for the Puerto Rican poor. Secondary-labor-market jobs on the island are of the same menial quality that exists on the mainland, but they pay less and are highly vulnerable to macroeconomic forces from outside the island. (For example, Puerto Rico was particularly hard hit during the recession of the 1970s.) In addition, many of the younger workers have been trained and educated for jobs that rarely exist either on the island or on the mainland. As the next chapters note, they have too much education for farm work. However, they may not have enough technical training for non-labor-intensive, highly automated jobs. When they do have such skills, they have difficulties competing with the sons and daughters of past immigrants. More and more second generation Puerto Ricans are coming to understand that they face fierce competition in occupations where mobility may be possible. In the case of the Puerto Rican, such competition is often with other minority group members. In New York, the scramble is primarily with blacks. In New England, Puerto Ricans are likely to compete with other Hispanics, as well.

NOTES

1. Felipe Rivera, "The Puerto Rican Farmer Worker," Unit 4 in Centro Taller de Migración, April, 1974, p. 12. Centro de Estudios Puertorriqueños, City University of New York.
2. Frank Zorilla, Secretary of Labor for the Commonwealth of Puerto Rico, in an address before the Eleventh Social Welfare Workshop sponsored by the School of Social Work of the University of Puerto Rico and the Migration Division of the Department of Labor of the Commonwealth of Puerto Rico. It was held on June 17, 1963, at the Normandie Hotel, San Juan, Puerto Rico. (Mimeo.)
3. National Migrant and Information Clearinghouse Migrant Programs in the Northeastern States (Austin, TX: Juarez Lincoln Center, 1974), p. 198.
4. Rivera, "Puerto Rican Farm Worker," p. 10.
5. Note that Zorilla, in the address listed in note 2, stated that from 1950 to 1962 employment in Puerto Rican tobacco farms declined by 9,000 jobs. I surmise that many of those jobless farmers on the island accepted jobs in New England fields.
6. See Enid J. Cruz, "The Puerto Rican Seasonal Farm Laborer: A Victim," Revista (Brooklyn College: Instituto de Estudios Puertorriqueños, Autumn 1972), p. 73.
7. Department of Employment Services, Annual Agricultural and Food Processing Report, 1951 (Boston: MA:

Department of Employment Services), p. 24.

8. Department of Employment Services, Annual Agricultural and Food Processing Report, 1953 (Boston, MA: Department of Employment Services), p. 8.

9. Ibid., p. 11.

10. Cruz, "Seasonal Farm Laborer," p. 74.

11. In 1964, 14,628 Puerto Rican agricultural workers were brought to the United States. In 1965, the number jumped to 17,385 and continued to increase steadily until 1969. After 1970, there was a decline in the number of contract workers. National Migrant and Information Clearinghouse, Migrant Programs.

12. Cruz, "Seasonal Farm Laborer," p. 73.

13. Ibid., p. 75.

14. The word "skips" is used to describe people who agree to the terms of the contract but break it by "disappearing" at the airport after they have obtained air transportation to the United States or by leaving the farms without completing the time that had been agreed to. The number of skips has usually been very small. However, when farmers have a great deal of competition for secondary workers, the number of skips tends to reflect such competition.

6

Waltham, Massachusetts: A Specific Elsewhere

DIALOGANDO CON "SUNCHA" SOBRE EL AYER

Con el propósito de saber quienes fueron las primeras familias en establecerse en Waltham, decidimos hacerle una entrevista a la Sra. Asunción Aviles, quien ha sido una de las primeras residentes Hispanas de Waltham. Muy atenta y cariñosa, como siempre, nos atendió Doña Suncha al enterarse de la razón de nuestra visita.

Luego de prender el abaníco en la sala ya que la temperatura estaba en los 90 grados, procedimos a preguntarle:

PREGUNTA:¿Bueno Suncha (como todo el mundo cariñosamenta la conoce)

SPEAKING WITH "SUNCHA" ABOUT YESTERDAY

Wanting to know about the first Hispanic families to settle in Waltham, we decided to interview Mrs. Asunción Aviles, who had been one of the first Hispanic residents of Waltham. Gracious and affectionate as always, Doña Suncha greeted and agreed to speak with us.

After she turned on the electric fan in her living room, since it was one of those 90 degree days, we proceeded to ask:

QUESTION: Doña Suncha, (as she is affectionately known to everyone), how

cuánto hace que resides en Waltham?

SUNCHA: Hace 17 años.

PREGUNTA: ¿Que te motivó a venir a vivir a Waltham?

SUNCHA: Resulta que el primo de mi esposo que trabajaba en la finca de tomates en Lexington le consiguió un trabajo con él. Entonces decidió cojer la oportunidad ya que la situación para aquélla época en la Isla de Puerto Rico estaba mala. A los 10 meses de haberse establecído me mandó a buscar y nos mudámos a Waltham.

PREGUNTA: ¿Cuántos puertorriqueños habián en Waltham en aquél tiempo?

SUNCHA: Que nos conocier-amos - solo cuatro familias. Estaba Paco Alicea, Marcelino Avilés, (primos de mi esposo), Cristóbal Picón, y Antonio Santiago. Las 5 familias éramos bien unidas y nos ayudábamos los unos a los otros como podíamos. Mas tarde mi esposo buscando mejor ambiente empezó a trabajar en una fábrica de metal y lleva ahí casi 18 años. Para ese entonces ganaba $1.25/la hora.

PREGUNTA: ¿Para que ano

long have you lived in Waltham?

SUNCHA: It's been 17 years.

QUESTION: What motivated you to come to live in Waltham?

SUNCHA: Well, it turns out that my husband's cousin who worked on a tomato farm in Lexington got a job for my husband in the same place. My husband decided to take the opportunity since at that time the working situation in Puerto Rico was bad. Ten months after my husband was established he sent for me and we moved to Waltham.

QUESTION: How many Puerto Ricans were in Waltham at that time?

SUNCHA: That knew each other?—Only four families. There was Paco Alicea, Marcelino Aviles (my husband's cousins), Cristóbal Picón, and Antonio Santiago. The five families were very close and we helped each other as best as we could. Later my husband, searching for something better, began working in a metal factory and he's been there almost 18 years. He was then paid $1.25 an hour.

QUESTION: At about what

más o menos crees que
empezó a crecer la
comunidad Hispana.

year, more or less, do
you think the Hispanic
community began to grow?

SUNCHA: Yo diría que para
despues del "60" cuando
muchos de los vecinos y
familiares del barrio
donde vivíamos en
Orocovis vinieron. Yo
tuve en mi casa viviendo
a un promedio de 100
personas. Me acuerdo
haber abierto la puerta
a las 11:00 P.M. y a
las 2:00 de la mañana
a gente llegando de
Puerto Rico con sus
maletas. Le llamabamos
el "Hogar del Nino."

SUNCHA: I would say that
it would be after 1960
when many of the neighbors
and their families
from the town where we
lived in Orocovis came.
I had approximately
100 persons living off
and on with us. I
remember opening the
door at 11:00 P.M. and
at 2:00 A.M. in the
morning to people who
were arriving, with
their suitcases, from
Puerto Rico. We used
to call our home
"House of the Children."

PREGUNTA: ¿Cual crees
tu fue la razón
principal para que
tantos Puertorriqueños
empezaran a emigrar
a Waltham?

QUESTION: What would you
say was the main reason
for so many Puerto
Ricans migrating
to Waltham?

SUNCHA: Yo diría que
buscando un mejor
ambiente. Para
aquel tiempo se
conseguía trabajo
fácil en las fábricas
y en los pastos. Y
cada uno nos ayudamos
unos a los otros.

SUNCHA: I would say their
search for a better
ambiance. At that time
(60's) one could rather
easily obtain work in
the factories or in
the farms. And we
would all help one
another.

PREGUNTA: ¿Cuantas
personas Hispanas
estimas que hay
actualmente?

QUESTION: How many
Hispanic persons would
you estimate presently
reside in Waltham?

SUNCHA: Alrededor de
2,000 o más personas.
Antes conocía a todo

SUNCHA: Around 2,000
or more. I used to
know everybody, but now

el mundo, pero ahora	I see many new faces
veo muchas caras	that I do not recognize
nuevas que no conózco	even though I know
aunque sé que son	they are Hispanics.
Hispanos.	

From El Coqui, community newspaper of El Programa Roberto Clemente (Waltham's Hispanic Agency), July, 1975.

The January 15 and 16, 1978, issues of the Boston Evening Globe carried a rather lengthy two-part series entitled: "Lure of Jobs Attract Puerto Ricans to the United States." The article's author, Anne L. Kirchheimer, noted that:

It's usually the well-employed Americans—those with money to spend in casinos, in poolside lounge chairs and rented cars who vacation in Puerto Rico. But it's the unemployed Puerto Ricans, unable to support their families, who leave the sun-drenched Caribbean island for the U.S. mainland in hopes of a job. . . .

Today, Massachusetts and Puerto Rico are intertwined as the state's Hispanic population of between 175,000 and 250,000 which is predominantly Puerto Rican, continues to grow. . . .

In fact, what happens in Puerto Rico—its unemployment rate, its cost of living, its rate of population growth and whether it becomes this nation's 51st state, an independent island or holds onto its commonwealth status—should, some authorities say, be a major concern to Massachusetts residents and planners.[1]

Kirchheimer claims that Puerto Ricans will often take any job, and quotes a Puerto Rican (Hector) who left the island for lack of employment there. He came to work on a tobacco farm,

believing that the trip would be temporary. . . . Hector was never able to afford to move back to the Island. In 1970 he was finally able to bring his wife and six children to Springfield . . . they eke out a living on Hector's $106 weekly take home wage when he has work, or $503 monthly welfare

> supplements (when he doesn't). For Hector, like
> so many other Puerto Ricans, the income difference
> between wages and welfare is negligible.[2]

Hector seems to have followed the pattern presented earlier
for the Massachusetts Puerto Rican population. He came
from the rural section of the island, worked initially on
farms in New England, and then moved to factory work
when he could find it. Later he sent for his loved ones.
The pattern holds true for several of the families I spoke
with in Waltham.

In an attempt to get at least one farmer's perspective
on this migration pattern, I interviewed Mr. D., a Waltham
farm owner.

INTERVIEW WITH MR. D.:
WALTHAM, MASSACHUSETTS

Mr. D. runs a medium-size roadside retail farm in Waltham
(Middlesex County), which sells vegetables, flowers,
plants, and trees. It is a nursery as well as a farming
operation. Planting in the nursery takes place as early as
February with a June to October harvest; farming vegetables begins in late April and lasts until November. The
produce is harvested between June and October. Mr. D.
used to employ from two to ten Puerto Rican workers at
various times of the year; two to farm during early and late
months and up to ten during harvesting. While Mr. D. told
me he had always had "good luck" with his Puerto Rican
workers, he also said it was best for him to hire dependable workers and keep them on full time. That Mr. D. is
able to accomplish this to some degree today is evidence of
the growth and diversification of his operation. Two of
these permanent employees are Puerto Rican workers who
along with their families have stayed on the farm over many
years, with Mr. D. providing housing and a trip to Puerto
Rico annually. Mr. D. told me his aim was to find dependable workers and then bypass contract arrangements by
hiring them directly either by mail, messenger, or in
person.

When asked how he became involved in hiring Puerto
Rican workers, Mr. D. responded that his involvement, as
well as that of other farmers in the area, began in the late
1940s. In that decade, Puerto Rican workers were brought
in to replace Jamaicans and Bahamians who had been working on the farms (via contracts) since the end of the war.
According to Mr. D., during the war, farms were worked

by prisoners of war. Prior to that, there had been a scarcity of people willing and able to do farm work, which was seasonal and offered little security. This situation led to the use of migrant labor, starting with war prisoners and Caribbean peoples. Mr. D. said that Puerto Ricans were recruited during the late 1940s because their citizen status made it easier to transport them than other groups and because employers were offered the encouragement and assistance of the Department of Employment Services in setting up contracts. The agricultural background of Puerto Rican migrants was a further advantage. Mr. D.'s farm has been using Puerto Rican laborers for 30 years, the peak years occurring between 1958–61.

At the beginning, Mr. D. used contract labor but soon switched to using noncontract labor by negotiating with "effective" workers directly. Up until 1964, these workers were housed in barracks on the farm. Since then, they have commuted from Boston or Waltham itself—a development Mr. D. attributes to the growth of the Hispanic communities in the Boston area. In recent years, the number of Puerto Rican workers from the island on Mr. D.'s farm has been reduced by the hiring of permanent workers, by the use of such modern farming methods as herbicides, weed cutters, and seeders, as well as the availability of Puerto Rican workers who settled in Waltham or nearby. The increased cost, due to regulatory standards for housing, health, and transportation, has also contributed to this trend. In response to a question about whether any of his workers might have settled in Waltham or been responsible for the Puerto Rican migration there, Mr. D. replied that he could only remember five individuals who had worked for him and were now living in town. He said he couldn't be sure that more of his workers had not migrated to Waltham but felt it was unlikely, emphasizing that his workers were seasonal and rarely lasted in Massachusetts more than six months (four to five months normally) due to homesickness for their families and Puerto Rico. Of course, he could not rule out the possibility that the workers would later return to Waltham with their families.

Mr. D. was unable to provide any specifics about other farms in the area that might have contributed to the growth of Waltham's Puerto Rican community. All he could say was that the other farms hired fewer workers than his (averaging three), and that the W Farms in Lexington had two to four workers who were permanent residents on the farm.[3] Most of the migrant workers on Mr. D.'s farm came from the same area of Puerto Rico, and many were related or had been friends and neighbors in Puerto Rico.

Mr. D. noted that the workers related well with main-
landers and that trouble, if any, arose between the Puerto
Rican workers themselves. However, he told us there
wasn't much interaction between his workers and the people
in Waltham and the surrounding environs. He again
stressed that in his experience the workers related
primarily to communities in Boston. He talked about the
older, reliable workers he had and said that they saved
their money for "their plans" in Puerto Rico and partici-
pated little in the community life of the area. The plans
often included buying property on the island and being able
to take better care of the financial needs of other family
members. Mr. D. also described his difficulties with
younger workers, many of whom had drinking problems and
were not good workers. It seemed that for Mr. D. the
viability of using "seasonal laborers" from Puerto Rico (as
he repeatedly emphasized, saying that his workers were not
"migrant") no longer made economic sense. However, it
was apparent that Mr. D. had profited substantially over
the years from an inexpensive Puerto Rican labor force.

Mr. D. does not entirely reject the possibilities of his
workers, or those of other farmers, settling down in
Waltham. He remembers the 1940s and early 1950s as a time
when workers went back to Puerto Rico. In that decade,
most migrant workers did just that. They were older
farmers who often worked during the farming season in
Puerto Rico and then migrated to the farms of the Northeast
to work at planting and/or harvesting there. As many
crops were harvested in New England, the growing cycle
began in Puerto Rico and vice versa. It was not until
later, as agriculture continued to decline on the island,
that some Puerto Ricans began to consider remaining in the
United States, often in cities near the farms that had
offered them seasonal employment. From discussions with
long-term Puerto Rican residents of Waltham, it appears as
though the initial "founding families," perhaps five of them
according to Doña Suncha, came to live in Waltham in the
mid- or late 1950s.[4] Suncha suggests that the men had
originally come to work on nearby farms, orchards, nurseries, or greenhouses. They were later lured into such
factories as the Tenneco factory. Some men moved into
rooming houses or in with relatives at first and later into
small apartments. They were joined by their immediate
families initially and then by friends and neighbors from
Orocovis or elsewhere in Borinquen.

The process of migration is a gradual back and forth
pattern of traveling to the new land for work and then
returning to the homeland as soon as possible. After a few

years, it becomes easier for the worker to stay on in the community for longer periods of time due not only to a familiarity with the area, but also to the growth of the local Hispanic community and the arrival of other family members. Michael Piore suggests that more permanent settlement is often by default; it simply becomes easier to stay.

For example (all names changed), Angel Luis had a Puerto Rican friend who worked on one of the small farms in Waltham, Massachusetts. Angel received a letter from his friend, Paquito, informing him of available work on that farm. So, he came in 1964, worked for a couple of weeks, and quit. He then went to work for Tenneco, a plastic-producing factory whose workers, by 1975, were mostly Puerto Rican. Tenneco, Angel states, was once called Lucien Plastics and was located in Waltham before moving to Newton. Angel sent for his wife and children. His sister, Ana, joined them in 1966. Her boyfriend, Carlos, followed. Ana and Carlos were married in 1967. In 1968, Carlos' two brothers, Jacinto and Israel, came to live with Ana and Carlos. Israel got a job as a custodian in a hospital in Wellesley. He hated that job and went to work in a factory before being hired by Raytheon (in Waltham), where he started as a custodian but later got a job inspecting parts. In 1969, Israel sent for his wife and two children. He now has four more children.

Mr. Mateo came in 1969 to work on a farm in Lexington. He went home to Orocovis, Puerto Rico, after the season ended but came back the following year. He met some Puerto Rican people in Waltham and that year did not return to the island. Instead, he found a job in Chesterbrook Restaurant as a kitchen aide. "Lots of Puerto Ricans worked there—dishwashers, table cleaners, and cooking aides—you know." Mateo has not gone back to that farm or to the island.

Don Pepe was living in Florida in 1971 when his brother-in-law from Waltham wrote to him. Pepe worked on a farm where he picked vegetables and fruits. He hated it, so he came to Waltham to join his sister and brother-in-law. He and his wife had good skills in farm work, but "every year it was harder to work so much for so little." Pepe and Lucy had four children when Pepe became very sick in 1973 and stopped working. Now he and his family are welfare recipients.

Doña Suncha, in an interview for El Coqui, a 1975 community newsletter for Waltham's Spanish-speaking community, stated that she had come to live in Waltham in 1958, ten months after her husband's cousin found a job for him on a tomato farm in Lexington. When she moved into the small four-room apartment her husband had acquired in Waltham, there were only four Puerto Rican families in town. They were all very close and helped each other a great deal. Later her husband got a job in a metal factory at 1.25 dollars an hour. According to Doña Suncha, after 1960 many of her friends and neighbors from Orocovis, Puerto Rico, came to Waltham. She claims to have sheltered more than 100 persons from the island. At times, "people just arrived at 2:00 A.M. with their suitcases and their kids." All of them were looking for a better environment. "At that time, one could get work real easy—in the factories or on the farms . . . and then we all helped each other."[5]

Today many families can trace their roots in Waltham to someone working on the neighboring farms even though few have actually worked on the farms themselves.

Throughout the last few chapters, I have noted a pattern I feel exists in Puerto Rican migration to New England. Initially recruited as migrant farm workers, Puerto Ricans were pulled into core industrial cities in an effort to escape the farms and find year-round employment. Such migration was made possible by the availability of "inexpensive" rental units, low-skill jobs in menial service positions, and marginal industries that had remained or relocated in these core cities.

Chapter 5 also documents, through the Department of Employment Services (DES) annual reports, manufacturers' recruitment of Puerto Ricans from the farms or directly from Puerto Rico. The DES reports often note the competition between the agricultural and industrial sectors for Puerto Rican workers.

Piore suggests that Puerto Ricans were actively recruited for jobs in marginal industries operating on a low profit margin.[6] He told me in an interview that he sees Puerto Rican recruitment as a response to the loss of second generation blacks. The 1960s civil rights movement had resulted in blacks becoming more articulate and aggressive and many in the "liberal" North perceiving blacks as threats. Blacks in turn saw themselves as deserving and having more power and thus were less willing to settle for dead end, low paying "dirty work." Puerto Ricans were recruited to fill the vacuum at the bottom. Piore, however, does not document this observation. His assumptions are based on his interviews with workers in the industries with which he or his associates were involved. Piore mentioned that at times even black foremen preferred the less aggressive Puerto Ricans to the more assertive black U.S. citizens, in the way that farmers tended to prefer Jamaicans and other West Indians to Puerto Ricans, especially to English-speaking Puerto Ricans from New York.

According to the 1970 Census, only 51 families in Waltham were identified as "Negro," so the census data does not provide mean or median income for the group. Most black families in Waltham, however, are seen as being middle class. They are often either professors or students at Brandeis University or Bentley College. None of the black families were receiving public assistance and none were categorized as families having a female head of household. Thirteen of the 51 families (15.5 percent) owned their own homes. In Waltham, Puerto Ricans are clearly not replacing blacks. They are replacing lower income whites as they move out of the secondary labor market.

The question left unanswered, however, is: what if Puerto Ricans had not been available? Would blacks have been recruited for the marginal industries in and around Waltham and for the secondary-market jobs such as those in hotels, restaurants, and landscaping establishments vacated by white ethnics?

My interest in looking at Waltham's Puerto Rican population stemmed from several factors. Waltham's Puerto Rican community is relatively recent. Waltham houses Brandeis University, and, during my student days at Brandeis, I became involved with its Puerto Rican and Hispanic community. Later I was instrumental in developing and directing on a part-time basis El Programa Roberto Clemente, a social service program that used advocacy techniques and tools to obtain resources and services for this population.

As director of El Programa Roberto Clemente, I was able to obtain money to implement a leadership-training project to prepare Puerto Ricans and other Hispanics in the community to enter social service jobs in that city. As part of their responsibilities, the trainees (and I) interviewed approximately 200 Hispanic families in the city (all the Hispanic families identified in a three-month period). A questionnaire was administered.[7] A preliminary questionnaire, administered to 100 families, had established Orocovis, Puerto Rico, as the town contributing most of Waltham's Hispanic population.

A list of Hispanic families was compiled by collecting names of families known to the Waltham Public School System, the department of Welfare, Project Health of the Waltham Hospital, the Family Counseling Services, and El Programa Roberto Clemente. The Waltham Directory was reviewed, and all persons with Spanish-sounding names were added to the list. As families were interviewed, they were asked to provide names of other Hispanic families.

Such a process yielded fewer and fewer new names as more and more interviews were made. The process was stopped after approximately 200 families were interviewed.

Answers to the following questions will be formulated from information gathered through the questionnaire.

- Where did the migrants come from?
- Why did they come to Waltham?
- What types of employment are they engaged in?
- What are the best predictors for employment—knowledge of English, length of residency in Waltham, level of formal education, a specific skill, other?
- Are non-Puerto Rican Hispanic families "better off" (income, language skills, housing, services) than Puerto Rican families? Do their perceptions about issues and problems differ?
- Are social services utilized by Puerto Ricans? To what extent? How do Puerto Ricans perceive the services? Are there agencies that rate higher than others?

This chapter is a study of Waltham's Hispanic community in the year 1975. It presents historical information as well as observations that I, as a resident of that city for four years, as the director of El Programa Roberto Clemente, and as a member of the Newton-Waltham Comprehensive Employment Training Act (CETA) Advisory Board, feel competent in making. This chapter will also provide statistical data from the original research discussed earlier.

LIMITATIONS OF THE STUDY

This study focuses only on Massachusetts and possible relationships between migration there and conditions in New York and on the island of Puerto Rico. Furthermore, primary data was gathered from Waltham only. One hundred ninety-six families were interviewed. However, some Puerto Rican or Hispanic families not known to the schools, the social services, or to the larger Hispanic community of Waltham may have been omitted. These might include men and women with two jobs who were not at home either during the day or evening when interviewers canvassed in Waltham with large numbers of Hispanic families.

Clearly, only information that respondents were willing to share with interviewers can be analyzed.

The study is also limited by the census information itself. Too often the census does not provide essential information on Puerto Ricans. It tends to provide information on blacks and whites that it fails to break down by more specific categories. Puerto Ricans may be in either group.

Information on Spanish-speaking or Hispanic populations does not break down the categories either. Statistics on Chicanos, Cubans, and South Americans may not reflect a true picture of the Puerto Rican population. For example, the New York Times carried a story called "Census Shows Hispanic Families Rising in Income Faster Than Other Groups." After making generalizations about families headed by persons of "Spanish-speaking ancestry" it shows that the optimistic picture, while being true for Cubans, Chicanos, and South Americans, is not true for Puerto Ricans.[8] The census often raises as many questions as it answers.

WALTHAM: A HISTORICAL PERSPECTIVE

Before presenting some of the results of the study, it may be appropriate to provide some information on the city of Waltham itself.[9] The Waltham Monograph based on 1970 census data, Howard Gitelman's Workingmen of Waltham,[10] and various publications and materials from the city's planning office form the basis for the following historical summary.

Initially, Waltham attracted fur trappers. In 1630, it was settled by Europeans seeking to establish an agricultural community in the fertile lowlands and marshes along the Charles River. During the late eighteenth and early nineteenth century, Waltham changed radically from an agricultural township to an industrial manufacturing center. The city's riverside location and the need of farmers to secure a year-round income led to the establishment of Waltham's mills and the manufacture of paper, cotton, and woolen goods. These goods, along with the town's agricultural products, were easily transported via the Charles River to Boston and beyond. In 1814, the Boston manufacturing textile mill was founded, which Gitelman calls "the single most important event to befall Waltham in the first one hundred years of its existence."[11]

It was during this period that Waltham's greatest industrial development took place. A railroad linking Waltham to Boston was built, the famous Waltham Watch Company was established in 1854, and 600 acres of riverfront land was purchased and earmarked for industry. Some of the industry attracted skilled native and male Canadian technicians. Industry also brought in the first waves of Irish immigrants.   Unskilled, uneducated, poor, and Catholic, they flooded into the mills of Waltham, replacing the women who had previously worked there.

Enormous social and political consequences came about from this first period of industrial growth, most of them resulting from the 400 percent population increase caused by the influx of two heterogeneous groups—skilled, well-paid, upwardly mobile Protestant technicians on the one hand and unskilled, miserably paid Irish Catholic mill hands on the other.   The technicians invested their savings in businesses and banks and, along with the factory owners and farmers, soon controlled much of the economic life of the town.   Their churches became centers of cultural, educational, and social activities, and their companies supported the churches, especially in their Protestant relief efforts.   The technicians despised the Irish for their lack of skill, ignorance, Catholicism, "criminality," and poverty and discriminated against them in employment and housing. By the late nineteenth century, Waltham had "Yankee" neighborhoods where the businessmen, bankers, and tech-nicians lived and Irish neighborhoods housing the factory workers and many newly elected aldermen, for in Waltham as elsewhere, politics became the Irishmen's point of entry into the establishment.   By 1870, 44 percent of Waltham's population was Irish.

As in New York, the Irish of Waltham initially were unskilled and categorized as peasants.   They would later look down at the Italians and French Canadians.   Much later, all of the above groups would continue the cen-turies-old pattern and belittle the Puerto Rican newcomers.

Waltham's industry and population continued to grow, comfortably absorbing a second wave of Irish immigrants, then the influx of Italians.   However, with the depression came severe economic problems, which were relieved only by the involvement of the United States in World War II.   After the war, Waltham's industries converted easily into peace-time production of small manufactured goods.   These in-dustries and Waltham's profitable retail businesses, which attracted shoppers from a wide geographic area, provided the city with a sound economic base.

The recession of the 1950s and the closing of the Waltham Watch Company served as powerful stimuli to business interests in town to aggressively seek solutions protecting the city from the decline in wartime production it had just overcome.   The Chamber of Commerce and ulti-mately local government officials chose to rescue Waltham's western sector along the newly constructed Route 128 for light industrial use, a decision that was to have economic, social, and political ramifications equal to those occurring in the 1840s and 1850s. This time, Waltham ceased to be an independent, self-contained city and became instead part of metropolitan Boston.

The Golden Horseshoe, as Waltham's Route 128 industrial park area is called, houses such major national and international electronics research and development corporations as Raytheon, Honeywell, GTE-Sylvania, Polaroid, Hewlett-Packard, Thermo-Electron, and Digital. Their establishment in Waltham produced an industrial spin-off effect as the old machinery manufacturing plants expanded and new metal-and-mica processing and pump-and-tire-producing firms were attracted to the riverfront factory area. This double-barreled industrial expansion resulted in more jobs, greater retail sales, and a solid industrial property tax base. It also produced a 25 percent rise in the city's population from 1950 to 1970, which strained many city resources, particularly the supply of housing available to low and moderate income families.[12] In addition, 50 percent of those working in the Golden Horseshoe are not Waltham residents, although they travel through the city daily, straining its capacity to accommodate the continual flow of commuter traffic and creating pollution, street safety, and parking problems for Waltham's residents.

Today, Waltham, in spite of its employment opportunities and history of economic growth, is rapidly decaying in many of its neighborhoods, most obviously in those with a heavy concentration of Puerto Ricans.

Waltham is bounded by one city, Newton, and five towns, Weston, Lincoln, Lexington, Belmont, and Watertown. All of these communities are popularly perceived to be upper- and upper-middle-class bedroom suburbs of Boston. Waltham, in contrast, is often seen as a deteriorating, lower-middle-class city with too much traffic, despite some similarities to its neighbors in median income levels, density levels, and even median housing values. None of the abutting towns, however, are high industrial centers, and they all outstrip Waltham in terms of college graduates. The neighboring towns have three to nine times (in percentage) more college graduates than Waltham, and the percentage of professionals living in those towns are strikingly higher.

Table 6.1 offers some specifics regarding a comparison between Waltham and the adjoining communities. All figures are taken from 1970 census materials. The professional worker category is obtained by combining the "professional, technical, kindred, and managers" categories from occupational figures of the census.

TABLE 6.1 Comparison of Waltham and Surrounding Towns

	Lincoln	Waltham	Weston	Newton	Watertown	Belmont	Lexington
Median Income ($)	13,733	11,523	23,530	15,381	9,875	11,578	15,593
Persons 25 years and older completing college (%)	44.5	5.1	45	14.7	15.9	27.1	37.2
Professional workers (%)	56	23	54	45	30	44	51

Waltham ranks well below its neighbors, with the possible exception of Watertown, in terms of income, education, and prestige. A sense of social and economic exclusivity pervades the other towns and isolates Waltham from them.

Waltham is located nine miles west of Boston in a central pivotal point of the greater Boston transportation network. Several major highways converge in the streets of Waltham. Rush hours create parking and traffic flow problems for its residents and retail customers, thus contributing to the city's image of congestion and pollution. Public transportation, both within Waltham and to nearby communities, is poor. Therefore, most transportation in the city is by car.

The impact of industrial and commercial development along Route 128 has been phenomenal. From 1950 to 1970, Waltham's population increased by 25 percent; retail sales soared from 68 million in 1954 to 200 million in 1975 (wholesale gains were of similar magnitude); and the work force increased by 20,000. However, in spite of the undoubtedly salubrious effects the 128 complex has had on the area, the downtown commercial and residential area has suffered a slow but steady decline in recent years. Housing decay and overpopulation caused by tremendous growth and the inability of retail establishments to compete with other suburban shopping centers have placed social, economic, and environmental hardships on residents of the area.

CHARACTERISTICS OF THE ECONOMY

Waltham's total assessed valuation in 1975 was 548,802,615 dollars, a figure roughly 18 million dollars more than in

1973. The city debt for 1975 was 13 million dollars, down 2 million dollars from 1971. Continued growth coupled with a declining city debt and a tax rate among the lowest in the state is a rare achievement in an inflationary period. One reason for this accomplishment is the conservative spending program the mayor, with city council approval, has overseen. The more significant reason for Waltham's prosperity is the continued growth of industry in the city, particularly in the Golden Horseshoe area, but also in the older industrial sector along the river front.

The Route 128 corporations are intimately connected with national and, in some cases, multinational defense programs and with the aerospace and nuclear technology industries. Many of these companies were sites of anti-Vietnam war demonstrations in the late 1960s and early 1970s. Although the war is over, defense needs continue as do federal contracts to develop the products to meet those needs—thus, the continued growth of these companies. As previously mentioned, they employ 20,000 people, but only 20 percent of them are Waltham residents. Townspeople attribute this fact primarily to the inability of the Waltham school system to prepare its graduates to compete for the highly skilled jobs required by the Route 128 industries. And just as the Waltham Watch Company attracted upwardly mobile, trained craftsmen from New England and abroad to produce what Waltham residents could not, so also do these Golden Horseshoe industries attract outsiders for identical reasons. Waltham Watch employees, however, became active investors in and residents of the town while 16,000 of the 20,000 Route 128 employees have not. Waltham's shortage of affordable family housing and its image as a less desirable place to live than its neighbors foster the reluctance of Golden Horseshoe employees to live in Waltham. Its congested traffic flow and parking problems prevent them from shopping, even for lunch, in the city. The result is that Waltham is denied the additional contributions to its tax base and stimulation to its downtown commercial area that the 128 employees could provide.

The manufacturing industries that occupy the old mill and factory sites fronting the Charles River are, like their predecessors, major employment areas for unskilled and semiskilled workers—formerly New England farmers or Irish, Italian, or French Canadian immigrants; presently, high school and vocational high school graduates without "space age" specialization. Twenty percent to 25 percent of Waltham's jobs are supplied by these industries, and 60 percent of their workers are Waltham residents. The negative impact that these industries have on the Waltham economy, according to city officials, is their location on land that could be developed for high property-tax yield, luxury housing with sites having riverfront views and within walking distance to Waltham's downtown commercial area.

Waltham's downtown consists of about 400 sundry retail outlets located along Main and Moody Streets on Waltham's residentially dense south side. This commercial center supplies 30 percent of the 40,000 jobs in the city and employs Waltham residents in 65 to 70 percent of them. Before the construction of Route 128, this area was the central suburban shopping area for metropolitan Boston. Retail companies such as Sears Roebuck, J.C. Penny, Gilchrists, Kennedy, Touraines, and Woolworth operated large prosperous branch stores along Moody Street, and Grover Cronin's promotions, especially at holiday time, rivaled those of Boston's major department stores. But with Route 128 came the shopping malls with easy highway access and plentiful parking, and one by one the large branch stores in Waltham relocated, taking their nonresident customers with them. Waltham's downtown is far from a commercial ghost town, but stores come and go with alarming regularity. The merchandise carried by most of them is of an inferior quality and is poorly displayed. Often traffic seems hardly to flow at all on Moody and Main Streets. Parking is practically nonexistent. Though revitalization of this area is a major concern of the city government, city officials and residents recognize and acknowledge that qualitative improvement is impossible until constricted traffic flow patterns and restrictive parking are alleviated.

Fifteen hundred and ninety acres, or 29 percent of Waltham's land, produce no property tax revenues for the city since it is owned by the state (Fernald State School, University of Massachusetts, Farm Bureau Field Station, Metropolitan State Hospital), by the federal government (Army Corps of Engineers, Federal Records Center), and by nonprofit corporations (Massachusetts Girls Scouts, Brandeis University, Bentley College). However, 4,000 to 6,000 jobs are generated by these service institutions. Many of the semiskilled and unskilled jobs are held by Waltham residents, many of them Puerto Ricans. These institutions must conform to affirmative action guidelines, and many of them do so by hiring unskilled Hispanics as janitors, repairmen, and dishwashers.

The people and the powers that be in the community feel ambivalent about these service institutions. For example, students do purchase community goods and services but they also exert pressures on the severely limited Waltham housing market because of their preference for living collectively in the community rather than on campus. They also prefer to pool resources and often pay far more for housing than a family with a single income could afford. Residents are also ambivalent about the deinstitutionalization programs that the Fernald State School and Metropolitan State Hospital are vigorously pursuing. Many Waltham residents regard the goal of deinstitutionalizaion as a worthy one but do not support the influx into their community of many former residents of these institutions who are sometimes released without adequate supervision and have no other place to go.

It is with Bentley and Brandeis students, with former residents of Waltham's many institutes, with low income persons wishing to live close to Waltham's places of employment, and with other Hispanics that Puerto Ricans often compete for housing. The white minorities who immigrated to Waltham since the Great Depression followed the pattern of white immigrants described in the first chapter of this book. The French Canadians were the last white group to occupy the lowest rung on the ladder of status until their numbers stabilized and a new threat to community homeostasis, the Puerto Ricans, replaced them as the "unworthy poor." The French Canadians are now incorporated into the wider white community. Puerto Ricans have had a different experience in Waltham, as indeed they have had everywhere in the United States. Their color difference and lack of valued skills prevent assimilation.

Puerto Ricans compose a statistically significant portion of Waltham's population. Their numbers are estimated at anywhere from 1,000 to 2,500 persons. They first came to the city in the late 1950s to work on the farms in and around Waltham and Lexington. Because many left rural mountain areas in Puerto Rico such as Orocovis to come directly to Waltham, they have been forced to learn skills for urban living in a foreign culture and in a foreign language. As a result, they were and continue to be prime targets for exploitation, discrimination, and harassment on the job, in the schools, and in their homes.

My family and I were the victims of Waltham's racism. My children were, on numerous occasions, verbally insulted by other children because they were "spics." Furthermore, our house was vandalized late one night while we were sleeping; we received hate mail; and twice we found dead snakes at our doorstep. The police told me that those incidents would probably not have happened if we had been living in the Puerto Rican section of the city. They suggested we make sure the house was heavily insured since the insurance company would be more likely to apprehend culprits than they would.

Other Puerto Rican families related many similar incidents to me. For example, Puerto Rican families often refused to live in either of Waltham's two public housing projects because in the past Puerto Rican tenants in them had been beaten and vandalized. One group of Puerto Rican youngsters recounted being "welcomed" to one of the town's junior high schools in September by a group of Waltham girls carrying signs stating "Spics go home."

Despite these obstacles, Puerto Ricans remain in Waltham, and the Puerto Rican community continues to grow. Between 1972 and 1974, the number of Spanish-speaking students who were part of the bilingual program increased by 165 and the number of Italian, and French-speaking youngsters declined by 21 and 85, respectively.

Waltham residents are aware that a significant Spanish-speaking population exists within their town. Most of these Hispanics are of Puerto Rican heritage. Most people in Waltham, however, do not know much about the Latino community. The 1970 census offers a figure of 529 persons of Spanish-speaking background. Since there were 289 youngsters needing bilingual education in 1974, that figure is very unrealistic. The Waltham City Planning Office and Project Health (which health-related services to Hispanics) used 1,200 as a figure in 1973, and in 1974 a memo from a former planner at City Hall estimated the number, based on the bilingual education program, at 1,700.

CHARACTERISTICS OF WALTHAM'S HISPANIC POPULATION

When I began my study of Waltham's Hispanic community, I found that data from previous community studies (notably the 1970 U.S. census and the 1974 Beaverbrook Study, a summary of which follows) often contradicted each other. The census figures, as a rule, tend to give a more optimistic portrayal of the Hispanic community than does the Beaverbrook Study. My data tend to agree more with the Beaverbrook findings, although at times my study reveals an even grimmer reality.[13]

On August 5, 1974, the Beaverbrook Guidance Center in Belmont complied a five-page demographic synthesis of the Spanish-speaking community of Waltham, Massachusetts, most of which is Puerto Rican. There are few facts known about the Puerto Rican population of Waltham in general and, although funding proposals and reports of agencies that serve this population have included some brief demographic descriptions, the information often has had wide gaps. The Beaverbrook study was simply an attempt to consolidate the available information.

It concluded that 86 percent of the Spanish-speaking population of Waltham was 35 or younger. Close to 20 percent fell between 15 and 24 and 23 percent between 25 and 34. Less than 11 percent of the population was older than 35. The Puerto Rican population of Waltham is young —composed primarily of young married couples and their children. This suggests that recent arrivals, from rural areas of Puerto Rico, may be more likely to be two-parent families than their second generation urban compatriots. In Waltham, there were slightly more males than females, which may be attributed to the fact that, compared to rural females, proportionately more young Puerto Rican rural males migrate to the United States in order to find employment. The median rent payment per month was approximately 125 dollars; also rent payments were higher in those tracts in which the majority of Puerto Ricans live than in any other areas of Waltham. One hundred percent of the housing in Spanish-speaking areas is renter occupied. The Beaverbrook Report theorizes that the lack of formal education, the general rural background of the Puerto Rican people of Waltham, and their inability to speak English force most of the Puerto Ricans to do menial labor. Approximately 75 percent of the Spanish-speaking population of Waltham was unskilled. Most of these people worked as landscapers, maintenance people, migrant laborers, and factory workers.[14]

The 1970 census accentuates the sex ratio differences in Waltham's Spanish-speaking population. According to the census, 61 percent of the Hispanic population was male and 39 percent female. Census data also indicates that 82.3 percent of Hispanic households were headed by both husband and wife.

According to the 1970 census, over one half of the Hispanics in Waltham had completed 8 years or more of schooling, and 11.5 years of schooling was the median for Hispanic families. These figures differ greatly with my findings. They are also in contradiction with the Puerto Rican Group Survey cited in the Beaverbrook Study, which stated that "50 percent of the adult Puerto Rican population had sixth grade education or less, 40 percent could not read or write in Spanish, and 71 percent could not carry on a conversation in English" (and therefore needed an interpreter).[15]

The 1970 census indicates that 33 percent of the Hispanic families live at a density of more than 1 person per room with a median of 3.5 persons per housing unit, in contrast to 2.5 persons per unit for the city of Waltham in general. It also revealed that 100 percent of Waltham's Hispanic families live in renter-occupied units. The Beaverbrook Study states that more than 75 percent of Spanish speakers in the city moved into their apartments since 1968 and that they tend to live (81.7 percent) in homes built before 1950. This was true for only 65 percent of the general population of Waltham.[16]

The 1970 census also indicates that only 4.4 percent of the Spanish-speaking males "in the labor force" were unemployed. This figure is very incongruent with the data I obtained.

Income statistics for Waltham's Hispanic population according to the Beaverbrook Study place the mean gross Puerto Rican family income at 91.37 dollars a week or 4,751 dollars a year (in 1974). These statistics, which are congruent with my findings, differ from the census data of 1970, which indicate a median income of 6,595 dollars a year for the Hispanic family. As another indicator of Hispanic economic status, the 1970 census found that, while in the general population of Waltham only 15.8 percent of the residents did not own a car, the figure for the Spanish-speaking population was 42.7 percent.

As bleak as the above statistics appear, the study I conducted not only supports such statistics, it actually demonstrates even greater poverty. Could it be that census takers are unable to obtain accurate information, or is it that initially the migrants are recruited for specific work and that those arriving later come to join families or friends but have no specific job offers or less possibility of finding employment? In all probability, both assumptions are true.

What follows are some of the demographic data revealed in my study. The material is generally divided into two categories—Puerto Ricans and non-Puerto Rican Hispanics. Some explanations regarding the disparity between the census figures and those of this study have already been discussed; others will be offered later.

AGE, SEX, AND BIRTHPLACE OF HEADS OF HOUSEHOLD

Sixty-two, or 31.6 percent, of the 196 heads of household in Waltham were below 24 years of age (see Table 6.2).

TABLE 6.2 General Characteristics of Population Sample

	For All Subjects		For Puerto Ricans		For Other Hispanics	
	Number	Percent	Number	Percent	Number	Percent
Sex of Heads of Household						
Male	139	70.9	117	68	22	91.7
Female	57	29.1	55	32	2	8.2
Age of Household Head*						
16–20			15	8.7	0	
21–24			44	25.5	3	12.5
25–30			31	17.0	13	54.3
30–35			24	13.9	5	20.9
39–40			18	10.5	0	
42–71			30	17.4	3	12.5

*Mean age for heads of household was 31.27 years. Median age for heads of households was 28.68 years. Range for heads of household was 16 to 72 years.

NOTE: N = 196 subjects; 172 (87.8%) Puerto Rican and 24 (12.2%) other Hispanics.

Fifteen (7.5 percent) were teenagers. All of the teenage household heads were Puerto Rican. Seventy-two of the 196 heads of household (36.7 percent) were between the ages of 25 and 34. Of these, 56 were Puerto Rican and 16 were other Hispanics. Thirty-four (11.5 percent) fell between the ages of 35 and 45 (3 Hispanics, 31 Puerto Ricans). Only 20 heads of households (10.2 percent) were older than 46 years of age.

One hundred and seventeen (68 percent) of the Puerto Rican heads of household were males and 55 (32 percent) female. For other Hispanics, 22 (91.7 percent) of the heads of household were men and 2 (8.3 percent) women.

Note that the 1970 census indicated that 82.2 percent of Hispanic households were headed by males and 8.9 percent by females. This study shows a much greater percentage (29.1) of the total Hispanic families headed by females. That percentage is much lower for non-Puerto Rican Hispanics (closer to the census figure) and higher for Puerto Ricans.

Fifty-two of the heads of household, or 30.2 percent, were born in Orocovis, Puerto Rico. Twenty-one, or 12.2 percent, were from Barranquitas, the neighboring municipality. Interestingly enough, however, in looking at other persons in the family (spouse, children), a much higher percentage of the families trace their origins to Orocovis. Sixty-two percent of all Puerto Rican families had one or more of their members born in the town of Orocovis. Only 5, or 2.9 percent, of the Puerto Rican household heads were born in the United States. Two of those had been reared in Puerto Rico. Five Puerto Rican heads of household stated that they had been born outside of the United States or Puerto Rico. All of the other Hispanics were born in a Latin American country. It becomes apparent that Waltham's Hispanic population is a first generation community facing a new environment and all the problems the first generation experience poses.

The educational attainment level is another area of discrepancy between census data and my statistics. The 1970 census indicates that more than 50 percent of the Hispanic families had completed 8 years or more of schooling. The median was 11.5 years. The median in this study is 6.7 years of schooling, and 61.2 percent of the total Hispanic population had 8 years of schooling or less. Other Hispanics had greater educational attainment levels and more proficiency in English. See Tables 6.3 and 6.4.

A summary of the general characteristics thus far presented reveals the following findings:

- There are many more female heads of household for Puerto Rican families than for other Hispanic families.
- Other Hispanics are more homogeneous with respect to age (87 percent of whom were between 21 and 35) than Puerto Ricans.
- Other Hispanics have more formal education and are more fluent in English than are Puerto Ricans.[17]

The 1970 census agrees with this study in terms of housing characteristics. The census revealed that 100 percent of all Hispanic families (Puerto Ricans and other Hispanics) lived in renter-occupied housing units. Note that 26 heads of household marked 0 for the number of rooms in their home. These people, it is my assumption, are renting space from a relative or friend and do not have their own apartment. I also assume that these people (22, or 12.8 percent, for Puerto Ricans and 4, or 16.7 percent, for other Hispanics) are less likely to give census takers information about their families for fear of retribution from

TABLE 6.3   English-Speaking Ability of Heads of Households

Degree of Proficiency	Total Population		Puerto Ricans		Other Hispanics	
	Number	Percent	Number	Percent	Number	Percent
Well	44	22.4	34	19.8	10	41.7
Fairly well	50	25.5	45	26.2	5	20.8
Very little	68	34.7	60	34.9	8	33.2
None	33	16.8	32	18.6	1	4.2
No response	1	.5	1	.6	0	

TABLE 6.4   Educational Attainment Level of Heads of Households

School Years Completed	Puerto Ricans		Other Hispanics	
	Number	Percent	Number	Percent
0	11	6.4	1	4.1
Grades 1-6	76	44.1	7	23.2
Junior High School, Grades 7-9	42	24.4	2	8.4
High School, Grades 10-12	40	23.3	10	41.6
College, Levels 13-20	3	1.8	4	16.7

landlords if they are boarders, or from welfare if they are welfare recipients and renters or boarders. Such fear leads to an undercount of persons of Latino heritage.

The unit-size varies from 0–8 rooms with the mean of 3.5 rooms. Of all Hispanics, 46.4 percent have fewer than 5 rooms. Although there is no significant difference between Puerto Ricans and other Hispanics, Puerto Ricans tend to have smaller apartments: 27 percent of the Puerto Rican families lived in apartments that had five rooms or more compared to 31.1 percent of the other Hispanics.

This study reveals the median gross rent for all Hispanics to be 160.27 dollars per month. The difference between the census and this study may be a function of time since 1975. The Beaverbrook Study concluded that, "the Spanish-speaking population tends to pay higher rent for older houses than the remainder of the Waltham population, as well as has less space available (per person)."[18]

Table 6.5 offers information on the amount of rent per unit for all Hispanics and compares the figures for Puerto Ricans and for non-Puerto Rican Hispanics. In general, it appears that non-Puerto Rican Hispanics could afford more expensive housing than Puerto Ricans.[19]

Table 6.5 Rent per Housing Unit

Rent (dollars)	Total		Puerto Ricans		Other Hispanics	
	Number	Percent	Number	Percent	Number	Percent
Under 75	7	3.6	7	4.2	0	
76-100	14	7.1	14	8.2	0	
101-125	17	8.7	14	8.2	3	33.2
126-150	38	19.4	35	20.3	3	12.6
151-200	100	51.0	88	51.1	12	50.0
210-360	20	10.2	14	8.2	6	25.2

NOTE: Mean = 157.980; median = 160.273.

The 1970 census shows Waltham's Hispanic community to be the result of a very recent migration with 59.4 percent of the Hispanics having moved there after 1965. It also emphasizes the high mobility of this population. Less than 10 percent (9.9 percent) of the Hispanic population lived in the same house in 1965 as they did in 1970.

The study I conducted in 1975 verifies that information. Ninety-four or 48 percent of the Hispanic heads of household interviewed in this study lived in Waltham prior to April of 1970. One hundred two (52 percent) came to Waltham after 1970. Sixty-three (32.1 percent) of the total group lived in the same housing unit for five years or longer. One hundred thirty-two (67.3 percent) had moved within a five-year period. Tables 6.6, 6.7, 6.8, and 6.9 summarize this information and offer comparisons between Puerto Ricans and other Hispanics. Most Hispanics interviewed moved within the city of Waltham, or from Puerto Rico to Waltham. These four tables provide a breakdown, by ethnic group, of migration patterns. They show fairly similar trends across both groups in terms of length of

TABLE 6.6 Patterns of Migration: Length of Residency in Waltham for All
Hispanics

	Total Population		Puerto Ricans		Other Hispanics	
	Number	Percent	Number	Percent	Number	Percent
Residency in Waltham before April 1970						
Yes	94	48	81	47.1	13	54.2
No	102	52	91	52.9	11	45.8
Same Locus from 1970 to 1975						
Yes	63	32.1	53	30.8	10	41.7
No	132	67.3	118	68.6	14	58.3

NOTE: Mean time in Waltham = 276 weeks; range = 1-998 weeks; median =
208 weeks; standard deviation = 238 weeks.

residency in Waltham, although non-Puerto Rican Hispanics
are somewhat more likely to have lived in the same dwelling
over the past five years than are Puerto Ricans.

Much has been written about Puerto Ricans' return to
Borinquen and the back and forth movement from the island
to the United States. This is at times cited by schools and
social service providers as a reason for community insta-
bility and often seen as a cause for problems children
encounter in school. The proximity of the United States to
Puerto Rico and the relatively inexpensive air fare coupled
with the fact that Puerto Ricans as citizens may travel
freely to or from Puerto Rico act as encouragement for back
and forth migration.

In the previous chapters, it was noted that most seasonal workers returned to Puerto Rico. It is my contention
that often Puerto Ricans will return to the island several
times before making a decision to stay in a U.S. city.
Much could be learned about communities and migration if
we could study the point at which migrants stop returning
to the Island and accept living in the United States as more
than just a temporary condition, thus establishing a sense
of community in their elsewheres.

When we asked Hispanics in Waltham if they had returned to Puerto Rico (or their original home) since living
in Waltham, 46.9 percent of the household heads said they
had and 51.5 percent stated that they had not. The per-

TABLE 6.7 Migration Pattern over Last Five Years

Category Label	Puerto Ricans		Other Hispanics	
	Number	Percent	Number	Percent
Most Recent Place of Residency Prior to Present One				
	1	.6	0	
Waltham	106	61.6	8	33.3
Puerto Rico/Latin America	43	25.0	2	8.3
New York	6	3.5	0	
Boston	4	2.3	0	
Other	9	5.2	13	54.2
NA	2	1.2	1	4.1
No response	1	.6	0	
Second Most Recent Place of Residency Prior to Present One				
Waltham	45	26.2	5	20.8
Puerto Rico/Latin America	94	54.7	6	8.3
New York	6	3.5	0	
Boston	4	2.3	0	
Other	9	5.2	13	54.2
NA	2	1.2	1	4.1
Third Most Recent Place of Residency Prior to Present One				
	2	1.2	0	
Waltham	20	11.6	1	4.2
Puerto Rico/Latin America	131	76.2	9	37.5
New York	5	2.9	0	
Other	3	1.7	10	41.7
NA	9	5.2	4	16.7
No response	2	1.2	0	

centage of Puerto Ricans returning was higher than that of Hispanics as a whole. The main reason offered, however, was not a doubt about living in Waltham but rather a desire to visit family. The range of the stay varied from a few days to 9 weeks with 1.4 weeks being the mean. An important aspect of these frequent trips to Puerto Rico, however, is the possibility it presents for those persons established in Waltham to convince loved ones to join them in their new elsewhere. Table 6.8 provides more detailed information on return trips.

Table 6.8 Migratory Patterns between Puerto Rico or Latin America and the
United States

	All Hispanics		Puerto Ricans		Other Hispanics	
	Number	Percent	Number	Percent	Number	Percent
Trips by Head of Household to Puerto Rico (or home of origin)						
Yes	92	46.9	83	48.3	9	37.5
No	101	51.5	87	50.6	14	58.3
No response	3	1.5	2	1.2	1	4.2
Reasons for Return Trips						
Family			64	37.2	6	25.0
Vacation			10	5.8	3	12.5
Job			8	4.7	1	4.2
Sickness			2	1.2		
Other			1	.6		
Did not return			87	50.6	14	58.3

NOTE: Number of return trips, mean = 1.046 return trips; standard
deviation = 1.54 return trips; range = 0-8 return trips. Length of return
trip, mean = 1.4 weeks; standard deviation = 2.1 weeks; range = 0-9 weeks.

When heads of household were asked if other members
of their families had returned home since they moved to
Waltham, the percentage of "yes" answers increased dras-
tically. One hundred and seventy-two, or 87.2 percent,
answered affirmatively. The reasons were similar to those
offered by the heads of household. These persons would
also attract others from home to join them in their new
location.

Being with family was one of the reasons for coming to
Waltham most cited by heads of households. Employment
was the only reason cited more frequently. Studies of
Boston[20] and Cambridge[21] also revealed these two factors
as the main reasons offered by Hispanics when asked why
they came to those cities. Table 6.9 offers the explanations
cited by Waltham. The table offers a comparison between
responses offered by Puerto Ricans and those offered by
other Hispanics. Note that the responses are similar.

There is no official policy in the Commonwealth of
Puerto Rico to either encourage or discourage the permanent migration of its citizens to the United States.

TABLE 6.9 Reasons for Settling in Waltham

	Puerto Ricans		Other Hispanics	
	Number	Percent	Number	Percent
Employment	77	44.8	10	41.7
Family	66	38.4	9	37.5
Friends	5	3.9	1	4.2
Health	7	4.1	0	0
Housing	7	4.1	2	8.3
Welfare	3	1.7	0	0
Education	1	.6	2	8.3
Other	5	2.9	0	0
No Response	1	.6	0	0

However, as previously seen, it tends to unofficially promote and certainly assist the process of outward migration. The media, government offices and bureaus, and educational programs influence people to leave. In Puerto Rico, the government offers orientation programs alerting the future migrant of job opportunities on the mainland, the weather on the East Coast, what to wear on the mainland, and documents needed for schools. Films and directions to find traveler's aid at mainland airports are taken around to various towns and villages. In 1960, there were 35 local mayor's committees on migrant orientation in towns and cities throughout Puerto Rico, and more were being organized. Twenty-nine radio stations on the island carry the program, "Guide to the Traveler," based on the experiences of successful migrants.[22] As early as 1936, the governor of Puerto Rico suggested that a "well-planned migration might relieve the pressures of population."[23] It has been suggested that many of the Puerto Rican government's efforts in Puerto Rico and the United States are not only to help Puerto Ricans adjust to a new environment, but also to assure that fewer of them return.[24]

The responses to previous questions demonstrate that they do, in fact, return but not necessarily to stay. I speculate that just by their returning to Waltham, however, they encourage friends and relatives to migrate and provide a specific elsewhere for that migration.

Government encouragement is not enough reason for people to uproot and leave Borinquen. The massive unemployment, especially in rural areas; the hope of employment

TABLE 6.10 Major Problems Identified by the Hispanic Community of Waltham

| | Puerto Ricans | | Other Hispanics | |
	Number	Percent	Number	Percent
Most Pressing Problem				
No response	2	1.2	0	
Housing	69	40.1	5	20.8
Employment	43	25.0	7	29.2
English	30	17.4	10	41.7
Drugs	7	4.1	1	4.2
Crime	4	2.3	0	
Lack of recreation	1	.6	0	
Discrimination	11	6.4	1	4.2
Education	2	1.2	0	
Other	3	1.7	0	
Second Most Pressing Problem				
No response	2	1.2	0	
Housing	40	23.3	7	29.2
Employment	42	24.4	6	25.0
English	34	19.2	6	25.0
Drugs	5	2.9	0	
Crime	2	1.2	0	
Lack of recreation	2	1.2	0	
Discrimination	35	20.3	1	4.2
Education	5	2.9	3	12.5
Other	6	3.5	1	4.2
Third Most Pressing Problem				
No response	6	3.5	0	
Housing	21	12.2	3	12.5
Employment	32	18.6	2	8.3
English	39	22.7	7	29.2
Drugs	8	4.7	1	4.2
Crime	5	2.9	0	
Lack of recreation	6	3.5	2	8.3
Discrimination	28	16.3	6	25.0
Education	13	7.6	23	8.3
Other	14	8.1	1	4.2

opportunities in the United States; and, in the 1950s and
1960s, the actual jobs offered form a major part of the
forceful push–pull dynamics leading to the migration.
Having relatives or friends in a specific city or town

narrows down the choice of destination for the Puerto Rican uprooted worker.

Puerto Ricans come to Waltham because they have the desire to work and the hope of finding a job. Too often a job is not found, and the conditions they encounter are much less promising than expected. The conditions found by Puerto Ricans in Waltham are similar to those faced by their compatriots in New York. Specific statistics describing the quality of life for Puerto Ricans and other Hispanics in Waltham follow.

When asked what the number one problem they confronted was, 40 percent of the Puerto Rican heads of household interviewed identified poor housing, 25 percent mentioned lack of employment, and 6 percent said discrimination. When asked to identify their second biggest problem, 24.4 percent said employment, 23.3 percent said housing, 20.3 percent said discrimination, and 14.2 said they inability to speak English. When asked their third most pressing problem, a total of 18.6 percent mentioned employment, 22.7 percent said lack of English skills, and 16.3 percent mentioned discrimination. (See Table 6.10.)

Combining the top four responses to major problems, Puerto Ricans ranked them as follows:[25]

	Number	Percent
Housing	130	25.2
Employment	117	22.7
English (lack of)	102	19.8
Discrimination	34	6.5

Non-Puerto Rican Hispanics ranked them differently:

	Number	Percent
English (lack of)	23	31.9
Employment	15	20.8
Housing	15	20.8
Discrimination	8	11.1

Hispanics, other than Puerto Ricans, were likely to feel that if they spoke better English, they would solve most of their problems. Puerto Ricans saw the need for better housing and greater employment opportunity as being more important to them than learning the English language. I see several reasons for these differences. First, non-

Puerto Rican Hispanics are not citizens, and learning English is necessary if they are to become U.S. citizens. Secondly, as we saw earlier, they are generally better educated and tend to spend more money on housing. The non-Puerto Rican Hispanics also tend to earn more and are more likely to be employed than the Puerto Ricans. Out of 196 heads of household interviewed in April to June of 1975, only 105 were employed full or part-time. The rest were either unemployed at that time or were receiving public assistance. The salaries of those working ranged from 159 dollars or less per month to 999 dollars per month. For the entire group, the mean income was 275 dollars per month (3,300 dollars per year).[26] Although there is no statistical significance in income, note that 76.6 percent of Puerto Ricans earned 500 dollars or less a month, whereas only 23.3 percent of other Hispanics earned 500 dollars or less a month.

Table 6.11 looks at the job status of all subjects and divides the information into full-time, part-time, and unemployed categories. Furthermore, it compares that information for Puerto Ricans with that for other Hispanics. In this comparison, there is statistical significance.[27] Non-Puerto Rican Hispanics are employed to a greater extent than Puerto Ricans.

TABLE 6.11 Job Status of Puerto Ricans and Other Hispanics

| | Puerto Ricans | | Other Hispanics | |
	Number	Percent	Number	Percent
Full-time	84	48.8	19	79.2
Part-time	2	1.2		
Unemployed	86	50.0	5	20.8
Total	172	100.0	24	100.0

The majority of unemployed persons were looking for employment. Some of those not looking expressed feelings of insecurity or hopelessness about getting a job. Others talked of moving away from Waltham and attempting to secure employment elsewhere. A few said they would try welfare, and others said perhaps they would wait for unemployment benefits to end before trying again since "no hay gran diferencia en ingreso." (There is not very much

difference in income between employment wages and unemployment benefits.)

Eight heads of household were recipients of Social
Security Insurance, 18 (10 percent) of the household heads
saw welfare as more than a temporary condition, and three
persons did not say what their source of income (if any)
was.

Tables 6.12 and 6.13 provide information on the type of
employment Hispanics hold. Note that the majority of
Puerto Ricans hold unskilled positions, while the majority of
other Hispanics are engaged in skilled work.[28]

Specific unskilled jobs most commonly cited by Puerto
Ricans include landscaping, farming, janitorial or custodial
work, dishwashing, clearing of tables, meat packing,
bundling packages, and working as a security guard.

I would like to emphasize that, while no significant
differences were found between other Hispanics and Puerto
Ricans in family income earned, differences were found in
levels of employment and types of jobs held. Non-Puerto
Rican Hispanics held jobs more often, and were more likely
to hold white collar and skilled jobs than were Puerto
Ricans.

In attempting to ascertain the relationships between
earned income, employment status, type of work, and
English-speaking ability, several cross tabulations were
computed. The correlation between educational attainment
and earned income suggest that income tends to increase
when educational attainment is higher.[29] Forty-two percent
of persons with grade school education hold full-time jobs,
70 percent of persons who attended high school had full-
time employment, and 85 percent of people with some college
had full-time work. Thus, the chances for full-time
employment increase as educational attainment increases.[30]
In addition, those who attended only grade school are more
likely to have unskilled jobs (27.7 percent) or be unemployed (50.6 percent) than to be employed at skilled jobs
(21.7 percent).

Data gathered form the study suggests that, while
education had almost no correlation with the type of work
held, it was moderately correlated to earned income and
employment status. The general trend in employment status
was for larger percentages to be employed as the level of
education rose and for more highly educated persons to be
more likely to hold white collar or skilled jobs.

When looking at English-speaking ability and earned
income, we find a moderate correlation between the ability
to speak English and a higher income.[31] Only six persons
or 5.7 percent of those employed spoke no English.

TABLE 6.12 Type of Employment

	White Collar	Skilled	Unskilled	Unemployed	Totals
Puerto Ricans					
Number	5	41	50	76	172
Percent	2.9	23.8	29.1	44.2	87.8
Other Hispanics					
Number	1	13	8	2	24
Percent	4.2	54.2	33.3	8.3	12.2
Totals					
Number	6	54	58	78	196
Percent	3.1	27.6	29.6	39.8	100.0

TABLE 6.13 Detailed Breakdown of Type of Work

	Puerto Ricans		Other Hispanics		Total	
	Number	Percent	Number	Percent	Number	Percent
No Response	15	8.7	0	0.0	15	7.7
Machine Operator	25	14.5	1	4.2	26	13.3
Electronic	10	5.8	9	37.5	19	9.7
Clerical	2	1.2	0	0.0	2	1.0
Janitor	17	9.9	1	4.2	18	9.2
Landscape	10	5.8	0	0.0	10	5.1
Social Service Trainee	3	1.7	1	4.2	4	2.0
Other Unskilled	23	13.4	7	29.2	30	15.3
Other Skilled	6	3.5	3	12.5	9	4.6
Unemployment	61	35.5	2	8.3	63	32.1
Total	172	87.8	24	12.2	196	100.0

Thirty-four persons or 32.4 percent of those employed spoke English well or fairly well.

Those who spoke English well or fairly well were more likely to hold full-time or part-time jobs than to be unemployed. The opposite held true for those who spoke no English. For those who spoke little English, 45 percent held full-time jobs and 54.4 percent held no jobs.[32]

Although the correlates are only moderate, the general trend in the data is that those who spoke no English are more likely to be unemployed. Those with little English ability are likely to be unemployed or hold less skilled jobs. Heads of household claiming to speak the English language well or fairly well tend to hold jobs more often and, compared to others, have more highly skilled jobs.

The evidence presented thus far clearly indicates that employment or the hope of employment is the main reason for Puerto Rican migration to Waltham. It also confirms the dual-market assertions that economists Rita Maldonado and Michael Piore present and that have been summarized in Chapter 4. It appears that Puerto Rican migrant workers may be willing to risk unemployment because they are aware of welfare entitlements.

The large percentage (33.2 percent) of Waltham's Hispanic heads of household receiving welfare payments can be explained as easily by their participation in the secondary labor force as by their inability to speak English or their lack of a high school education.

We asked the heads of household to tell us specifically the types of jobs they did for payment in the last three years (1972–75). What follows are the answers to that question. Some persons, having held more than one job in three years, gave us two, three, and, at times, four answers. All of the following are unskilled and generally very poorly paid jobs and clearly in the secondary sector:

Machine operator (in a factory or plant)	48
Factory (mostly assembly work)	41
Janitor	22
Hotel or restaurant personnel (usually dishwasher, waiter, or kitchen aide)	13
Landscaping or farming	12
Housekeeper	3
Truck or bus driver (part-time)	3
Security guard	2
Painter	1
Construction work	1
Total	146

The number of professional, skilled, or semi-skilled jobs performed according to the survey is very small by comparison:

Skilled worker (usually working with electronics machines at Raytheon, and other 128 electric and communication firms)	12
Semi-skilled worker (soldering, working with chemicals, drilling, and grinding)	6
Social Services - often as translators	6
Secretary, office clerk	4
Salespersons	3
Manager	2
Teacher	2
Construction work	1
Total	35

Puerto Ricans in Waltham are very much at the survival stage—that is, their main concerns are food, shelter, and clothing. Thus, the social service agencies coming into most contact with Puerto Ricans are those related to public welfare; for example, Aid to Families with Dependent Children, Food Stamps, and Medicaid. As easily seen in Table 6.14, Puerto Ricans showed particularly high utilization rates of welfare, medicaid, and food stamps relative to other Hispanics. However, since other Hispanics are not always citizens, they may not be entitled to these services.

TABLE 6.14 Public Assistance Utilization Rates

	Puerto Ricans		Other Hispanics		Total	
	Number	Percent	Number	Percent	Number	Percent
Welfare*	62	36.0	3	12.5	65	33.2
Medicaid*	90	52.3	7	29.2	97	49.5
Food Stamps*	83	48.3	6	25.0	89	45.4
Social Security Insurance	8	4.7	0		8	4.1
Social Security**	1	.6	0		1	.5

*Areas of substantial differences between Puerto Ricans and other Hispanics.

**Hispanics, especially Puerto Ricans, often refer to unemployment benefits as "social security."

Puerto Ricans had greater contact with the Department of Welfare, the Department of Education, the Housing Authority, City Hall, and the Police Department. The most utilized program was Roberto Clemente, with both groups showing high utilization rates. (See Table 6.15.)

TABLE 6.15 Utilization Rates of Selected Institutions

	Puerto Ricans		Other Hispanics		Total	
	Number	Percent	Number	Percent	Number	Percent
Boston College						
Legal Aid	26	15.1	3	12.5	29	14.8
Social Security	44	25.6	6	25.6	50	25.5
Department of Bilingual						
Education	38	22.1	3	12.5	41	20.9
Department of Welfare	94	54.7	4	16.7	98	50.0
Housing Authority	38	22.1	3	12.5	41	20.9
Police	21	12.2	0		21	10.7
Fire	6	3.5	1	4.2	7	3.6
City Hall	36	20.9	3	12.5	39	19.9
Roberto Clemente	102	59.3	14	58.4	116	58.4

In general, mental health or counseling services were not used to any great extent by either Puerto Ricans or other Hispanics interviewed with the exception of Project Health[33] and the Community Mental Health Program at Waltham Hospital, which was mainly used by Puerto Ricans. It should be noted that both of these services utilize Hispanics or Anglo Spanish-speaking staff.

Services to Puerto Ricans and Hispanics follow the migrations. It is not until a significant population of Puerto Ricans and other Hispanics are residents of a specific town and advocates begin clamoring for services that social service agencies begin to address that population.

In Waltham, it was Hispanic Brandeis students and some faculty who initially provided enough impetus to support community leaders in their request for Spanish language services at Waltham Hospital. They were able to obtain Project Health, which was initially staffed by a non-Puerto Rican Hispanic and a Spanish-speaking Anglo worker. Project Health continues as part of Waltham Hospital. In contrast, a Hispanic neighborhood center (El Centro) died when funding for it stopped. Its demise was followed by the establishment of El Programa Roberto Clemente in 1974.

El Programa Roberto Clemente negotiated for services and greater employment and housing opportunities for Puerto Ricans and Hispanics in the city and surrounding area. Responses to the questionnaire tend to indicate that Puerto Ricans did not use services other than welfare and the hospital prior to 1974. Social services were utilized to a greater extent after 1974. This is attributed to El Programa's successful advocacy for the hiring of Spanish-speaking workers in such agencies and in mandating priority in CETA slots for Hispanic service providers. By 1975, Hispanics began to see city services as possible networks of support and used the facilities listed in Table 6.16 to the indicated extent.

TABLE 6.16 Utilization of Health and Mental Health Organizations and Institutions

	Puerto Ricans		Other Hispanics		Total	
	Number	Percent	Number	Percent	Number	Percent
Metropolitan State Hospital	11	6.4	1	4.2	12	6.1
Beaverbrook Guidance	3	1.7	0		3	1.5
Fernald State School	5	2.9	0		5	2.6
Family Youth Resource	2	1.2	2	1.2	2	1.0
Family Counseling	9	5.2	0		9	4.6
Project Health, Waltham Hospital	87	50.6	7	29.2	94	48.0
Community Mental Health, Waltham Hospital	16	9.3	0		16	8.2

El Programa Roberto Clemente was clearly the most utilized service by Waltham's Hispanic population at the time of this study. People often came to El Programa for help in filling out forms, getting letters translated to and from English, help in job placement, translation services with welfare, doctors and lawyers, and English language classes.

A very active youth group, a tenants rights group, and a civil rights group were organized.

Recreational activities in the area, even when known, were not generally used. Most who claimed to participate began doing so after 1974. The YMCA is a good example. Almost everyone involved in some Y activity claimed they began that involvement after 1974. In general, people using the services rated them as excellent or good. The main reasons for not using services were lack of transportation, lack of money, or lack of awareness. The more culturally and physically accessible a facility was, the more likely it was to be used. The recreational patterns of Waltham's Hispanic population duplicate the pattern of most poor persons. The chief uses of free time involve relatively small investments of money.

An important indicator of the quality of life for any group of people is their use of leisure time and the activities they identify as recreational. In looking at recreational patterns of the Hispanic population in Waltham as a measure of the acceptance of Waltham as their new elsewhere, we asked the heads of household several questions. What did they and members of their families do for recreation? What recreational activities would they like for themselves and their families? Which recreational facilities in Waltham were known to them? We also requested a rating (excellent, good, or poor) of those facilities. My assumption was that recreational facilities, like social service agencies, would have been used to a greater extent after 1974 for two reasons. After 1974, there were more Hispanic families in Waltham, and, more importantly, the facilities (through El Programa Roberto Clemente) had been urged to make the use of their services easier and more attractive for Hispanic families.

The families questioned indicated that men and young men used recreational facilities to a much greater extent than women, young women, and children. Men were almost twice as likely to see socials and dances as recreational possibilities. Sixty-three households identified these as activities that men attended as compared to 35 households identifying them as women's activities.

Visiting relatives and friends was mentioned as the most frequent recreational activity for women and children—less so for male or female youth. This activity may be a cultural mechanism of support but is possibly strengthened by an economic factor; that is, such visits do not cost money. Car rides (outings) and walks were seen as recreation for all family members. Few Hispanic families owned cars, compared to the general Waltham population, but friends and neighbors often took each other on outings.

Watching television ranked very high as a use of leisure time for all family members, and attending church-related activities (coffee and doughnuts after mass) was also seen as desirable by almost 75 percent of the families interviewed.

Participating in sports was seen as a recreational activity for the young men and adult males. It was not then an option for the women and girls, although most families expressed a desire for both their male and female children to be active in summer and winter sports.

Men considered "hanging around" and visiting the neighborhood bars as recreational activities. Women and youth were less likely to use their leisure time in this way.

The Boys Club was the best known recreational facility, with parks in the city being less known and less used. Parents would like to see summer camp facilities for their male and female children. They also thought a Hispanic social club that would plan dances and other cultural and recreational activities would be desirable.

Waltham, having farms within its boundaries (and also an office for migrant workers), having more jobs in the 1960s than people to fill these jobs, having a certain amount of low-income housing and some public transportation (within it as well as to and from it), may very well be a good example of the type of city where Puerto Ricans have migrated. The available jobs in the Route 128 complex described earlier attracted French Canadians and other poor white persons, but some of the dirty work they had previously done (in farms, factories, hotels, and restaurants) may have been left in need of workers. Puerto Ricans moved first to the farms and then to the factories and other nonfarm secondary employment in and around Waltham.

The work to which they moved is unstable and low paying. It is work that inevitably becomes less available. First generation Puerto Rican workers became more numerous as they attempted to secure such jobs and join their relatives. The competition for jobs is among the unskilled workers in the city, among Puerto Ricans themselves, and with other Hispanics. The question raised is, who will succeed in the attainment of jobs—and especially of jobs that are better paying and offer the possibility of security?

In comparing education, ability to speak English, length of residency in Waltham, and citizenship (Puerto Ricans as opposed to other Hispanics) as predictors of income (the dependent variable), the following statistical analysis suggests that the most important independent variable is citizenship. Essentially one is more likely to have a higher

income if one is a Hispanic rather than a Puerto Rican.
The ability to speak English is the second strongest
predictor. The number of weeks in Waltham and the amount
of education are slightly less important than the first two
independent variables.

My study attempts to predict the importance of the
previously mentioned independent variables (education,
ability to speak English, length of residency in Waltham,
and citizenship—Puerto Rican or other Hispanic) on job
status as the dependent variable. The regression analysis
suggests that the order of importance of the independent
variables for predicting type of work held are:

- ability to speak English;
- citizenship;
- length of residency;
- education

The evidence seems to indicate that the Waltham Spanish
speakers who are not Puerto Rican tend to have better
paying jobs, greater educational attainment, and are able to
pay higher rents than Puerto Ricans. In Waltham, most of
the other Hispanics are also poor, and thus they compete
with Puerto Ricans for the more desirable jobs. In many
other towns with large Hispanic populations such as Newton, the majority of the Hispanics are non-Puerto Rican and
tend to be skilled workers and professionals. Thus, there
is little competition of the type seen in Waltham. And yet,
social service providers and affirmative action programs
tend to categorize all Hispanics as if their needs were
similar. Chapter 9 attempts to show that the needs of
Puerto Ricans are usually different from the needs of other
Hispanics. Although Puerto Ricans make up the majority of
Hispanics in New York and New England, they most often
are overshadowed by non-Puerto Rican Hispanics.

NOTES

1. Anne L. Kirchheimer, "Lure of Jobs Attract Puerto
Ricans to U.S.," Boston Globe, January 16, 1978, p. 16.
2. Ibid.
3. The W Farms is a specific farm in Lexington, MA.
4. See brief interview with Suncha in this chapter.
5. Ibid.
6. Michael J. Piore, "The Role of Immigration in
Industrial Growth: A Case Study of the Origins and Character of Puerto Rican Migration to Boston," (working paper,
Department of Economics, Massachusetts Institute of Tech-

nology, May 1973).

7. The trainees and I were given instructions in how best to use the questionnaire by Dr. Rocina Becerra and Dr. Fernando Torres-Gil, both Hispanic graduates of Brandeis' Heller School.

8. "Census Shows Hispanic Families Rising in Income Faster Than Other Groups," New York Times, September 7, 1975, p. 30.

9. Massachusetts Department of Commerce and Development, "City and Town—City of Waltham Monograph," mimeograph. March, (Boston, 1972).

10. Howard Gitelman, Workingmen of Waltham (Baltimore: Johns Hopkins University Press, 1974).

11. Ibid., p. 12.

12. The population began to decrease as of 1970, coinciding with the influx of greater numbers of Puerto Ricans.

13. In fairness to both the census and the Beaverbrook study, the reasons for the disparities may be that poorer persons have settled in Waltham and that the job market changed since those studies were done.

14. Beaverbrook Guidance Center, "The Spanish Population of Waltham," mimeographed (Belmont, MA: Beaverbrook Guidance Center, 1974).

15. Ibid., p. 2.

16. Ibid., p. 3.

17. The statistical differences between the groups on grade completed are: $\chi^2 = 19.12$; df3; p = .003; R = .22.

18. Beaverbrook Guidance Center, "Spanish Population," p. 3.

19. χ^2 for rent paid by Puerto Ricans compared to other Hispanics approaches significance. ($\chi^2 = 9.56$; p = .0885.)

20. Adriana Gianturco and Norman Aronin, Boston's Spanish Speaking Community (Boston: Action for Boston Community Development, October 1971), p. 12.

21. Susan E. Brown, The Hispano Population of Cambridge: A Research Report (Cambridge, MA: Cambridge Spanish Council, 1973), p. 51.

22. David J. Rintel, "Some Reasons Why Puerto Ricans Migrate to the United States" (unpublished work, Somerville, MA., 1975), p. 29.

23. Ibid. Note that Rintel obtains much of his documentation from William C. Baggs, "Puerto Rico Showcase of Development," reprint from the 1962 Britannica Book of the Year (New York: Encyclopedia Britannica, Inc., 1962; and Clarence Senior, The Puerto Ricans—Strangers—Then Neighbors (Chicago: Quandrangle Books, 1961).

24. Rintel, "Why Puerto Ricans Migrate."

25. Percentages do not add up to 100 percent since other problems were selected at times.

26. I want to stress that this figure refers to net income for head of household, not family income. When the heads of household were asked their earnings, they always gave "take home pay" figures.

27. $\chi^2 = 7.82$ and $p = .02$.

28. $\chi^2 = 14.07$ and $p = .002$.

29. $\chi^2 = 31.120$ and $p = .006$. The correlation coefficient is .289.

30. $\chi^2 = 14.61$ and $p = .023$ with a correlation coefficient of .23.

31. $\chi^2 = 32.07$ and $p = .042$; correlation coefficient = .23.

32. Note $\chi^2 = 41.46$ and $p = .00001$ with a correlation coefficient of .30.

33. Project Health or Projecto Salud was founded in the early 1970s largely as a result of advocacy efforts by L. Orlando Izaza, a Hispanic (Colombian) student at Brandeis who was its first director. The project is housed in Waltham Hospital and has become integrated into the hospital. The staff (two persons) provide translation services and advocacy on health related issues.

7

From Orocovis, Puerto Rico, to Elsewhere

"Pero negrito, después de carreteras y estudios, quien diablo siembra guineos?" ("But my dear, after roads and schooling, who the hell will plant bananas?")

> From an interview with
> Mrs. Ofelia Torres de Melendez
> Mayor of Orocovis, Puerto Rico

"Pero la necesidad del empleo los echa afuera, afuera. La pena es que venden lo que tienen para irse y van con la idea de que van a progresar. Cuando sufren allá, no tienen nada a que regresar aquí porque han vendido lo poquito que tenían. Sufren aquí y sufren allá." ("But the need for employment pushes them out, out. The pity is that they sell all they have so they can leave. They go with the idea that they will make progress. When they suffer over there, they have nothing here to return to because they have sold what little they had. They suffer here and they suffer there.")

> From an interview with
> Nimia Lugo de Morales
> Pharmacist, Orocovis, Puerto Rico

The Puerto Ricans migrating to New York City in the 1940s and 1950s were first generation migrants. The typical pattern was one in which the family was uprooted twice. First there was a movement from Puerto Rican rural towns

to slums in Puerto Rican cities.[1]   Unable to secure employment in those cities, Puerto Ricans often moved to
slums in New York.   They were thus pushed out of Borinquen while being pulled to New York City.

The 1976 report of the U.S. Commission on Civil
Rights, Puerto Ricans in the Continental United States: An
Uncertain Future, describes three distinct trends in Puerto
Rican migration to the United States.   "All three," the
report asserts, "have responded to job opportunities on the
mainland and the Island."[2]

During the first stage, in the 1950s, an average of
40,000 Puerto Ricans migrated each year.   Job recruiters
often came to the island in a process that resembled the
recruitment of European peasants and southern blacks
discussed earlier.   In the 1950s, according to the report,
Puerto Rican "farm workers were affected by unemployment
or had seasonal work (such as sugar cane cultivation) that
left them idle for several months of a year."   On the other
hand, the U.S. economy was booming and Puerto Ricans
were in demand in the "sweatshops in the needlework
industry. . . . Puerto Rico unlike the mainland, offered
few urban jobs, particularly in factories, that could serve
as a social step upward in comparison to field labor."[3]
Approximately 20 percent (400,000) of Puerto Rico's population migrated to the United States during this stage.

During the second stage of migration in the 1960s,
hundreds of factories opened on the island as a result of
the industrialization process in Puerto Rico.   Nevertheless,
even with the factories, workers could not be absorbed,
and according to the Civil Rights report, "neither could all
of the young persons entering the labor force nor the farm
workers idled by the shrinking of agricultural jobs."[4]   The
1960s averaged a yearly migration of 20,000 persons from
Puerto Rico to the United States.

The third stage—the 1970s—marked the third trend.
Unemployment in the United States became widespread, and
factories in many U.S. cities closed.   Despite the fact that
Puerto Rico's unemployment rate soared to 19 percent by
1975, the migration slowed down, and at times there was a
reverse migration.[5]   This trend, nevertheless, appears to
have been temporary.   Table 7.1 depicts travel to and from
the United States from 1970–83.   Please note that the
figures do not always agree with the figures provided in
Table 8 of Puerto Ricans in the Continental United States
- - An Uncertain Future[6] or with those found in Latino
Migration Under Capitalization.[7]   All tables obtain their data
from the Puerto Rican Planning Board.   Not all those
leaving or arriving in Puerto Rico are necessarily Puerto

TABLE 7.1   Puerto Rico Net Migration: Fiscal 1970-83

Year	Inbound Passengers	Outbound Passengers	Balance*
1970-71	2,088,544	2,091,069	- 2,525
1971-72	2,329,872	2,306,224	23,648
1972-73	2,470,076	2,507,145	-37,069
1973-74	2,497,170	2,522,141	-24,971
1974-75	2,329,452	2,334,882	- 5,430
1975-76	2,317,034	2,280,833	36,201
1976-77	2,341,174	2,346,784	- 4,610
1977-78	2,538,671	2,558,953	-20,282
1978-79	2,853,324	2,859,402	- 6,078
1979-80	2,741,798	2,757,899	-16,101
1980-81	2,645,430	2,645,890	-10,460
1981-82	2,660,153	2,693,450	-33,297
1982-83	2,575,967	2,620,400	-44,433

*A negative balance indicates an outflow of people from the Island.
Source: Data from Commonwealth of Puerto Rico Planning Board. Printed in National Puerto Rican Coalition, "Puerto Ricans in the United States and on the Island--1970-1980," mimeographed (Washington, DC: October 15, 1984).

Ricans or persons of Puerto Rican heritage. Some of the persons may be Anglo-Americans or members of other Hispanic groups. As previously discussed, the latter may prefer to live or seek a home in a place where a Hispanic culture still dominates and where Spanish is the native tongue. There is generally little information on the income level, skills, and educational attainment of those persons who return to Borinquen, or any indication of how long they remain there without again migrating to the United States. "Some observers have perceived the two Puerto Rican communities (on the Island and on the mainland) as two parts of the same organism, linked by a highway in the air. By 1970, the combined population of Puerto Ricans on the Island and the United States mainland was in excess of 4.1 million, with 66 percent residing in Puerto Rico, 20 percent in New York City, and 14 percent living elsewhere on the United States mainland."[8]
    According to the 1980 census, the Puerto Rican popu-lation in the United States totaled more than 2,004,961 persons, an increase of 41 percent over 1970. Puerto

Ricans on the island totaled 3.1 million, an increase of 17.8 percent over 1970. Puerto Ricans in the United States comprise 13.8 percent of the Hispanic population in this country. The combined Puerto Rican population (island and United States) represents 29 percent of the 1980 U.S. Hispanic population. Between 1970 and 1980, the Puerto Rican population in Texas increased by 262 percent, in Ohio by 60 percent, in Massachusetts by 227 percent, in Connecticut by 135 percent, in Pennsylvania by 107 percent, in California by 47 percent, in New Jersey by 75 percent, and in New York State by 8 percent.

The Migration Division of the Commonwealth of Puerto Rico distinguishes Puerto Ricans visiting or residing in the United States from those who come to work as migrant workers.

> In addition to the 1.7 million year-round Puerto Rican residents of the U.S. mainland, several thousand migratory workers come each spring and summer, to fill seasonal farm labor shortages in many states along the Eastern seaboard and in the Midwest. Most of these workers return to Puerto Rico at the end of the farm season. Since the slack season in sugar cane (which is the winter crop in Puerto Rico) coincides with the peak of the farm season in the United States, this arrangement enables U.S. farmers to obtain much needed manpower; it also enables Puerto Rican agricultural workers who might otherwise be unemployed during the summer months, to obtain work. Last year in New Jersey alone, Puerto Rican farm workers harvested crops worth more than $100 million.[9]

According to Joseph Fitzpatrick, Puerto Ricans have always had an excellent reputation for being superior farmers. Early in the 1940s, U.S. employers came to Puerto Rico and hired Puerto Ricans. Because of the tendency of U.S. farmers to exploit the migrant workers and the large numbers of newspaper accounts in both Puerto Rico and the United States depicting such exploitation, Puerto Rico passed two laws in 1947 and 1948 in an attempt to regulate the recruitment of Puerto Rican laborers.[10] Puerto Ricans recruited in Borinquen had to be guaranteed employment for 160 hours at the wage level identified in the contract; provisions for transportation, housing, food, medical care, and death benefits were also stipulated. The Office of the Commonwealth of Puerto Rico established branch offices on the mainland for monitoring the contract.[11]

In 1971, Joseph Fitzpatrick claimed that an average of 29,000 contract workers have come to the mainland year after year. "They harvest sugar beets in Michigan, tobacco in Connecticut, garden crops in New Jersey, potatoes in Long Island and a range of other crops from Massachusetts to Illinois."[12] More recently, Puerto Rican migrant workers are being used in New Hampshire and Maine as well. I posit that, especially since the late 1960s, the Puerto Rican migrant worker, with or without contract, has played a major role in the Puerto Rican migration to places other than New York City. Fitzpatrick states the following:

> In some cases a contract farm laborer and his employer would come to know each other, and the Puerto Rican worker would either stay on in the United States after the contract expired, or return later without a contract as a permanent employee. In many other cases, the contract farm workers do not return to Puerto Rico, but simply stay on in the area where they were working or move to a nearby city and establish a permanent residence. Many of the original Puerto Rican communities, such as those in Camden or Trenton, New Jersey, Springfield, Massachusetts, Detroit, Michigan, and Suffolk County on eastern Long Island, New York, began with small clusters of farm contract workers who remained on the mainland. Once established, these clusters attracted relatives directly from Puerto Rico and the urban Puerto Rican communities in these cities began to develop.[13]

In Massachusetts, the Puerto Rican communities traced to migrant workers are numerous. It is possible to view the Puerto Rican population of Boston as one of these communities. The initial newcomers are joined not only by friends and relatives from their hometowns in Puerto Rico, but later by friends, relatives, and strangers from other places on the island and at times from New York City.

This has been the case of Waltham, Massachusetts. It was the nearby small farms, orchards, and nurseries of Lexington, Concord, and Waltham itself that first brought Puerto Ricans there. The majority of these Puerto Rican migrants came and are still coming from the rural town of Orocovis.

Migrants from rural areas of the island still resemble the migrants of the 1950s when the exodus was to large cities. Those cities, however, may not be San Juan or New York but such cities as Waltham.

Because, as documented earlier, the largest number of Puerto Ricans in Waltham migrated from Orocovis, Puerto Rico, the rest of this chapter will highlight various interviews that I conducted in that Puerto Rican municipality in July of 1975 in an effort to better understand the Puerto Rican migration process that starts in Orocovis and ends in Waltham.

INTERVIEW WITH
MRS. OFELIA TORRES DE MELÉNDEZ,
MAYOR OF OROCOVIS, PUERTO RICO

It was a hot and sunny July morning in 1975 when I began my journey from my parents' home in Vega Baja, Puerto Rico, to the mountainous rural town of Orocovis. A preliminary questionnaire to approximately 90 Hispanics in Waltham had revealed that almost 50 percent of them had come from that Puerto Rican municipality. I was planning to speak with the town's mayor, Mrs. Ofelia Torres de Meléndez, and to the Morales family (no relation), owners of the Farmacia Orocovis and the Orocovis Travel Agency. I had also anticipated visiting the local church, the nearby factories, and other places and persons that could help explain the large number of persons from Orocovis, Puerto Rico, living in Waltham, Massachusetts.

The Orocovis mountains and the surrounding countryside were beautiful. Along the way, I passed homes precariously perched on stilts in the rear because of the steep incline. The vegetation was lush. I couldn't help but be reminded how different this was from the Charles–Felton neighborhood in Waltham where hundreds of this town's inhabitants were living.

I arrived about 10:00 A.M. and asked an old gentleman for instructions to the mayor's office. I had made a tentative appointment for 1:00 P.M. but was prepared to come back the next day or any time that was more convenient for Mrs. Torres se Meléndez. I walked into the Orocovis Town Hall, headed for the mayor's office, and confirmed my appointment. There were many people waiting to see Her Honor. I then drove around town, made a few appointments for later on that day or the next, had a cold drink, and returned to City Hall a few minutes before 1:00 P.M.

The mayor was eating fried chicken when I knocked on her door. She reached for a paper napkin, cleaned her hands, and extended them to me, very pleased to spend some time speaking with a Puerto Rican doctoral student from the United States. "A ver si te encuentro un hueco por aqui [Let me see if I can find a place for you around here]," she said. Five women and four men were still waiting to see her. She had seen 20 people already. I asked if I could just sit and observe. "That way," I said, "you can go on seeing your public." She was delighted. She introduced me to the people as they came in, and I was granted permission to take notes.

Mrs. Torres de Meléndez did basic intake. She took people's names and addresses and asked them how she could be of help. If they were looking for work, she inquired about their formal education, their skills, and the type of work they wanted to find. Most did come asking for her support in securing employment for their relatives or for themselves. They also, at times, asked for her aid in securing a parcela, government land on which to farm and/or build a home. One older, blue-eyed, white-haired woman wanted some help in burying her son.

Her Honor gave advice freely. With one man in his fifties she went over regulations for food stamps. To a younger man who had been arrested for carrying a dangerous weapon and disturbing the peace, she said, "If you have a lawyer, do as he suggests." As he told her he had no lawyer, her grandson came in. Mrs. Torres de Meléndez hugged him and sent someone out to get some more fried chicken for the eight-year-old boy. She continued eating and loudly reminded those waiting, "I'll take care of all of you." Going back to the young man she said, "What you need is some orientation, and I am going to offer it to you now. When the judge calls on you, you tell him that you don't have a lawyer and that you want one before the trial. Have the trial suspended and I'll get you one [a lawyer]." He said, "OK," and thanked her. She replied, "A tus ordenes, mi amor [You're welcome, my love]."

Another man entered, and she promised to help him get a job with the crew fixing the streets. A second elderly woman was called in. Very well dressed, she also had light colored eyes and was fair skinned. This woman complained about the terrible conditions of the street on which she lived. She wanted the road paved, the holes covered, and the garbage collected. The mayor agreed that something had to be done. She told the woman that she had visited that street. "It's the one with all those dogs," then

added, "I haven't forgotten . . . pero son muchos los
hermanos del muerto [the brothers and sisters of the de-
ceased are many]," meaning that the problems and requests
are too numerous.

The elderly woman thanked Doña Ofelia and asked for
"otro favor." She had a daughter who completed two years
of college. Her daughter needed work. "If she does not
get work soon, she will have to move elsewhere—perhaps
leave Puerto Rico altogether." Mrs. Torres de Meléndez
said she would put the woman's daughter's name on a list,
but she wanted to see the young lady herself.

Doña Ofelia, as many call the mayor, was a big,
motherly woman who spiced her language with a few curse
words. She looked at the statue of Saint Jude that was on
her desk. She repeated, almost to herself, but loud
enough for me to hear, "Ay! son muchos los hermanos del
muerto." Turning to me she said, in Spanish, "Now there
is a great deal of academic preparation but little employment. There is work on the land but people do not
want to toil it. . . . What the hell is the use of finishing
twelve years of schooling so that later you can go back to
the farms . . . and do the same thing that you would have
done without schooling. . . . In truth, it's not just
. . . but the thing is to work . . . even if it's collecting
papers in the streets. One has to earn a living. I guess
if not here—elsewhere."

Another young man entered. He complained of poor
sanitation in his barrio (neighborhood) and of lots of
garbage all over the place. He said that people were
burning the garbage in the streets and that she must do
something. He was angry. Obviously, Her Honor knew
that man. She also reacted angrily. "I'll take care of
you," she said. "Don't start out with your political
rhetoric. We are all brothers and sisters. . . . I'll take
care of you despite your political ideology. I'm grateful for
your concerns. I'll look into it. I'll also take care of the
holes. Can you do something about all those dogs?"
Evidently, the young man did not agree with Her Honor's
politics, and he lived on the street that the second elderly
woman complained about.

She turned and asked me how I was doing. "Fine," I
answered. "Gracias." She continued seeing people until
they were all gone. It was then almost 3:00 P.M.

Mrs. Torres de Meléndez told me that she had 17
grandchildren. She often had to see them the way she had
seen her grandson earlier. "They like to be with me.
Sometimes they all stay at my house at once."

"Orocovis," she went on, "has 17 barrios, as many

barrios as I have grandchildren. The town itself is in the middle. Orocovis is in the middle of the island. It's the heart of Puerto Rico . . . the third largest municipality in terms of territory, only Utuado and Ponce are larger." She remembered traveling on horseback around Orocovis' hills in the 1940s. "The roads were nonexistent, but 30 years ago people were not leaving. They managed. They were farmers and they loved the land. They grew platanos, bananas, coffee, sweet potatoes, pumpkins, mangos, and other vegetables. Today the roads are real roads, and people complain about a small hole. They're graduating from high school now, and they don't want to work the farms anymore. Only the old ones do that. They still do it with love, but who will take their place?" She paused, "If there were other types of work, perhaps more would stay. But the factories here do not offer enough employment and the farms are not seen as desirable work places for those who have aspirations of doing better work."

She removed some paper from a chair near the wall, pulled the chair closer to where I was sitting, and sat on it. "In 1941," she went on, "I used to have a bakery. I couldn't deliver bread if the river grew. Sometimes I would try for days to take the bread around. . . . In those days men and women would bathe in the creeks. There was no water system. People would sell water for two cents a big can. We had no hospitals—no roads, bridges, running water. But people still need to better themselves. They need jobs. Agriculture was the source of strength in the 1940s. Farms were worked on by entire families. . . . Pero negrito,[14] despues de carreteras y estudios quien diablo siembra guineós? [But my dear, after roads and schooling who the hell will plant bananas?]"

Her Honor explained that approximately 200 youngsters graduated from Orocovis High School every year. Twenty percent of them have ususally gone on to college in Puerto Rico. The others needed work—but there was none. So some went to San Juan, but many went to the United States. Some families, afraid of their children leaving after high school by themselves, went to the United States before the children finished.

In 1975 there were three factories in Orocovis: Rico Banana, Socks and Stockings, and La Pionera. Rico Banana canned gandules (green pigeon peas) and other native products. It also canned baby food. It only employed 50 people because it was capital rather than labor intensive.

Socks and Stockings, the second factory, was U.S.- owned and employed 200 men and women. La Pionera, another U.S.-owned factory, manufactured underwear and employed 250 to 300 people.

Her Honor continued, "What we have," she said, "is not enough. If we had ten more factories, we would fill them with workers, and perhaps there would be happier families around here. Aquí siempre hay alguien llorando porque algún ser querido se está yendo para otro sitio. [There is always someone crying around here because a loved one is going elsewhere.]"

I asked Doña Ofelia about farm workers from Orocovis migrating to the Boston area. She said, "In the 50s, local workers were getting 30 to 40 cents an hour in Puerto Rico. They got 95 cents an hour in the United States. Naturally, they went and some are still going. As a matter of fact, at first most of the men leaving here were going to work on farms. Most would come back but would go again to the same farms or others. Later they started going to the factories as well as the farms. Year after year the numbers increased. Since 1971, there is a 10 percent increase every year." She added that at times entire families left without knowing if there was work over there. "They go to live with friends and relatives hoping to work, but if worse comes to worse, Morales, there is always welfare." She thought for a while, then continued, "There is welfare here too now. . . . It's in the form of food stamps. People have to eat. Without them more people would go elsewhere."

REFLECTIONS ON THE INTERVIEW
WITH DOÑA OFELIA

Despite the trend of the early 1970s toward a reverse migration, Doña Ofelia spoke of a 10 percent increase in out-migration from Orocovis since 1971. That Orocovis was one of Puerto Rico's poorest municipalities explained its inability to hold on to its people. They were forced to leave for places of possible employment. Rural areas have traditionally been poorer than urban centers on the island.

As a whole the mean family income for 1963 in rural areas was $1,447 compared with a mean of $2,534 in urban centers. This comparison is better shown by taking a more detailed distribution of incomes while regarding the abstraction of the "mean." In a detailed distribution we find such extremes as a per capita income of $2,142 in San Juan on the one

hand, and a per capita income of $232 in Orocovis
on the other.[15]

Luis Nieves Falcón describes Puerto Rican municipalities
such as Orocovis as "municipalities which have remained
marginal to the process of economic development and are
characterized by a high rate of emigration of its young
adult population and slow increases in income."[16] Table 7.2
enumerates the municipalities with the highest unemployment
rates on the island as of 1969:[17]

TABLE 7.2 Municipalities in Puerto Rico with High Unemployment rates: 1969

Municipality	Unemployment Annual Rate of	Municipality	Unemployment Annual Rate of
Adjuntas	23.3	Manati	23.3
Aguada	24.0	Maricao	24.0
Aguadilla	24.0	Maunabo	27.9
Anasco	24.0	Moca	24.0
Arroyo	20.1	Morovis	23.3
Barceloneta	23.3	Naguabo	24.1
Cabo Rojo	21.0	Orocovis	23.3
Ciales	23.3	Patillas	20.1
Comerio	23.3	Quebradillas	22.9
Culebra	23.9	Rincon	24.0
Guayama	20.1	Sabana Grande	21.0
Hormigueros	21.0	Salinas	25.0
Humacao	23.9	San German	21.0
Isabela	24.0	Toa Alta	25.3
Jayuya	23.3	Utuado	23.3
Lajas	21.0	Vega Alta	29.0
Lares	23.3	Vega Baja	23.7
Las Marias	24.0	Vieques	23.9
Las Piedras	23.9	Uabucoa	23.9

Interestingly enough, Doña Ofelia recounted that it was
not in the 1940s that her people left Orocovis, but later,
especially the 1960s and 1970s. Other persons and families
interviewed supported this claim. They also spoke of
people in government trucks recruiting farm workers from
Orocovis to migrate as laborers to the United States.

Unemployment, according to Doña Ofelia, causes the
people to continue leaving Orocovis. Note that she also
validated Piore's assumption that the younger generation,

with more schooling than their parents, would refuse the hard work and low wages associated with farming. Factory work was seen as superior and as better paying. Mr. Guzmán and Mr. Avilés of the Corporation for Rural Development elaborated on this theme. Unlike Doña Ofelia, however, these gentlemen also stressed automation and the seasonal nature of farm work as important variables in explaining unemployment and out-migration.

I went back to Orocovis five times after my meeting with Mrs. Ofelia Torres de Meléndez. I spent time talking to people in the streets, in the stores and in their homes. Several had relatives in Waltham. Everyone to whom I spoke knew of several families living in New York, New Jersey, Pennsylvania, or the Boston area.

I spent a few days with the Morales family, going over their records of ticket sales from Orocovis to the United States. Summaries of these records will follow as will excerpts from my meetings with police officers and with Lieutenant Eduardo Pinto; hospital administrator Luis Alberto Díaz; Catholic clergymen, Father Victor Mastalerz, who is pastor of the town's Catholic church, Father William J. Joyce, and Father Julian Camino; representatives of Orocovis' three factories; and Mr. Guzmán and Mr. Avilés of the Corporation for Rural Developments.

INTERVIEW WITH MR. GUZMÁN AND MR. TORRES AVILÉS, CORPORATION FOR RURAL DEVELOPMENT

Mr. Guzmán and Mr. Torres Avilés were extremely hospitable. They began our conversation by stating that agriculture has always been the most important source of employment in Orocovis. "It was in the past and it continues to be now," Mr. Guzmán emphasized. According to these gentlemen, however, one of the problems in 1975 was that there was more and more efficiency in farming, more technology, and less need for human muscles. The fact that farming was seasonal also was problematic, especially for workers who did not own land. Production continued to increase, but the number of workers necessary for such production steadily decreased. They also quickly added that this may have been a blessing since the workers were getting older and the younger people were less interested in farming and more interested in moving to the cities. They offered me copies of two studies of farming in Orocovis, done by the University of Puerto Rico's College of Agriculture Sciences. One of the studies was done in 1963 and the other in 1975.

The reports bear out the trends that Mr. Guzmán described. In 1963, there were 823 farms (see Table 7.3). In 1975, there were 1,199 (see Table 7.4). However, in 1975, the farms were smaller and tended to be owned by the families that worked them. Guzmán repeated that Orocovis was one of the few towns in Puerto Rico that greatly depended on agriculture for its economic life and that the overwhelming majority of the farm laborers earned, as was the case in all of the mountainous areas of Puerto Rico, very low wages. They generally operated small farms with very sloped and rugged topography, which produced only enough for autoconsumption.[18]

TABLE 7.3 Classification of Farms by Size: 1963

Size in Cords	Numbers of Farms	Percent of Total	Area of Farms (Cords)	Percent of Total
3-9	238	28.91	1,441.42	5.16
10-19	209	25.39	2,879.74	10.32
20-29	116	14.09	2,775.70	9.94
30-39	68	8.26	2,284.06	8.18
40-49	61	7.41	2,707.43	9.70
50-43	88	10.69	5,942.40	21.29
100 or more	43	5.22	9,869.20	35.37
Totals	823	99.97	27,899.95	99.96

Note: A cord is slightly smaller than an acre.
Source: Servicio de Extensión Agrícola de la Universidad de Puerto Rico, Estudio de la Situación en el Area de Orocovis, Julio 1963, p. 2.

In 1965, the average age for farm workers in Puerto Rico was 52.6 years of age. In 1975, it was 56.4 years. In 1975, only 11.5 percent of the farmers were younger than 40 years old and only 2.4 percent younger than 30 years of age. On the other hand, 43.4 percent of the farmers were 60 years or older. Two hundred and three of them were 70 years or older. It may be that farming will die in Puerto Rico as these older men die. The farmers in Orocovis, as a whole, were younger than the others on the island. (See Table 7.5.)

"Farming in general is paid very poorly, is hard work, and is seasonal. Thus, it is, justly perhaps, seen as very undesirable, unsteady work," said Guzmán. He added,

TABLE 7.4 Classification of Farms by Size: 1975

Size in Cords	Numbers of Farms	Percent of Total	Area of Farms (Cords)	Percent of Total
3-9	497	41.45	2,849.82	8.13
10-19	280	23.35	3,852.78	10.99
20-29	132	11.00	3,118.65	8.89
30-39	80	6.67	2,696.25	7.69
40-49	71	5.92	3,112.68	8.88
50-99	89	7.42	5,931.70	16.92
100 or more	50	4.17	13,487.56	37.48
Totals	1,199	99.98	35,049.44	99.98

Note: A cord is slightly smaller than an acre.
Source: Universidad de Puerto Rico Colegio de Ciencias Agrícolas, Servicio de Extensión Agrícola, La Agricultura de Orocovis, Sección de Economía Agrícola, 1975, p. 3.

"It's usually people who own and love the land who continue in the industry."

In order to attract younger people to farming, as well as to avoid the exodus of the people from the rural areas to

TABLE 7.5 Age of Farmers: 1975

Age (Years)	Number	Percent of Total
Less than 30 years	28	2.44
30-39	104	9.08
40-49	228	19.91
50-59	288	25.15
60-69	294	25.67
70 years or more	203	17.72
Total	1,145	99.97

Source: Universidad de Puerto Rico Colegio de Ciencias Agrícolas, Servicio de Extensión Agrícola, La Agricultura de Orocovis, Sección de Economía Agrícola, 1975, p. 8.

the city, the government was giving families two and three cords of farming land. "We," said Guzmán, meaning the Corporation for Rural Development, "buy the larger farms and distribute them. Twenty families will be receiving farms in Orocovis for the first time this year [1975]. By next year, we hope to distribute 36,000 cords throughout Puerto Rico."

TABLE 7.6 Educational Level of Farmers

Years of School Completed	Number	Percent of Total
0	147	13.17
1-4	479	41.92
5-8	337	30.19
9-12	120	10.75
13-16	28	2.50
More than 16	5	0.44
Total	1,116	98.97

Source: Universidad de Puerto Rico Colegio de Ciencias Agrícolas, Servicio de Extensión Agrícola, La Agricultura de Orocovis, Seccion de Economía Agrícola, 1975, p. 8.

When I asked Mr. Guzmán and Mr. Torres about migrant workers from Orocovis going to the United States, they answered that in Puerto Rico the largest number of farm hands were employed in October, November, December, and January—the least in August and September. Many farm hands were accustomed to leaving for the United States in May or June and returning in October. "Poverty here," they added, "is great. People must go elsewhere." Mr. Guzmán quoted the 1975 study he had offered me earlier. "The typical average nuclear Puerto Rican farm family in the early 60s had 7.08 members. In 1975, it is 6.53. It is 4.6 for Puerto Rico in 1975."[19]

The farm hands used to leave in May and return in October. They would use their farming skills in farms in the northeastern part of the United States. They sent money home. The younger ones would come home the first and second year. The third year they would often not return. "They are poor here, they are poor there." He continued, "The people from Puerto Rico and especially from here (in Orocovis) are still migrating."

FACTORY PERSONNEL

In an effort to understand more about the relationships between Orocovis' factories and the town itself, I interviewed administrative personnel from all three factories that Mrs. Orfelia Torres de Meléndez had mentioned.

All the persons to whom I spoke were, in general, delighted with their workers. Their employees averaged 1.90 dollars an hour (76 dollars a week) in one factory, 2 dollars an hour (80 dollars a week) in the second, and 2.22 dollars an hour (88 dollars a week) in the third. The turnover rate in all three factories was very low, with the majority of workers remaining at the job for more than five years. Because of this stability, out-migration was not feared by the factories' administrators. The three interviews follow.

Interview with Héctor Sánchez,
Assistant Manager of the Orocovis
Manufacturing Corporation (La Pionera)

According to Mr. Sánchez, 200 people were employed at this factory.[20] The minimum wage (July 1975) was 1.84 dollars an hour, but 2 dollars an hour was the average wage. Many employees had been with the firm since it opened in 1966. The average worker was around 30 years of age and was female. Approximately 30 percent of the workers had finished high school. Mr. Sánchez added that all workers were literate, and some had finished college.

Despite the fact that his workers were stable and that the turnover rate was very low, Mr. Sánchez complained that food stamps discouraged people from working. He also felt that too often people were drawn to the United States. "Yes, there should be more work here—but it's really a mental thing—we are programmed from the day we are born to think that the United States is a place with lots of money, lots of facilities, and good paying work."

Interview with Orlando Irlanda, Personnel Manager,
and José Rivera - Foreman (gerente) of Orocovis
Hosiery Mills (Socks and Stockings)

This factory relocated here from the United States in 1967 and has manufactured socks for men. In 1975 it employed between 180 and 190 persons on three shifts. The minimum wage in this industry was 1.62 dollars per hour, but the average wage in this factory was 1.92 dollars. The male employees moved the socks in and out of the machines. The females did the sewing.

Most people working the first and second shifts had been employed for six, seven, or eight years, and there was very little, if any, turnover there. However, even though the hourly wage was slightly higher in the third shift (very late at night to very early in the morning), the turnover rate was high. Those who stayed in that (third) shift the longest were the young, single men. They averaged 90 dollars a week pay. All employees had medical benefits and death insurance.[21]

I asked him why he thought people left Orocovis. He agreed with Mr. Irlanda. "We do not have enough work. We now have food coupons. Maybe that's why fewer people are leaving. As long as they can eat they prefer to stay. Those that leave have a specific job in mind or a friend or a relative that promises them that they can get a job. Once the wage earner has a job over there, the family usually follows."

"Those who return from New York," said Rivera, "speak very badly about it. It's hard to raise children in New York. They say that their children, like our socks, leave Orocovis clean—almost pure—natural. And then, like our socks, they get tinted and used over there. . . . I do not agree or disagree with them. Maybe it's true. I do know that those who came back here after New York try not to go back to New York. If they return to the United States, they often try elsewhere."

Interview with Eduardo Carro,
Vice President, Rico Banana Canning Company

In 1975, Rico Banana employed 42 persons. Mr. Carro explained that in the past they had employed as many as 60. It was a slow season, but the lower number of employees was also due to the larger number of packaging machines. Things were done faster with fewer people. Two-thirds of the employees were male, one third were female. Ninety percent of the employees had been with the company for more than three years, 80 percent for five or more, and 50 percent had been employed at Rico Banana for more than 15 years. As in the other two factories, turnover rate was low. The minimum wage at this factory was 2 dollars an hour; the average wage was 2.22 dollars an hour.

Rico Banana had been in Orocovis since 1949. It was

the only one of the three factories that was Puerto Rican-owned. It established itself in Orocovis to insure proximity to the agricultural products it cans. Canning requires a great deal of water. Orocovis provides an ample supply of fresh water. In 1975, the company produced over 2 million dollars in products a year. Price control, Mr. Carro said, kept him from producing more. He bought his raw produce from the local farmers. His number one canning crop was pigeon peas (gandules).

INTERVIEW WITH LUIS ALBERTO DÍAZ, OROCOVIS HOSPITAL

Luis Alberto Díaz was the administrator of Orocovis Hospital. He told me that his beds were filled at least 70 percent of the time. The hospital employed two doctors, six registered nurses, and nine practical nurses. The employees were paid by the Orocovis municipality or by the government of Puerto Rico.

"No one using the hospital pays for the services," said Mr. Díaz, "everyone here qualifies for Medicaid. We see 100 to 150 persons a day. The majority of them are women and children. When the mothers come to bring their children for a check-up or a vaccine, they take the opportunity for a check-up for themselves. The cancer rate here is high. We get a lot of people with the flu. Diabetes, asthma, and bronchitis are common illnesses. Once in a while, we get cases of anemia in some children. When we cannot handle a case, we send the person to the hospital in Ponce or Aibonito."

Mr. Díaz was born and raised in Orocovis. He had relatives in Delaware. When I asked him why people left Orocovis, he replied, "Employment is the big issue." He thought that when people came back to visit, they seemed to be well off. They had nice clothing and brought presents; others, especially those without jobs, wanted to go also.

Mr. Díaz talked to a large number of patients and claimed they all had close relatives in the United States. He said, "They tell me what kind of work they do. . . . In Pennsylvania, it's mushrooms they work with. In Hartford, they work on tobacco farms. On Long Island, they do gardening. In Waltham, they do gardening, too, and some work in factories. In Newark, it's vegetables, and in New York state, it's gardening and factories." He added, "They do a lot of farming over there; that's what we can do best."

INTERVIEW WITH EDUARDO PINTO,
LIEUTENANT, OROCOVIS POLICE DEPARTMENT

In 1975, Orocovis employed 15 male police officers and 1 female. "That's plenty," said Eduardo Pinto, "we usually get less than three or four arrests a week. . . . The most common crimes are really accident related—or disturbing the peace. A few are due to heavy drinking."

Migrant workers had to come to the police department for fingerprints before they left. "We're getting fewer and fewer. Perhaps it's because less are migrating to farms . . . more are going to cities. . . . They do not have to come here for that."

"The reason they leave," continued Lieutenant Pinto, "is to get jobs. . . . They still tend to leave in May and June."

INTERVIEW WITH FATHER VICTOR MASTALERZ,
FATHER WILLIAM J. JOYCE, AND PADRE JULIAN CAMINO
OF THE HOLY SPIRIT CATHOLIC CHURCH

There were four priests in the Holy Spirit Parish of Orocovis Center; two were North Americans and two were Spaniards.[22] Three were assigned on a full-time basis to the parish, and one of them was assigned on weekends. I spoke with the three gentlemen who were at the parish on a full-time basis.

Father Victor Mastalerz had been a priest in Puerto Rico for ten and a half years as of July of 1975. He had been at the Holy Spirit Church for five of those years. Father Joyce had been in Orocovis for two years and Padre Camino for six.

I explained that I was in Orocovis to try to understand why so many of its inhabitants were living in the Boston area. I told them my background and asked them to chat with me. They said they were delighted to do so and I, too, enjoyed the visit.

In response to my question about why people left, Father Joyce said, "People leave for economic reasons and return for sentimental or cultural reasons. Anyone who leaves Orocovis does not do so because of the people who live here or because of the climate. The reason is purely economic."

Fathers Mastalerz and Camino agreed. "A lot of people," said Camino, "put themselves or their relatives and friends down. They complain of the food stamp program— of people being lazy, but if we had more employment in factories or stores or other work, they would not hesitate to go get the jobs. If they were lazy, they would not risk moving to a strange land hoping for jobs."

Father Mastalerz said his parishioners often talked of the United States. "They talk about the family members they have in America. They talk of differences in climates, about being curious about what's over there, of wanting to see and feel snow, of getting jobs." He continued, "Our people here are not divorced from the mainland. Most, if not all, have relatives in the United States. As a matter of fact, most of the people in Orocovis get financial aid from relatives in the United States."

There were three parishes in Orocovis: Holy Spirit, Misión Noel, and Fátima. In the town section of Orocovis, there were 14,000 people with 2,500 receiving communion weekly. "Protestants," said the Fathers, "have not made a significant inroad in Orocovis."

"The other priests, from the other parishes," said Father Camino, "would make the same types of comments as we are making."

Father William was impressed with the fact that so many of the persons leaving Orocovis were settling in Waltham, Massachusetts. "It seems," he said, "that 60 percent of those persons that I know who have left have gone to Waltham." "Why Waltham," I asked. "Why not?" they said. "Those leaving with families have heard horror stories about New York. They want to go somewhere else. They usually have friends and family in Waltham," said Father Mastalerz.[23]

They, too, mentioned that food stamps helped to curb the out-migration. "Unfortunately, if one earns a little money he can't get food stamps. If they want benefits they can't work. Sometimes a seasonal job is worse than no job at all."

INTERVIEW WITH THE MORALES FAMILY

The Morales were a well-established, respected family in Orocovis. La Señora Nímia Lugo de Morales was a licensed pharmacist. She and her husband Egberto managed Orocovis' largest drug store. They both owned land and were in the agricultural industry. Egberto Junior and his wife ran the Morales travel agency from the drug store, which was in the center of town near City Hall.

I wandered into the Morales Pharmacy the first time I went to Orocovis. I introduced myself and asked Mrs. Nímia Lugo de Morales if she would have time to speak with me about the town and about the people who leave it. She said she gladly would as long as she wasn't busy. She also suggested that I include her husband and her son in the discussions. Her daughter-in-law was pregnant and was not around for our talks. I am very grateful to this family. for their enthusiasm and willingness to share their ideas and experiences.

The Morales were an attractive group of people. They were considered a part of the power structure in the town and recognized as leaders. They acknowledged the respect that was given them and took leadership in issues affecting the town.

Mrs. Morales was articulate and often was elected spokesperson by community groups. She saw the migration as a forced one. "People are obligated to leave," she said. "It used to be that in the 50s and 60s the government trucks would go around Orocovis' sectors recruiting farm hands to migrate as seasonal workers. The men really had no choice. . . . The biggest problem their leaving created was that it left so many families fatherless for months. At times, it was not just their specific (nuclear) family that missed them. It was often their sisters, nephews, and parents who also felt a lack of leadership and a general void by the absence of the family's most respected male . . . the advice giver."

She went on, "And then so many people just left their own homes in Orocovis' barrios (neighborhoods). They moved to the town center. The whole countryside appeared to have come to the town itself.[24]

"The trucks don't come now as much as they did in the late 60s and early 70s. But people keep leaving. They prefer to stay here, especially if they live in the town's center, closer to schools and public transportation. Pero la necesidad, del empleo los echa afuera—afuera. La pena es que vénden lo que tienen para irse y van con la idea de que van a progresar. Cuando súfren alla, no tienen nada a que regresar aquí porque han vendído lo póquito que tenían. Sufren aquí y sufren allá. [But the need for employment pushes them out—out. The pity is that they sell all they have so they can leave. They go with the idea that they will make progress. When they suffer over there, they have nothing here to return to because they have sold what little they had. They suffer here and they suffer there.][25]

"Lo que pasa es que los viejos vuelven pero sus hijos se quédan. [What happens is that the older ones return but their children remain]," Mr. Morales added.

"Was there a time when the people of Orocovis migrated

in large numbers?" I asked. Mrs. Morales replied, "They
have always left, but in the late 1960s many more left,
[porque aqui la agricultura cayi cayó entonces y mas tarde]
because here agriculture almost collapsed then and during
the few years that followed." "They leave more frequently
in May and June," said Morales, Jr. He confirmed the
statements articulated earlier by Guzmán and Torres Avilés
of the Corporation for Rural Development. His statements
were also congruent with the figures of the 1975 report of
the University of Puerto Rico.[26] Generally, paid workers
were utilized during the fall and winter months. By comparison, few were utilized during the spring or summer.[27]

TABLE 7.7   Month of the Year in which Paid Farm Workers Are Most Utilized

Month	Total	General	Vegetables and Grains	Coffee
January	119	--	89	27
February	68	--	56	4
March	705	1	63	1
April	53	--	18	--
May	58	--	45	12
June	84	--	49	24
July	55	--	18	23
August	46	--	20	8
September	39	--	35	4
October	131	--	65	42
November	240	--	121	84
December	186	--	102	60

Source: Universidad de Puerto Rico Colegio de Ciencias Agrícolas,
Servicio de Extensión Agrícola, La Agricultura de Orocovis, Sección de
Economía Agrícola, 1975, p. 31.

Table 7.7 clearly documents this. It also shows that
workers were less utilized in April, May, June, July,
August, and September—the months when Puerto Rican
migrant workers were used most in the United States for
the harvesting of summer crops.
I spoke further to the family. They offered their
travel agency records for me to examine. Their records
were not complete, but the pattern of more persons
migrating in May, June, and July than at any other time
held for every year, regardless of destination. Mr.

Morales, Jr., sold tickets through Delta, Trans Caribbean, Caribair, Avianca, Eastern, Air France, and Pan American. His records did not reflect the purchase of tickets outside Orocovis. Through the ticket records, we can determine if the traveler was male or female, paying full fare (older than 12), or half (under 12). Figure 7.1 gives us a picture of the migration to New York City in 1972. It bears out the commentaries of several residents of Orocovis—that workers left during the inactive farm season on the island. Table 7.8 is interesting in that it charts numbers of tickets sold to different destinations in the United States during the peak travel months of the years 1972–75. The figures correspond directly with Mr. Díaz' (hospital administrator) description of where people with whom he speaks say their relatives have gone.

Morales, Jr., said that those that leave in March, April, and May usually have a specific job in mind. Working in green houses and people's gardens was popular then. "They know where they are going and the boss is usually ready for them."

Mrs. Morales spoke to many of the people who return to Orocovis for Christmas or to visit sick relatives "or on

Figure 7.1 Sale of Airline Tickets from Orocovis to New York City by Month: 1972

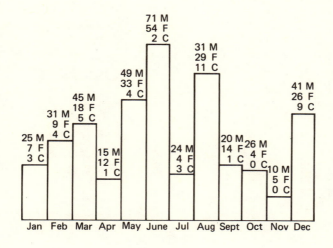

TABLE 7.8 Destinations of Travelers to the United States from Orocovis, Puerto Rico, during Months of Peak Travel

City	1972 MAY M	F	C	JUNE M	F	C	JULY M	F	C	1973 MAY M	F	C	JUNE M	F	C	JULY M	F	C	1974 MAY M	F	C	JUNE M	F	C	JULY M	F	C	1975 MAY M	F	C	JUNE M	F	C	JULY M	F	C	Subtotal M	F	C	TOTAL
Atlanta																																3							3	3
Baltimore	4	1		5			1	1		3	1		9			5	2		2			2			7	1		6			1						44	6		50
Boston	16	8	2	30	17	2	8	6	1	6	1	1	13	11		20	18	5	26	16	4	10	13	2	11			8			9	8					164	113	17	294
Buffalo																			1																		2	1		3
Chicago	3	3	4	5	2	3				2	4		3	4	2	3	4	1	5			7			4	4		6	10		3	2					41	33	17	91
Cleveland													1						2																		3			3
Washington													1					1				1	4						1	4	3						2	6	8	16
Grand Rapids																			4	2																	4	2		6
Hartford	7	4	3	4	6					4	2	1	1	6	4	3			6	10		2	1		2	1		3	4		3	6					35	41	13	89
Los Angeles													3	1					1	1																	3	2	1	6
Miami	3	1		1	4		1	1		3	1								2	5		1			1			1			2	4					13	18	1	32
Newark	23	12	1	30	34	3	2			18	15	5	18	12	3	13	28	7	13	21	4	7	10	2	16	7		16	7		10	13					157	162	25	344
New York	49	33	4	71	54	2	24	4	3	44	41	1	40	28	3	62	28	3	67	36	12	35	32	2	31	1		35	31	1	29	24	7				509	348	39	896
Philadelphia	38	20	2	23	23	2	5		3	18	13	5	15	6	2	12	6	7	37	14	3	13	10	5	12	7	1	13	10		15	7	2				200	117	30	347
Rochester	1									1	1		6			2	1																				10	2		12
Syracuse																			4																		5			5
Other*												2	1									1			1						1	3					1	3		4

*Other cities and total travelers include Detroit (1), New Orleans (1), and Pittsburgh (2).

156

vacation during their unemployment in the States. . . .
Many take their mothers or mothers-in-law with them to the
U.S. so they will care for the children while both husband
and wife work. Some leave their children here and send
for them later. . . . They all have to get used to the
English language and to the cold weather. . . . They really
have a lot of nerve. . . . Many are people who have gone
to Waltham as the elsewhere."

NOTES

1. For a fictional account of the pattern, see René
Marqués, The Oxcart (New York: Scribner's, 1969). See
also Joseph P. Fitzpatrick, Puerto Rican Americans: The
Meaning of Migration to the Mainland (Englewood Cliffs,
N.J.: Prentice-Hall, 1971); and Elena Padilla, Up From
Puerto Rico (New York: Columbia University Press, 1958).
2. U.S. Commission on Civil Rights, Puerto Ricans in
the Continental United States: An Uncertain Future
(Washington, D.C.: Government Printing Office, October
1976), p. 25.
3. Ibid.
4. Ibid.
5. Ibid.
6. Ibid., pp. 26–27.
7. Centro de Estudios Puertorriqueños, Labor Migration Under Capitalism (New York: Research Foundation of
the City University of New York, 1979), pp. 186–87.
8. Ibid.
9. Commonwealth of Puerto Rico, Department of Labor,
Migration Division, Puerto Ricans in the United States,
pamphlet, 1975.
10. See Fitzpatrick, Puerto Rican Americans, p. 16.
11. For more information on this contract, which had to
be approved by the Department of Labor of Puerto Rico,
see Chapter 5.
12. Fitzpatrick, Puerto Rican Americans, p. 17.
13. Ibid.
14. In Puerto Rico, "negrito," literally meaning little
black one, is used as a term showing affection and en-
dearment and has nothing to do with one's color. I
translate it as "my dear."
15. Gamiel Pérez, "A New Approach to the Puerto Rican
in His Society," in A New Look at the Puerto Ricans and
Their Society, ed. The Institute of Puerto Rican Studies,
Brooklyn College (New York: Brooklyn College, 1972), p.
27.

16. Luis Niéves Falcón, "Social Class and Power Structure in Puerto Rican Society," in A New Look at the Puerto Ricans and Their Society, ed. The Institute of Puerto Rican Studies, Brooklyn College (New York: Brooklyn College, 1972), p. 118.

17. Ibid., p. 123.

18. See Universidad de Puerto Rico, Recinto de Mayaguez, Colegio de Ciencias Agricolas, Servicio de Extension Agricola, la Agricultura de Orocovis, 1975, p. 2.

19. Ibid., p. 10.

20. Note that Dona Ofelia said 250 to 300.

21. What is known in this country as life insurance is often called "death insurance" in Puerto Rico. Part of the policy's benefits includes provision of funeral arrangements for the policy holder.

22. Non-Puerto Rican priests are much more numerous in Puerto Rico (and Puerto Rican communities in the United States) than Puerto Rican priests. Perhaps, because of its colonial status, Borinquen has yet to develop a native Catholic clergy.

23. Note that Father Leon Bouvais of Waltham's Saint Mary's Church has often visited and said Mass in Orocovis. He has told me of meeting former parishioners there.

24. Universidad de Puerto Rico, Servicio de Extensión Agrícola, Estudio de la Situación Agrícola en el Area de Orocovis, 1963, p. 4, also describes this process.

25. All of the interviews in Orocovis were conducted in Spanish. I chose to keep some of the Spanish in the text to give the bilingual reader a flavor of the interview.

26. Universidad de Puerto Rico, La Agricultura de Orocovis, p.9.

27. Ibid., p. 31.

8

The Puerto Rican Migration
From New York
to Elsewhere

Poverty, like the color of one's skin, is inherited.   Unlike
skin color, however, poverty is not a function of genetics.
Julio Morales

Oh, but if those who picked cotton could've joined hands
with those who cut sugar cane.
Statement of Latins United
for Political Action,
February 11, 1985
Village Voice, February 19, 1985

My father had been a sugar cane cutter in Vieques, Puerto
Rico, and had often been unemployed.   My mother was a
homemaker, raising her own four children and, more often
than not, nieces, nephews, or the children of neighbors or
close friends, as well.   In 1950, we left Vieques and joined
my mother's relatives in New York City.   For approximately
one year, my parents, my brother, my sister Ruth, and I
lived with my maternal grandparents, several cousins, and
some aunts and uncles in a three-bedroom apartment in an
integrated neighborhood immediately northwest of Central
Park.   During this time, my sister Teresa stayed with one
of my aunts, her husband, and their hija de crianza ["foster daugher" is the closest translation of this culturally
unique institution] in an apartment in the next building.
My grandparents' apartment, like Suncha's in Waltham,
hosted hundreds of people from Puerto Rico.   As the new-

159

comers obtained employment, they left my grandparents' quarters and secured their own housing. In 1951, my parents and their four children moved to a one-bedroom apartment on the sixth floor of a rundown building on 109th Street between Second and Third Avenues. While there, we too found ourselves welcoming other families from Vieques. Fires were frequent, lack of heat and hot water were every day occurrences, and rats and roaches shared our space. Gang fights between the Italian and Puerto Rican youngsters were numerous. While in the third grade, I was beaten up, as I left school, by a group of Italian kids out to hurt a "Spic." It was not unusual to see dope addicts shooting up in the hallways of our building. People bolted their doors with many locks and their windows with iron gates to prevent being robbed.

As were almost every other family living at 309 East 109th Street, we were robbed of our few possessions on at least one occasion. As did many other children in the building, my siblings and I often played on the roof. Since we lived on the top floor, my mother could hear us moving around and frequently would call up from the kitchen window to ask how we were doing. Playing on the roof was safer than playing on the streets, she would often say. My father worked at a factory and earned 28 dollars a week. We qualified for government surplus food.

When we became sick or needed a dentist, we went to the emergency room of the nearest hospital. In the Bronx we used the emergency room at Lincoln Hospital, frequently referred to as the Butcher's Place—La Carneceria.

We were miserably poor but had a sense that in time things would get better. We had no television set, but the Spanish radio station was on almost all day. We visited neighbors often. They visited us. We shared a lot of leftovers.

We took the subway to public beaches and parks in the summer, but winters were spent inside very crowded quarters. Our extended family and neighbors provided us with clothing that their children had outgrown, and we, in turn, passed our clothing on to others. Family and friends shared advice, experiences, and love even more often than leftovers or clothing.

During holidays, my grandparents' home was like a magnet attracting my mother's family, consisting of her four sisters, four brothers, their partners, and children.

After living in East Harlem for two years, we moved to a two-bedroom apartment in the South Bronx, but in less than two years the building was condemned. We were temporarily relocated to another apartment a few streets away and within three months were offered a three-bedroom apartment in a housing project in Black Harlem. For us, the project was upward mobility. No more rats, fewer roaches, no more being without heat or hot water, and no more fire escapes to bar with huge iron gates to protect ourselves and our property.

In the mid-1950s, my father's relatives started arriving in New York from Vieques and had our support. We had to be careful about letting relatives stay with us in the projects because the Housing Authority only permitted immediate families in their apartments. New York City Housing Authority personnel would visit the apartment once in a while and inspect. My mother would clean even more carefully than usual and would make sure that no cots or other signs of extended family members were visible.

One of my father's three sisters and three of his four brothers migrated to New York City in the 1950s. All of my mother's brothers and sisters had done so in the 1940s. All of my aunts and uncles had children. They all worked. None were unemployed for long. Their older children also found work, but in general they were poor. I understood early in life that poor people worked but would remain poor as long as they were paid poorly for their labor. Poverty, like the color of one's skin, is inherited. Unlike skin color, however, poverty is not a function of genetics.

Before 1955, members of my extended family began leaving New York City for elsewhere. One of my mother's sisters moved to New Haven and later back to Puerto Rico. Her younger children left with her. The older ones followed. Two of my uncles went to Philadelphia and another to Florida. One of my aunts moved to Pittsburgh, because the lamp factory that employed her husband moved there. Some of my relatives are living in New Jersey, some in California. Today none of my aunts or uncles and only one of my cousins lives in the Statue of Liberty City. My parents, as did most of their brothers and sisters, moved back home to the island. My brother and sisters moved to Westchester County in New York, and I lived in Massachusetts before moving to Connecticut.

Some of my relatives succeeded in their new elsewheres. Some did not. If asked why they left New York, most would answer "fear." They did not feel safe in their apartments, in the subways, or walking to the grocery stores. Those who went back home to Puerto Rico would also add that they were tired of the winters. Most would talk of discrimination. Almost all would mention the likelihood of a better paying job or the dream of owning a home and starting a small business. When I think of my family and what wonderful, hardworking, and caring people they are, I feel anger, sadness, and despair about U.S. racism. Neither my relatives, friends, not I deserve the hostility and humiliation that we and most Puerto Ricans in this country too often confront. Because of sheer numbers, Puerto Ricans in New York City have more clout and power than elsewhere. And yet we are leaving and risking greater alienation in other cities. Perhaps it is Puerto Rican poverty in the Statue of Liberty City that drives us elsewhere. Competing for jobs that undocumented workers have will keep us poor, and yet we lose in our competition with blacks, whites, and other Hispanics for jobs in the primary labor market.

Between 1970 and 1980, New York City's population decreased by 10.4 percent; from a population of 7,894,862 persons to 7,071,639. The city's black population increased by 7 percent in that ten-year period, and by 1980 blacks made up 25.2 percent of the people of New York City, as compared to 21.1 percent in 1970. The Asian population increased by 145 percent between 1970 and 1980. This heterogeneous grouping includes persons of Japanese, Chinese, Filipino, Korean, Asian Indian, Vietnamese, Hawaiian, Guamian, and Samoan heritage. In 1980, that grouping accounted for 3.3 percent of New York City's population, up from 1.2 percent in 1970. The Native American, Eskimo, and Aleut population also showed an increase of 14.1 percent, comprising .02 percent of the city's total. Persons of Hispanic origin increased by 16.9 percent, comprising 19.9 percent of the city's people. In 1970, Hispanics numbered 1,202,281; in 1980, 1,406,024. It is imperative to stress again that the poor in general have been undercounted by the census. Minorities are even more likely to be undercounted, and Hispanics may be the most seriously undercounted by the census since they are often poor, lack English-speaking ability, and especially since many are undocumented workers who do not wish to be counted for fear of deportation. Note that, in August of 1980, the City and State of New York, along with other plaintiffs, filed suit against the United States Bureau of the Census. The plaintiffs argued that the population of the city and state had been undercounted. The Federal District Court agreed with the plaintiffs. The finding was appealed and reversed on procedural grounds. The litigation continues.[1] It is believed that the city's Hispanic population was more heavily undernumerated in the 1980 census than many other groups.[2]

From 1940 to 1970, the majority of Hispanics arriving in New York were migrants from Puerto Rico. From 1970 to

1980, however, the tide of Puerto Rican in-migration subsided, and the immigration of non-Puerto Rican Hispanics increased. Although classified under the Hispanic cultural banner, the newer non-Puerto Rican immigrants come from a variety of cultural and socioeconomic backgrounds, all quite different from that of Puerto Ricans.[3]

As of 1980, Puerto Ricans represented 60.6 percent of the 1,406,024 Hispanics counted in New York City by the Bureau of the Census; that is, 861,000 of the Hispanics are of Puerto Rican heritage, and 462,000 are "other Hispanics." Mann and Salvo calculated "a very small net out migration from the City to Puerto Rico for the entire 1970–1980 period. At the same time, several other states, including New Jersey and Connecticut experienced large increases in their Puerto Rican population. They had increases combining out-migrants from New York State as well as recent direct in-migrants from Puerto Rico."[4]

Numerous magazine and newspaper articles have raised questions regarding the number of Puerto Ricans arriving in New York after the 1980 census. For example, The Caribbean Business Magazine carried an article on December 22, 1982, (p. 48) written by Karl Wagenheim, predicting major out-migration for Puerto Rico, based on analysis of three months of data in 1982. "During the same period two years ago, Puerto Rico showed a reverse trend—a net immigration of 9,167 persons. The same was true last year, with a net immigration of 779 persons." The article acknowledges the difficulty in accurate data since "many of the persons thought to be 'migrants' from the Island may not, in fact, be Puerto Rican. . . . Evidence shows that the Island is used as a 'bridge' by foreigners who enter Puerto Rico and, once inside U.S. territory, they migrate to the 50 states."

The San Juan Star carried an article on February 1, 1982, that detailed the migration of the Puerto Rican retiree. One of the retirees interviewed, José deJesus, and his wife, Sara, said that the political bickering, the crime rate, and the economic life in Puerto Rico may not be good for the elderly. Mr. and Mrs. deJesus are moving to California.

The Daily News in January 31, 1982, (p. 39) had a story called "From Puerto Rico—with Skills," which highlights the large number of young people leaving Puerto Rico in the 1980s. El Mundo of October 4, 1984, expresses concern about the large numbers of Puerto Ricans (44,000 in 1983) leaving the island. El Nuevo Dia of May 7, 1984, also explores the new Puerto Rican exodus from the island. New York magazine of May 17, 1982, contained a two-page article entitled, "The New Wave From Puerto Rico." All the articles attribute the new migration to economic and political problems on the island.

For example, Dave Lindorft's article in New York maga-zine looks at the 1977 recession in Puerto Rico.

> Moreover, with 95 percent of Island exports coming to the United States and nearly everything imported from here, the American tailspin of the last few months has dragged Puerto Rico's economy even deeper into the hole . . . the economic collapse is only part of the problem. What's really causing the Island's exodus . . . is Reaganomics. Last fall . . . Puerto Rico lost its entire CETA program, throwing 25,000 to 30,000 municipal employees out of work . . . the Island's allotment (of food stamps) is being cut by 25 percent as of July 1. . . . For many Islanders, left with no job and no "safety net" there seems to be only one response. Unlike Cuban boat people or Haitian refugees, Puerto Ricans are born full United States citizens, they do not have to sneak into the United States and work in the underground economy—or avoid seeking social services. They have every right to be here. (P. 12)

The Puerto Rican Planning Board discusses the increas-ing Puerto Rican migration from Puerto Rico to elsewhere during the year.[5] Twenty percent of the people over 16 years of age who leave do so, the report states, because they have a job or the possibility of a job; 16.6 percent claim that they leave to study in the United States; 5.7 percent go into the military; 35.2 percent leave looking for employment; 2.1 leave to retire; and 20.5 leave for other reasons.

Without a doubt, more Puerto Ricans are leaving Puerto Rico. The question is, "Will they go to New York City or try elsewhere?" Obviously, as a group they will do both.

Of the 172 Puerto Rican families interviewed in Waltham, the overwhelming majority had come directly from Puerto Rico to Waltham, most of them from Orocovis. However, 17 families had lived in New York before Waltham.

Commenting on New York's Puerto Rican community, the Mann and Salvo report states that "only 48 percent of all New York families had own children under 18 but 68.9 percent of Puerto Rican families and 64.8 percent of 'other Hispanic' families had own children . . . almost half (49.8 percent) of families among Puerto Ricans were female headed, compared with 34.9 percent for 'other Hispanics,' about on the same level as for all City families (33.3)."[6] Puerto Rican families averaged 3.03 children, other Hispanics 2.35.[7] On the average, the male "other Hispanics" were 3.4 years older than the Puerto Ricans and other Hispanic females 2.4 years older than Puerto Ricans. The median age for the city's overall population was 32.6 years. It was 26.7 for "other Hispanics" and 23.7 for Puerto Ricans.[8] The report also documents lower levels of formal education for Puerto Ricans and significant difference in household incomes. "Over 23 percent of 'other Hispanic' males went on to college, with 9.8 percent graduating compared to only 13.3 and 4.3 percent for Puerto Ricans respectively. . . . About 16 percent of 'other Hispanic' females had gone to college with 6.3 percent graduating. Among Puerto Rican females, only 10.6 percent went from high school into college with 3.1 percent graduating."[9]

In 1980, the ratio of Puerto Ricans earned approximately 70 percent of what "other Hispanics" earned, or about 8,200 and 12,000 dollars, respectively. Over 47 percent of Puerto Rican households received under 7,500 dollars per year compared to 32 percent for other Hispanic households.

The differences between the Hispanic groups is often as great as the differences between the Puerto Ricans and "other Hispanics." For example, in comparing immigrants from the Dominican Republic and Colombia, Mann and Salvo conclude, "Apart from being recent immigrants, there was little that the two groups had in common."[10] For example, Colombian females were much more likely to be employed than Dominican females (59 percent as compared to 47 percent). "Median household income for Dominicans was about two thirds the level of Colombians. . . . Over 23 percent of Dominican households drew public assistance income, compared to 7 percent of Colombian households."[11] With the exception of the uncounted and undocumented Hispanic workers, Dominicans may be at the bottom of the "other Hispanic" category in terms of socioeconomic indicators. Perhaps since, as a group, Dominicans are darker than other Hispanics, racism may explain their condition. However, Dominicans are also darker than Puerto Ricans, and yet they appear to be doing better.

Dominicans have lower levels of formal education, have poorer English-speaking ability than do Puerto Ricans, and are concentrated in many of the same occupations. However, the 1980 census reveals that Dominicans have not replaced Puerto Ricans in the lowest rung of the economic ladder. On the contrary, as a group, they were economically better off than Puerto Ricans. Dominican labor force participation totals were on par with all New York City residents and well above those for Puerto Ricans. As in Waltham, English language skills and educational attainment are less significant than citizenship status for predicting higher employment and higher income. Again, such noncitizens as Dominicans and most other Hispanics do better than citizens who are Puerto Ricans.

When I asked Waltham Puerto Rican residents why they had migrated to Waltham, they often answered that economic conditions were so bad in their previous homes that they simply had to try elsewhere. Obviously, the search for economic betterment explains the outflow of Puerto Ricans from Puerto Rico and New York. Potential employment and/or having family or friends in a specific elsewhere explain where Puerto Ricans try next.

New York City's Puerto Rican population did not grow significantly between 1970 and 1980. Since Puerto Rican families are the largest of any identifiable group in the city and since Puerto Ricans are the youngest of the city's ethnics, the population should have dramatically increased in the ten-year period.[12]

In a recent (April 1985) conference, "Latinos in the United States: Cultural Notes and Present Diversity," held at Rhode Island's Brown University, Ricardo Campos from Hunter College's Center for Puerto Rican Studies stressed that Puerto Ricans are "always kept on the move—from the Island to New York to another United States city, and possibly another city—perhaps back to Puerto Rico and often back to the United States." Campos explains this observation by what he calls, "a pattern of exporting labor, importing labor, exporting capital, exporting profits on investments."[13]

Obviously, the Puerto Rican migration is interconnected to Puerto Rican poverty in Puerto Rico and in the United States. "Two thirds of the Puerto Rican population depends on some form of federal transfer payments, especially food stamps; the official unemployment rate is 25 percent, the real jobless rate is 40 percent; and 65 percent of the population is below the poverty level.[14]

In 1980, the Puerto Rican population under the poverty level in Hartford, Connecticut, according to the U.S. census, was about 50 percent. More than 50 percent (50.5 percent) of all Puerto Rican families in the United States earn less than 10,000 dollars per year, and half of those families had incomes under 5,000 dollars a year. Puerto Rican poverty and migration are both dramatically demonstrated by the 1980 census. Most Puerto Ricans are moving because of poverty—trying elsewheres hoping to diminish the misery, powerlessness, pain, and alienation felt while living in a society that boasts of comfort and affluence.

I asked several people why they thought Puerto Ricans were leaving New York City. The 17 Puerto Rican families in Waltham, who had lived in New York City, identified the crime rate, the lack of meaningful jobs, poor education, and poor housing as reasons for having left. Having friends or relatives in Waltham was also expressed as an important reason. A 25-year-old Puerto Rican migrant to Waltham from New York City thought that he might have a better opportunity for education in the universities in and around Waltham. He felt that the competition with other Puerto Ricans for financial aid might be better where there were significant Puerto Rican populations but very few Puerto Rican college students.

Another young Puerto Rican who had lived in New York but was a Waltham resident struck a similar note. She told me that getting a paraprofessional job in social services in New York was harder than it was in Waltham, because there was more competition for those jobs in New York City. The social service network in Waltham and elsewhere eventually seeks service providers who are bilingual. New York City, while utilizing bilingual personnel, has more contenders for such jobs than Waltham or other communities with recent Puerto Rican populations.

In the 1950s and 1960s, many of the service providers for New York's Puerto Rican population were imported directly from the island. The Board of Education, the Social Service industry, and colleges, for example, often recruited Puerto Rican teachers, social workers, and professors in Puerto Rico. Those New England communities with significant Puerto Rican populations also recruit such persons in Puerto Rico but are equally likely to recruit Puerto Ricans in New York City. The leadership in such cities as Boston, Springfield, and Hartford are often persons who have lived in New York City. These professionals understand the needs and aspirations of the Puerto Rican communities living in the United States and how to handle the problems that come from dealing with U.S. bureaucracies and participating in the political system. They have often had first-hand experience with Puerto Rican poverty. In the 1950s and 1960s, the professionals coming from the island tended to be more middle class in income, aspirations, and values than the constituency they served in the United States. Although professionals or students recruited from Puerto Rico today are closer to the Puerto Rican migrants in New England in terms of culture and language, they are, of course, new to the Puerto Rican experience in the United States. Furthermore, their English is not as proficient as that of their more acculturated New York-raised counterparts. Puerto Rican professionals from New York City then may follow the growth of Puerto Rican communities to their new elsewheres.

In the course of writing this book, I spoke with a number of people I hoped would shed more light on the reason behind the Puerto Rican exodus from New York to elsewhere.

INTERVIEW WITH
DAVID M. WERTHEIMER

David M. Wertheimer is presently Coordinator of the Lesbian and Gay Services at the Victims Services Agency in New York City and Lecturer in Pastoral Theology at Yale Divinity School. I met with David early in the morning. A lifetime New Yorker, he holds a master's degree in social work from the University of Connecticut School of Social Work and a master's in divinity from Yale Divinity School. He is knowledgeable, energetic, sensitive, and articulate. He sees the Puerto Rican population of New York City as an oppressed marginal community forced to compete with other communities. From his work with the Victims Service Agency/Travelers Aid, a nonprofit agency funded through government and private funds, David concludes that affluent crime victims tend to rely on private counseling. It is, therefore, the poorer members of society that are served by this agency at a rate of about 100,000 clients a year, most of them women.

"Is crime one of the reasons that people, in general, leave New York City?" I asked David. He replied that "a lot of people say they will leave New York after they have been victims of crime, but there is no documentation to verify this as far as I know." He is convinced that the less economically advanced members of racial minorities are the likeliest victims of crime. David thinks that there may be considerably more crime than is reported to authorities. "For law enforcers, an unreported crime is a crime that never happened. Victims feel that they may be revictimized in the process of reporting crimes, especially if they are poor or of color. It's true for women and gays as well."

Crime is one issue, but lack of housing and jobs may be more related to the Puerto Rican exodus. David explained that poor housing services, fires, and gentrification may explain why Puerto Ricans and other poor people are forced to leave. He gave numerous examples. The Alphabet City area of New York City (Avenues A, B, C, etc.) had a very large Puerto Rican population that is being replaced by the young upwardly mobile. The lower east side is another area where large numbers of Hispanics are being pushed out by gentrification. The same is true for the garment district and the Tribeca area (the triangle beneath Canal Street, South of Canal and West of Broadway). These areas have traditionally had small industries that were able to provide entry level jobs for the poor. These industries that employed the poor, like the buildings that housed them, are also victims of gentrification. Fires in older housing in which the poor live drive the tenants out. The buildings are them often condemned, at times left boarded up for a while, bought by investors, renovated, and sold as coops. Larger apartments are often converted into smaller units and rented at rates that the poor cannot afford. Greater police power is frequently demanded to clean out the social pathology that too often thrives in and around slum areas—prostitution, gambling, and the sale of drugs. David cited "Operation Pressure Point" in the Alphabet City area as an example of this phenomenon. This was seen as a police effort to rid several blocks of the "undesirable element" in order to facilitate gentrification. The areas are thus safer and more attractive to those willing to rent apartments in downtown Manhattan and to those who purchase condominiums or cooperatives that will sell for 100,000 dollars or more in Manhattan. The same process is taking place in Spanish Harlem. To make it more attractive, realtors are calling Spanish Harlem, "Upper Yorkville." The affluent neighborhood of Yorkville is definitely spilling into nearby Spanish Harlem. Perhaps the areas that housed Hispanic communities that have been bulldozed in the Bronx will also come back as neighborhoods for the affluent. Many of the buildings in the South Bronx have already been bought by speculators who board them up, do nothing but pay taxes for about five years, and then sell them to those looking to rehabilitate older buildings. Renovating a few buildings often begins the gentrification process for a whole block and eventually beyond. In neighborhoods that are shared by the Yuppies and the poor, one notices dilapidated buildings next to attractive and newly rehabilitated ones. "Ironically, the

Yuppies sometimes bring more thieves into the poorer neighborhoods," noted David.

"At times," said Mr. Wertheimer, "the poor communities resent the Lesbian and Gay roommates or couples who pool their economic resources in order to live in Manhattan. Gays, even when sharing apartments, become rent slaves. At times, they buy up old homes and rehabilitate them. In this process, they replace the poor in New York and elsewhere. It's one example of how one oppressed group perhaps unconsciously takes part in the oppression of other oppressed people." David suspects that the poor living in low-income housing projects may be more stabilized city residents. He added that currently there is a two-year waiting list for the city's low-income housing projects. "The welfare poor and the lower middle class outside of subsidized housing or projects may eventually disappear from New York's Manhattan," observed Mr. Wertheimer.

"The middle-class young worker, gay or heterosexual, does not generally live alone in New York. They can't afford it," he went on. "They need roommates, lovers, or spouses. Very often they must share even studio apartments. They also have to give up eating out, the theater, and children. Look through the real estate section of the New York Times on Sundays. One bedroom apartments going for 1,500 dollars a month are very common . . . and they get rented—or bought. People buy VCRs (video cassette recorders) or they go to movies, but it's the tourists and the very wealthy who eat out or go to Broadway regularly. When people want to start a family, they move to the suburbs." He added, "The small store operators, the bodegas (Spanish grocery stores), the small cleaners, the delis, the laundromats, doughnut shops, the small tailor shops are disappearing or at least leaving the city. Art galleries and other expensive tourist-oriented industries are coming in."

The impression that I get from David and others is that the upper middle class, the rich, and the undocumented workers are coming into New York in larger numbers. The lower middle class is leaving, but the welfare poor are trapped. David offered an example of ethnic competition when he noted that the Mom and Pop Jewish greengrocery stores of the past are becoming the domain of the very hard-working but more affluent Asian refugees from Korea, China, and Vietnam. "Not too long ago," he told me, "the New York Times ran a story about the growing conflict of these refugees and Harlem's black population." Nat Quiñones, Chancellor of New York City's Board of Education expanded on this issue.

INTERVIEW WITH CHANCELLOR NATHAN QUIÑONES

In 1968, I served on the I.S. 201 Community School Board, one of New York City's experimental school districts testing the concept of decentralization of the city's school system. In 1970, I was elected to the school board of District 9 in the Bronx, following New York City's school decentralization edict, which called for elected local boards of education. Chancellor Quinones remembered visiting my home in the Bronx after a school board activity that I hosted and asked about my children. The approximately two-hour interview that followed was pleasant and informative. He provided me with charts, and I have incorporated some of the information in those charts to complement the interview.

I first asked the chancellor if New York City's public school system had more Puerto Rican children in 1985 than in 1975. He replied that there has been a steady increase in the number of Puerto Rican youngsters, in the number of other Hispanic children, and in the number of Asian pupils, specifically Korean, Vietnamese, and Chinese children. The numbers of black and white youngsters, however, is declining. Approximately 32 percent of the city's public school population is Hispanic, compared with 33 percent black, 3 to 5 percent Asian, and less than 30 percent other. In 1968, Asians made up 1.3 percent of the city's school population, Puerto Ricans were 21.5 percent, other Hispanics 2.7 percent, blacks 32.2 percent, and whites 42.3 percent. There were a total of 1,121,922 students in New York City's public schools that year. By 1976, the figures had changed significantly. The number of Asian youngsters had doubled, to 2.6 percent of the total public school's population, while the Puerto Ricans' share rose to 23.6 percent. Other Hispanics had also doubled to 5.4 percent of the total. The percentage of black children had increased by more than 5 percent (37.4 percent), while the percentage of white youngsters had decreased by 11.8 percent and made up 30.5 percent of the 1,077,191 children that year. Note that the total number of children in the public school system had decreased by close to 45,000 youngsters. After 1976, the percentage and number of black and white youngsters have decreased every year while the number of Hispanic and Asian children has increased. In 1983, Hispanics comprised 40.6 percent of the children in prekindergarten and 36.9 percent of those in first grade. By the twelfth grade, they comprised only 22.8 percent of the school population. The Asian, white, and black populations do not show the same pattern of decline after the first grade. Blacks accounted for 21.7

percent of the children in kindergarten that year, 31.5 percent of those in first grade, and 35.6 percent of those in grade 12. Whites were 33.2, 26.2, and 34.8, respectively, and Asians 4.5, 5.4, and 6.7.

I asked the chancellor how Puerto Rican youngsters as a whole fared academically compared to other youths. "Proportionately, Puerto Ricans drop out to a greater extent than all other groups, including the other Hispanics, a pattern that has not changed." according to Quiñones, since the 1960s. "This is especially true for Puerto Rican boys. The girls do better. Compared to the 60s and early 70s, Puerto Rican youngsters do somewhat better, but all youngsters are doing better." He feels that today there is more concern for all children. "Programs for all children automatically benefit Puerto Rican children. . . . Programs for pregnant girls, for the disabled, for drop out prevention are good for Puerto Ricans since Puerto Ricans fall into all these categories." His impression is that large numbers of Puerto Ricans and other Hispanic children are entering kindergarten without speaking the English language. They also tend to be overrepresented in the over-age category as they enter high school. There is a high correlation between being over age (older) and dropping out of high school. "The Dominicans are not doing much better," he added. "But the Argentinians, the Colombians, the Bolivians and Ecuadorians are doing well. It's often an issue of class." His feeling is that the children of undocumented workers, such as those of the Dominicans, are at the same level as the Puerto Ricans. "The tremendous mobility of the Puerto Ricans limits them, but the real issue is poverty. If you add discrimination by class and add discrimination by color and culture, the obstacles are clear."

He spoke of a press conference announcing a Coca Cola grant that he had attended during the morning. "The thrust of the press conference was drop out prevention and more research on the problems and the program that may help. The mayor was present at the press conference held at Morris High School in the Bronx. ASPIRA is involved in the program . . . coalitions to work on programs attacking the drop out problem are essential."

I asked the chancellor if the number and percentage of Puerto Rican teachers and administrators are proportionately higher today, for Puerto Ricans, than they were in the early 1970s. He thinks so but Puerto Ricans are very underrepresented as teachers and as administrators. "Most Puerto Rican teachers are either in bilingual education programs or teaching Spanish."

"In 1967, there were only six Puerto Rican administrators in all of New York's public school system." He
started to name them "Joe, René, Mike, Loyda, Carmen.
. . . It wasn't until 1971 that we had our first Puerto
Rican principal—Marco Henández. In 1972, I became a high
school principal. There were none in the high schools in
1977. Today, there are five or six high school principals
of Puerto Rican heritage."

I asked about the ethnic competition. "It's there," he
said, "Recently I heard a weak allegation from a group of
Jewish leaders who felt that Jews were losing ground on
supervisory and administrative jobs." In 1977, there were
104 high school principals. Ninety-four of them or 90.3
percent were white, eight or 7.6 percent were black, two
or 1.9 percent were Hispanic. None were Asians. As of
November 1983, the number of white high school principals
had not changed much: 91 instead of 94 were white. There
were a few more blacks and Hispanics and two Asians, but
the number of high schools has increased to 110. Blacks
made up 9.1 percent of the high school principals, Puerto
Ricans and other Hispanics 6.3 percent, and Asians a little
under 2 percent. Considering the number of Puerto Rican
children in the schools, Puerto Ricans may be the least
represented population at the staffing level.

I asked Nat which Puerto Ricans leave the city for
elsewhere. He's not sure. He knows that entire families
go back home. His father came from Puerto Rico in 1912.
His mother in 1918. He remembers his family talking of
other Puerto Ricans coming and finding jobs and communities taking root. He generalized that "some leave because
of the lack of housing or unemployment, the crime, the
noise, or the nostalgia. I really do not know who leaves or
where they go, but I do know that gentrification and
poverty have created holy hell for Puerto Ricans." He
talked of Puerto Ricans being burned out of their
apartments and of 3,000 children, most of them Puerto
Ricans, living in old but expensive welfare hotels. "The
irony is that the city often pays as much or more to house
these children in those hotels as some families pay to live in
luxurious housing. Hotel families may pay 1,500 dollars a
month for a dirty hotel room. Exploiting hotel families is
big business." He doesn't think that the Asian immigrants
are as poor as the Hispanic undocumented workers or as
poor as Puerto Ricans. "They bring cash and establish
green stores and stationery stores. They often pay cash, I
have often been told."

As we ended the interview, he remarked that the recent
budget cuts have hurt all children. "Between federal years

80 and 84, adjusting for inflation, there has been a decline in federal support for urban schools amounting to 25 percent per child. There are 35 major urban school systems in the country. Combined, they have 4.2 million inner city youngsters—11 percent of the nation's enrollment, 21 percent of the nation's black children, 21 percent of the nation's Asian children, and 27 percent of the Hispanics." He concluded, "Eighty-one percent of all English-limited children of the state of New York are in New York City. Only 30 percent of the state's education budget goes to the city even though the state proportion of children attending New York City public schools is much higher. Our needs are greater, but proportionately we get less money. There is less money in general, especially for minority children. As the Reagan forces are more entrenched, this pattern becomes more clear."

INTERVIEW WITH YOLANDA SÁNCHEZ

Ms. Sánchez is a black New York City-born Puerto Rican woman who has been professionally involved in New York's Puerto Rican community since the mid-1950s. She helped to organize the National Puerto Rican Women's Caucus, worked for ASPIRA when the agency was first created, and was president of the Puerto Rican Association for Community Affairs (PRACA) in the early 1960s. Ms. Sanchez has taught at the City University, at Columbia University School of Social Work, New York University, and currently is acting chief executive officer of PRACA.

Is the Puerto Rican community of New York City shrinking, I asked Yolanda. She shook her head and said, "No." She thinks that "the census continues to miss us when they count. Many of us are still being counted as whites or blacks, or other." Is there a way to determine which Puerto Ricans have left New York? The people she knows who left did so in the late 1960s and early 1970s as a result of a career—either to get more professional training or to follow job opportunities. Most have not come back to the city. Yolanda also stressed gentrification, talked of welfare hotels, competition with other groups for jobs and services, and the search for better opportunities. "All these issues drive Puerto Ricans to move within New York City and out."

The comparison with other groups again arises. Yolanda referred to the more recent immigrants of color living in New York. "Other Hispanics and Asians now compete with blacks and Puerto Ricans."

Since 1980, an even greater number of Asians and Hispanics have been arriving in New York City. According to Ms. Sánchez, "It's not the poorer Asian who immigrates. For example, it appears to be the middle class technicians from Vietnam—those who supported American interests during the Vietnam era who are here . . . and you've got to give them credit. They have bought and run the green groceries as family businesses. They work long hours and, because they are run as a family enterprise, they include their children. But they are of an entrepreneur class and come in as entrepreneurs. Puerto Ricans as a group are workers, conditioned as such by a colonial system in Puerto Rico and a capitalistic system that needs cheap labor in the United States."

"How about the black–Puerto Rican conflict of the 60s? Does it continue today?" I asked. She replied, "Blacks and Puerto Ricans were figuratively battling it out in the streets during the 60s. Today we are more sophisticated but are still battling it out against each other for meager resources. The Badillo thing has not helped." This is in reference to an arrangement that blacks, Puerto Ricans, and liberals had made relative to the upcoming (1985) mayoral race. Herman Badillo, the nation's first Puerto Rican Congressperson, a former New York City commissioner, a former deputy mayor, and a mayoral candidate in the past, was to have received the support of the black leadership. However, after the agreement, a group of blacks refused to support Herman Badillo, insisting they would support only another black. They are urging blacks to rally around their candidate, Denny Farrell, insuring that both Badillo and Farrell will lose to current Mayor Edward Koch. Some New York Puerto Ricans are feeling betrayed. Other Puerto Ricans throughout the country are also taking note of the black–Puerto Rican split. In an editorial in the Hartford Courant of April 18, 1985, for example, Edwin Vargas, Jr., executive vice president, and José Laluz, leadership training coordinator for the Connecticut State Federation of Teachers, discuss the political support that Puerto Ricans have given black candidates. "Unfortunately today, this mutually beneficial coalition is at a low point. This is due in large measure to personality clashes that have little to do with programs or politics. . . . As the federal budget defines less assistance to urban areas, the fight over patronage and spoils intensifies among the poor. . . . In Chicago, many Latino activists have openly expressed disappointment that despite their support for Harold Washington as the first black mayor of that City, their influence on policy is now less than when the mayor's office was controlled by whites and that there are fewer Hispanic appointments than under Mayor Jane M. Byrne.[15] The common problem we face must be addressed by mutually developed programs . . . the keen competition for the few resources remaining in an era of scarcity induced by Reagan policies cannot be allowed to pit our communities against one another."[16]

"Blacks in New York and elsewhere," said Yolanda, "do not know what to make of the Puerto Ricans. Approximately 15 years ago, they wanted all of us to identify as black. We refused. Publicly, the issue went away—but it's not necessarily finished. In America there is no such thing as a little black blood. If that's the case, one is black. If Puerto Ricans are racially mixed, then they are black. If they are white, then they, too, are the oppressors, is the thinking of many blacks. We, as Puerto Ricans, light or dark, do not have the inner anger, rage, and fury that blacks as a community have. Puerto Ricans do not feel the same degree of white oppression. Partly because in Puerto Rico the visible authority continues being Puerto Rican. We have yet to understand our oppression, and blacks have yet to understand us. They do not distinguish us from other Hispanics, and they see more Puerto Rican success in a shorter time. The black and Puerto Rican Caucus at the state level is two-thirds black and one-third Puerto Rican, but blacks are numerically a larger community and have been in New York for 350 years. Puerto Ricans for less than 50 years. Blacks feel that Puerto Ricans are moving faster than they have moved."

The competition, according to Ms. Sánchez, is also around services for the poor. "Puerto Ricans rank lowest in the poverty scale. As such, we are threats to the institutions that work with the poor in the urban settings because we insist on bilingual, bicultural service delivery and often insist on being hired as social service providers and administrators.

"Government programs reward the very poor and the very wealthy. If one earns 10 to 15 thousand dollars a year, one gets little federal aid. If one earns less than 7,000 dollars, one is eligible for public housing or housing subsidy programs, for food stamps, medical care, etc., as a way of compensating for the very low income. It's a way of helping those who employ the very poor also. Blacks and Puerto Ricans compete for the dubious honor of being worse off and we compete for jobs."

Yolanda sees the coalition building as a possible way out of this no-win competition. She feels that, in the last year or two, black and Puerto Rican women have begun to organize and to address important issues for both groups. "We do not necessarily belong to the National Organization of Women (NOW), but we are working with the same theories. Sexism means that women regardless of their worth are viewed as inferior to men regardless of their worth. However, there is a refinement of the feminist philosophy within the feminist black and Puerto Rican women's groups. There is less arguing amongst ourselves. We know that too often poverty in our communities is caused by the lack of support that women have in raising children." She stopped and said, "You know how hard that is since you raised youngsters: but most men don't. In the United States, 40 percent of Puerto Rican families are headed by women. The statistics are similar in black America. Black and Puerto Rican women can make a difference in black and Puerto Rican poverty if we work together and get other women to fight against the feminization of poverty. We are starting to do that."

Ms. Sánchez addressed another area of competition, that of Puerto Ricans with other Hispanic groups. She, too, talked of differences between the Hispanic groups. "Argentinians, Equadorians, Chileans, Colombians, Cubans, are not hurting like Puerto Ricans, Dominicans, and the Latino-Indian-looking undocumented Hispanic worker who gets off the subway station in our Puerto Rican neighborhoods are hurting. The more Hispanics look European, the more acceptable they are to white Americans. The other Hispanics often see themselves as superior to us. For example, they think that their Spanish is better than ours because we mix Spanish and English. They do not realize that soon their kids will be speaking 'Spanglish,' too." Yolanda thinks that, although there is racism in the Hispanic communities, dark Hispanics like the Dominicans will continue identifying as Latinos. "The cultural bonds are great. More visibility of the black, mulatto, or dark-complexion Hispanic may help us in the efforts to build bridges with black Americans. It's all so crazy, the system is schizophrenic, isn't it?"

I asked Yolanda Sánchez one more question. "Compared to the 60s, are things today better or worse for Puerto Ricans in New York?" She has obviously been asked this question before, for she answers quickly, "Some of us are better off. Most of us are worse off!" She expanded, "Unemployment is higher; the per capita income is lower, the housing is poorer, more dilapidated. The subway system is now almost impossible. The city in general has deteriorated more, the education system seems unable to inspire our students. It's continued to deteriorate. More important, our sense of self is less. Generations of poverty leads to a poor self image. We used to live with the illusion that Puerto Rican kids were not dropping out of school in Puerto Rico. But they are. The school system there also has difficulty teaching lower-income children. The University of Puerto Rico still tends to educate the children of the middle class. In Puerto Rico, in New York, in New Jersey, Connecticut, Massachusetts, and everywhere else, we have been programmed for failure. I think that that failure continues into the 80s. Now we compete with many other groups who are willing to work for less in the poor jobs, and we compete with many groups who have greater support from system institutions and thus get the better jobs. I think we're worse off. Don't you?" I sadly nodded my head. "Yes, I think so, too," I answered.

A BRIEF CONVERSATION
WITH MARIA ROJAS

Ms. Rojas is of Colombian heritage. I met her as I left the PRACA office. Ms. Rojas is a reporter for Enfoque Nacional, an Hispanic National Public Radio program that airs out of San Diego and provides information on the national Hispanic scene. I explained my interest in comparing the Puerto Rican from New York City with other Hispanics. I asked if she feels that Colombians in New York City are generally middle class. "They are working class," she replied. "Today Colombian immigrants are probably poorer than in the past," she explained. "However, they get a lot of support from other Colombians who are already established and generally feel that eventually they will be able to afford homes. There is not the low self esteem that the Puerto Rican often has. The undocumented Colombians have it much harder."

Undocumented workers play a key role in Puerto Rican poverty. These workers enter the United States, or remain in the United States, without proper authorization from either their own country or from the U.S. Bureau of Immigration. Because of their illegal status, they are often forced to work for poorer wages than other workers, including Puerto Ricans. In order to offer more information on the undocumented workers, I interviewed several persons who have first-hand knowledge of the plight of a diverse group of people who can be viewed, depending on one's perspective, either as hard workers or as criminals. Persons who employ the undocumented workers know this reality and use it to exploit them.

INTERVIEW WITH
MR. MARIO TÁPIA

Mr. Mario Tápia is part-time director of the Immigration
Assistance Service of the Catholic Diocese of Metuchen, New
Jersey, and is the Hispanic access coordinator for the New
York Vocation and Community Services for the Blind. I met
Mr. Tápia in San Antonio, Texas, in November of 1984,
while participating in a conference on the Hispanic elderly.
Mr. Tápia has been involved in the provision of services to
undocumented workers for seven years.

As a Chilean, Mario personally identifies with the
weariness that Hispanics feel at being viewed as if we are
all alike. He reminded me of something that Antonia
Pantoja, founder of PRACA, ASPIRA, the Puerto Rican
Community Development Project, and the Puerto Rican
Forum once said. "There is no huge place called Hispania
from which Hispanics come." Mario told me that his clients,
regardless of their place of origin, are usually seen as
Puerto Ricans. "In the [U.S.] West, all Hispanics are seen
as Mexicans. . . . Initially, the undocumented worker is in
culture shock. Those who speak no English feel as if they
are in a coma, helpless and with others in control of their
lives."

Mr. Tápia stressed that his work with the Catholic
Church involves counseling Hispanics on how to obtain
citizenship or working visas if they qualify. He does not
give them false hope. The program does not bring undocumented workers to New Jersey; they are already there.
Persons working in Mario's program are trained by the
Department of Immigration.

The undocumented workers come because they are
needed here. They get jobs at minimum wage and less at
times. They work long hours, often graveyard shifts, and
put in overtime. They take jobs that citizens reject. They
work in New York City hotels as maids, wash dishes in
restaurants, park cars in parking lots, handle dangerous
chemicals in chemical plants, work in factories that are
reminiscent of the sweatshops at the turn of the century,
and serve as housekeepers and baby sitters for the affluent. They rarely get asked for working papers (green
cards), and if they get caught the employers know that
they can get others to replace them. They pay taxes but
do not use services out of fear of being discovered as
illegal residents. Mr. Tápia stated that the number of
undocumented workers in the United States is estimated at
anywhere between 2 and 10 million. He thinks that as many
as 200,000 may live in New York City.

Often, as in El Norte, the 1984 film about the struggles of a Guatamalean brother and sister who enter the United States through Mexico, the illegal entry is a function of both politics and poverty. Undocumented workers may also enter legally as tourists or students but remain in the country without proper authorization. In a series of articles in the June–July 1983 Nuestro magazine, the horrors faced by the illegal workers are explored. "As a result of the civil wars in Central America, an estimated 600,000 or more persons from that region are in the United States illegally, most of them Salvadorians."[17] "It often doesn't matter if the ruling government is leftist, center, or right wing. Every time a government changes, people must change their political ideology or face loss of jobs and the possibility of harassment or imprisonment," said Mr. Tápia. At times, the support of the United States for a particular type of government leads those opposing it to immigrate legally or illegally. Hispanics who enter legally, who are European looking, and who have formal education beyond high school tend to do well in the United States. However, those who do not speak English, lack formal education, enter illegally or remain after their visas expire, and are Indian looking or dark skinned end up working for minimum wage or less, are in tremendous debt, share their living quarters with many people who may be family, friends, or strangers, and live in fear of being arrested or deported.

The illegal workers are either supplied phony social security cards here, have bought them before, or simply work without them and get paid under the table. Most have been financially supported for their journey by friends and relatives at home and have promised to pay the money back. "Even when they are overwhelmed by their oppression and when their souls are back home, they do not dare to return out of fear of punishment when they return or out of fear of humiliation, of being seen as a failure, by those who helped to finance their trip. A round trip fare costs approximately 500 dollars for those coming from Colombia and over 1,000 dollars for those coming from Chile or Argentina. Getting a visa may cost 300 dollars. If they enter illegally, it may cost more to pay those who smuggle the immigrants and who profit from their plight. In order to get and keep living quarters, they need money for rent security in advance. Then there is the expense of food and transportation to the job and clothing. They earn about 100 dollars a week after deductions and are spending over 400 dollars or more every month. They work overtime on Saturdays and go unnoticed in their neighborhood because they are either working or sleeping."

Mr. Tápia echoed the numerous stories of the exploitation of the undocumented workers that I have heard. A
recent newspaper account suggests middle-class status for
some workers "such as the Asians who arrive from higher
income communities or settle into relative affluent life styles
but . . . In a city that prides itself on its technological
and intellectual progress, the abuse, sweatshops and sub-
standard living conditions that prevailed in the 'old world'
of immigrants have not vanished. . . . A resurgence in
sweatshop working conditions has occurred within the last
ten years . . . community assistance programs . . . report
some of the worst exploitation of newcomers in desperate
need."[18]

These are jobs that many Puerto Ricans may compete
for. Should U.S. citizens take these jobs? Should employers be forced to pay decent wages? The undocumented
workers through their cheap labor obviously keep some
firms from folding and help others make larger profits. In
a 1984 study on undocumented workers by Courtenay
Slater, a Washington consultant and former chief economist
for the Commerce Department, Ms. Slater finds that "many
illegal aliens are men in the 15 to 35 age group, which
makes them likely to be active in the job market . . . by
providing an ample supply of low wage labor, aliens helped
attract industry and jobs. . . . Their willingness to accept
low paying positions will tend to hold down pay in some
areas. . . . New York had the nation's second largest
concentration of illegal aliens calculated at 234,000."[19] To
a large extent, the undocumented workers help to keep
restaurant and hotel prices, vegetable prices, and the
prices of other goods and services lower for the U.S.
public. Obviously, the interests of many are served by
people who are often "at once immensely vulnerable and
immensely strong."[20] They are also victims of laws that
criminalize them as workers.

Mr. Tápia told of people with false social security cards
forced to give their children the names that appear on
those cards. They are afraid of going back to their actual
names because they and their families may lose health and
other insurance benefits. Although Mario praised the
lawyers with whom he works, I have heard numerous stories
of undocumented workers exploited by lawyers who charge
them a great deal of money to "start working on papers,"
at times knowing that the individuals involved have no
chance of obtaining citizenship. "They are strong people,
these undocumented workers. . . . They take tremendous
risks. . . . Mentally and physically they are healthy.

They have much to contribute. . . . Unfortunately, so many North Americans are of the opinion that only the European immigrant could do that." Mario added, "These oppressed souls have the illusion that some day they and/or their children will be better off. All they need to do is wait and learn the English language, become citizens, and get a better job."

Puerto Ricans are citizens, many know the language, but the hope of a better job is just an illusion. And yes, poverty and suffering is relative. Compared to the undocumented worker, Puerto Ricans may be better off; compared to other Hispanics, Asians, and blacks they are not.

Blacks today are mayors in approximately 300 cities, including Hartford, Philadelphia, the District of Columbia, Atlanta, Los Angeles, Newark, Detroit, Chicago, and New Orleans. The number of black elected officials totaled 4,890 in 1980. In 1981, there were 18 black Congressmen.[21] In 1984, Jesse Jackson, a black man, ran for president. Blacks are increasingly visible on television and in movies. They are presidents of more than 120 colleges in the United States. Compared to Puerto Ricans, they have power. Compared to whites, they are powerless. Only by sharing power and coalescing with each other can the various oppressed groups break the cycle of oppression that perpetuates misery. There really is enough to go around. Justice and equality for all is possible.

NOTES

1. Evelyn S. Mann and Joseph J. Salvo, "Characteristics of New Hispanic Immigrants to New York City. A Comparison of Puerto Ricans and non-Puerto Rican Hispanics," mimeographed (Paper presented at the Annual Meeting of the Population Associates of America, Minneapolis, Minnesota, May 3, 1984). The authors are, respectively, Director and Senior Demographer, Population Division, New York City Department of City Planning.
2. Ibid., p. 3.
3. Ibid., (abstract page).
4. Ibid., p. 4.
5. Puerto Rico Planning Board, Informe Economico Al Gobernador, 1982–83, Vol. 2 (San Juan: Puerto Rico Planning Board, 1984).
6. Ibid., p. 5.
7. Ibid., p. 8.
8. Ibid., p. 6.

9. Ibid., p. 9.

10. Ibid., p. 17.

11. Ibid., p. 19.

12. Ibid., p. 22. Much material used in this chapter was supplied by the staff of the Office of Hispanic Affairs of the City of New York, Office of the Mayor. I wish to especially thank Ms. Hulda Ramos for her cooperation.

13. "Future of Hispanics in U.S. Looks Somber," Rhode Island Journal—Bulletin, April 14, 1985, p. C9.

14. Ibid.

15. Ms. Byrne was mayor of Chicago before Mr. Harold Washington.

16. "Join Hispanics in Teaching Shared Goals," Hartford Courant, April 18, 1985, p. D9.

17. Richard Salvatierra, "U.S. Must Set a Limit on Refugees," Nuestro 7 (June/July 1983):19.

18. "New Wave of Immigrant Changing New York Society," Hartford Courant, October 25, 1982, p. C16.

19. "Illegal Aliens Called Benefit to Cities," Hartford Courant, December 28, 1984.

20. Aurora Camacho de Schmidt, "The INS & Sojourners from Y a Laj," Nuestro 7 (June/July 1983):20.

21. Robert Wood, "Urban Agenda Should Include State-house," Hartford Courant, April 17, 1985, p. B9.

9

Competition with Others and Relative Inequality: The Same Story Elsewhere

It is obvious that Puerto Ricans will tend to settle areas where low income housing is more available, and those cities would be the ones with declining urban populations. As the more affluent white ethnics move out, they leave the poorer housing, at times the dirty jobs, and often the problems to the less affluent minority group members.
Julio Morales

What has made certain towns in New England more accessible to Puerto Ricans than others? In an attempt to answer this question, I looked at certain variables in sixteen Massachusetts towns that had Puerto Rican populations of 300 or more as of the 1970 census. Twelve of the cities had over 50,000 inhabitants, and four had between 10,000 and 50,000 people. I compared these cities with others that do not have established Puerto Rican communities yet matched closely in terms of population statistics and are geographically scattered in the same pattern as the cities with Puerto Rican communities.[1]

The variables that I analyzed are population characteristics, housing, employment opportunities, proximity to farms, and the availability of transportation and social services. It is clear that no one factor can predict a Puerto Rican settlement. However, the set of variables interrelate to form an urban picture puzzle that may be useful in predicting the elsewheres that pull Puerto Ricans toward them.

184

Demographically half of the cities with large Puerto Rican settlements had declining populations from 1960 to 1970. As affluent white ethnics from these cities moved to the suburbs, housing became more available. One of the prime predictors of Puerto Rican settlements is the number of rental units as opposed to owner units. The rental units outnumbered the owner units by a ratio of 1.6 to 1.0 in the towns with Puerto Rican communities. The more rental units available, the greater the probability of Puerto Rican settlements. In 1970, the median rent was lower in the towns with Puerto Rican populations (85 dollars a month as opposed to 116 dollars per month).[2]

Looking at the Puerto Rican cities in terms of the jobs they provide, I found that Puerto Ricans seem to settle initially where entry-level unskilled jobs are available. Farm workers are more likely to find work in marginal industries. The cities that have a larger number of less technical industries than highly technical or skilled unionized industries have a larger Puerto Rican population.

The municipalities with established Puerto Rican communities share a proximity to farms that recruit migrant workers. See Figure 9.1. A prime example of this is the area surrounding Lawrence. Workers from the apple and vegetable farms may have moved to the textile factories. The Springfield–Holyoke–Chicopee area is another example of housing settlements by farm workers. Public transportation is probably another important variable influencing Puerto Rican settlements. For example, Boston, Cambridge, and Chelsea have a public system of buses and trains. Worcester, New Bedford, and Waltham have public buses that run close to the Puerto Rican neighborhoods.

Cities with declining populations, quantities of rental housing, and availability of entry level jobs are the ones that attract low socioeconomic groups. Public social services are also much more available in these cities because the poverty level is higher. I originally thought that the availability of social services would be a predicting variable of Puerto Rican settlement; however, I found that organizational life specifically geared toward Hispanics tends to follow the migrants. A list of Hispanic agencies found in a 1976 "Directory of Ethnic Organizations in Massachusetts" does coincide with the list of Puerto Rican cities, thus verifying that these communities are growing.

Unfortunately, Puerto Ricans in Massachusetts towns and cities experience the same tragic, grinding poverty as their relatives in New York City, for many of the same reasons: youth, lack of formal education, large families, lack of marketable skills, cultural and linguistic barriers,

Figure 9.1 Locations of Migrant Camps and Target Cities in Massachusetts

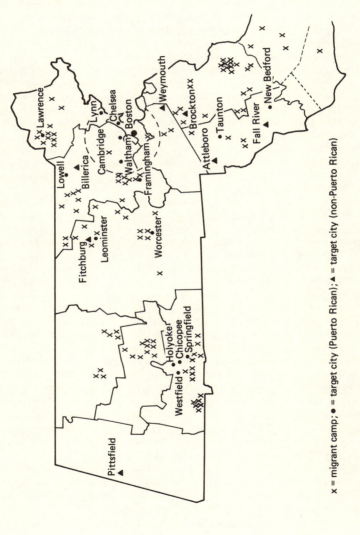

x = migrant camp; ● = target city (Puerto Rican); ▲ = target city (non-Puerto Rican)

Source: Migrant Programs in the Northeastern States, (Austin, Texas: Juarez Lincoln Center, 1974), pp. 41-43.

186

discrimination, racism, and social isolation. Furthermore, the present occupational and industrial distribution of jobs in Massachusetts, as in New York and elsewhere, tends to relegate Puerto Ricans to entry jobs with little if any security or opportunity for advancement. In addition, Massachusetts Puerto Rican communities are composed of recently arrived, mostly rural people who lack many of the resources and know-how of their New York counterparts.

Puerto Ricans in Massachusetts and the rest of New England not only have to adjust to major social, cultural, and linguistic obstacles, but to the complexity of urban life, as well. Many of the newly formed Puerto Rican communities lack the cohesiveness and organization necessary to negotiate effectively in the political arena and to combat racial and ethnic discrimination encountered in such areas as employment, housing, and education. Furthermore, the rapid influx of Puerto Ricans into various parts of the state has at times strained the capacity of helping professions to provide needed services. Discrimination, the economic burdens of the poorer cities where Puerto Ricans have settled, and insufficient priority given to the problems of the newest arrivals further prevent adequate services. Even when cities and towns see the necessity for services, a communication gap between providers and consumers is usually apparent. For example, a large percentage of Puerto Rican heads of families in Waltham could not speak English. The 1973 study of Cambridge's Hispanic population found that 70 percent of the Puerto Ricans living there could not carry on a conversation in English without the assistance of a translator.[3] Unfortunately, non-Puerto Rican interpreters are often incapable of interpreting cultural nuances.

In an effort to provide services in Spanish to Puerto Ricans, social service agencies, schools, and government bureaucracies have often resorted to using either non-Puerto Rican Hispanics, or black or white U.S. citizens who have learned some Spanish. Thus, the Puerto Rican poor help in providing employment for non-Puerto Rican service providers. In Waltham (1975), none of the social service providers who spoke Spanish in Project Health, the Department of Welfare, Family Service Association, or Waltham Hospital were Puerto Rican. They were overwhelmingly non-Puerto Rican Hispanics.

Affirmative action programs tend not to distinguish between Hispanic group categories, and Puerto Ricans in New England are too often missing from affirmative action programs. Although Spanish speakers in New England may come from Europe (Spain), the Caribbean (Cuba, the

Dominican Republic, Puerto Rico, etc), Mexico, or any one of the many Spanish-speaking countries of Central or South America, all are usually categorized under the rubric of Hispanics. Social service agencies, school systems, federal bureaucracies, and employers in general feel comfortable in hiring non-Puerto Rican Hispanics and blacks to meet affirmative action goals. Chuck Miller, director of the Newton–Waltham CETA programs in 1975, informed me that employers did not know and perhaps did not care about such differences. "It is easier," he said, "to hire blacks and non-Puerto Rican Hispanics for affirmative action purposes. . . . In Massachusetts, non-Puerto Rican Spanish speakers often have both skills and fluency in English." He added that several employers are under the impression that they have fulfilled their affirmative action responsibilities if they hire blacks.

The consensus among agencies providing services to Hispanic communities, including the Division of the Bilingual Information Center, is that poor Spanish-speaking communities in Massachusetts are overwhelmingly Puerto Rican. However, data concerning their plight have been incomplete and misleading since the studies of Hispanic populations in the state are usually based on the 1970 U.S. census, which, in addition to undercounting the Hispanic populations, also includes the Puerto Rican population under the inclusive heading of "Hispanic" or "Spanish speaking." Spanish-speaking families (other than Puerto Rican) are much more affluent than Puerto Rican families. These statistics of Cubans, Colombians, and other more affluent Hispanics, especially in Massachusetts where such individuals come for higher education, give a spurious impression about Puerto Ricans.

Only at the state level does the 1970 census contrast the Puerto Rican population in terms of general social, economic, and housing characteristics with the Spanish-speaking category, as well as with other groups in the state. From this data, clearer evidence of the Puerto Rican population's suffering at the very bottom of Massachusetts socioeconomic strata emerges.

Table 9.1 shows that, unlike the general population or black population, the percentage of Puerto Rican males greatly surpasses the percentage of Puerto Rican females. This again may be a function of the agricultural migrant workers who were recruited to New England. These workers have traditionally been male. Furthermore, men often migrate without their families and send for them as they secure employment and housing.

TABLE 9.1 Comparison of Selected General Characteristics by Population

General Characteristics	General Population	Black Population	Persons of Spanish Language*	Persons of Puerto Rican Birth or Parentage
Male (%)	47.0	46.9	50.2	52.0
Female (%)	52.2	53.1	49.0	48.0
Median age (years)	29.0	21.9	20.5	16.9
Size of families (number)	3.62	3.86	4.23	4.7

*This category includes Puerto Ricans. If it were Hispanics or Persons of Spanish language other than Puerto Ricans, the characteristics would resemble those of the general population.

Source: U.S. Department of Commerce, Bureau of the Census, Puerto Ricans in the United States, PC(2), IE, Washington, D.C., 1970; U.S. Department of Commerce, Bureau of the Census, Characteristics of the Population, Massachusetts, Vol. 1, Part 23, Washington, D.C., 1979.

Although conditions may have changed in the last 14 years, the Massachusetts Department of Public Welfare in Boston had 1,200 workers; only 49 were Spanish-speaking in 1973. Only 12 of 1,200 were Puerto Rican. All 12 were employed in the nonprofessional category. None were case workers or administrators. In the same year, the Boston school district had no Puerto Rican headmasters, principals, teachers, counselors, clerical workers, or maintenance personnel.[4]

Tables 9.2 and 9.3 document that Puerto Ricans are more disadvantaged than members of the category, "Persons of Spanish Language." They are also more disadvantaged than the black and the general population, as well. However, I contend that in Massachusetts, should it be possible to extract all Puerto Ricans from the more inclusive Spanish-speaking persons category, non-Puerto Rican Hispanics would then show an even greater advantage than blacks and, at times, an advantage over the general population. Tables 9.4 and 9.5 attempt to demonstrate the above by looking at available statistics for Spanish-speaking persons in towns where Puerto Ricans are few in number

TABLE 9.2 Comparison of Selected Social and Economic Characteristics by Population

Social and Economic Characteristics	General Population	Black Population	Persons of Spanish Language	Persons of Puerto Rican Birth or Parentage
Median income of families ($)	10,981	6,855	7,689	5,233
Mean income of families ($)	12,223	7,698	9,105	6,128
Per capita income ($)	3,438	2,155	2,920	1,499
Families/poverty level (%)	6.2	22.4	20.1	36.9
Families on public assistance (%)	6.1	26.4	17.7	32.8
Median school years (completed)	12.2	11.7	11.8	7.7
Unemployed (%)	3.8	6.7	6.5	10.3

Source: U.S. Department of Commerce, Bureau of the Census, Puerto Ricans in the United States, PC(2), IE, Washington, D.C.; U.S. Department of Commerce, Bureau of the Census, Characteristics of the Population, Massachusetts, Vol. 1, Part 23, Washington, D.C., 1970.

and 9.5 show that towns where other Hispanics outnumber Puerto Ricans are clearly more affluent than those where the concentration of Puerto Ricans is higher.

The 1975 census report, Persons of Spanish Origin in the United States, notes that large numbers of Cubans entered the country in the 1960s.[6] Cubans are the third largest HIspanic group in the United States.[7] Cubans and other documented Hispanic immigrants in this country have not confronted the tremendous poverty that Puerto Ricans and Chicanos (persons of Mexican origin) have faced. On the contrary, Tables 10.3 and 10.4 of the following chapter shows Cubans to be more affluent than Chicanos and Puerto Ricans. Nationwide, relative inequality, even among Hispanic groups, is consistent.

Comparing Puerto Rican to other Hispanics, the Bureau of the Census determined the median age for all Hispanics in the United States to be 20.7 in 1975. For Mexican U.S. citizens, the median age was 19.8; for Cubans, 37.3; for

TABLE 9.3 Comparison of Selected Occupational Groups by Population

Occupational Groups*	General Population (%)	Black Population (%)	Persons of Spanish Language* (%)	Persons of Puerto Rican Birth or Parentage (%)
Professional, technical, and kindred	17.4	11.5	16.8	7.02
Managers	8.3	3.5	5.9	1.9
Sales	7.0	2.9	3.9	2.82
Clerical	19.9	19.8	15.1	8.05
Craftsmen, foremen	13.1	9.7	10.5	13.07
Operatives	17.6	23.7	28.8	44.3
Laborers	3.5	5.1	4.0	6.6
Service workers	12.5	23.0	12.8	11.3

*Excluding farm laborers
Source: U.S. Department of Commerce, Bureau of the Census, Puerto Ricans in the United States, PC(2), 1E, Washington, D.C., 1970; U.S. Department of Commerce, Bureau of the Census, Characteristics of the Population, Massachusetts, Vol. 1, Part 23, Washington, D.C., 1970.

Central or South American Hispanics, 24.6; for other Spanish speakers, 20.2. For Puerto Ricans, the median age was 19.4. The median age for the general population was 28.6.[8] The census also revealed that 51.5 percent of all Cubans over 25 years of age in the United States had completed four years of high school or more. Thirty-one percent of Mexican U.S. citizens had also done so, but for Puerto Ricans the rate was only 28.7 percent.[9] "According to the 1980 Census, U.S. Puerto Rican families had the lowest median income of any ethnic group. The 1980 reported median family income of $10,704 for U.S. Puerto Rican families; $19,917 for the general population. . . .

TABLE 9.4 Comparative Incomes for Towns of Over 50,000 Having More Than 400 Persons of Spanish Language Background with Puerto Rican Populations of Less Than 200

Town	Persons of Spanish Language*	Puerto Ricans	Hispanic Median Income	Hispanic Mean Income	General Population Median Income	General Population Mean Income	Black Median Income	Black Mean Income
Brockton	936	166	8,214	8,971	10,377	11,169	7,667	9,109
Brookline	667	46	18,751**	9,500	13,701	18,888	NA	NA
Medford	437	20	12,742**	12,632**	11,145	12,101	11,800	11,608
Newton	1,333	199	19,174**	17,130	15,381	19,668	13,045	16,086
Quincy	564	34	9,374	7,587	11,094	12,111	NA	NA
Somerville	701	40	8,005	7,769	9,594	10,265	9,400	9,763

*Persons of Spanish Language are defined by the census as persons for whom Spanish is the mother tongue and all other persons in families in which the husband or wife reported Spanish as his or her mother tongue. In these towns, the majority of Spanish-speaking persons are non-Puerto Rican Hispanics. The second column gives the specific number of Puerto Ricans.

**Please note that these figures are higher than corresponding figures for the general population.

Source: U.S. Department of Commerce, Bureau of the Census, Puerto Ricans in the United States, PC(2), IE, Washington, D.C., 1970; U.S. Department of Commerce, Bureau of the Census, Characteristics of Population, Massachusetts, Vol. 1, Part 23, Washington, D.C., 1970.

TABLE 9.5 Comparative Income of Rural Nonfarm Communities by Race

	White	Black	Persons of Spanish Language	Total
By families				
Median income	11,297	9,490	11,756*	11,287
Mean income	12,906	9,973	12,699	12,888
Unrelated individuals				
Median income	2,982	1,862	3,167*	2,960
Mean income	4,382	2,589	4,493*	4,357
All families and unrelated individuals				
Median income	10,082	6,746	10,345*	10,061
Mean income	11,333	7,543	10,049	11,304

Note: Rural nonfarm communities in Massachusetts are usually characterized as desirable and affluent communities. None of them contain significant numbers of Puerto Ricans. Spanish-speaking persons in these towns are overwhelmingly non-Puerto Rican Hispanics.

*These figures are higher than corresponding figures for the general population.

Source: U.S. Department of Commerce, Bureau of the Census, Puerto Ricans in the United States, PC(2), IE, Washington, D.C., 1970; U.S. Department of Commerce, Bureau of the Census, Characteristics of the Population, Massachusetts, Vol. 1, Part 23, Washington, D.C., 1970.

Puerto Rican families in the Island fared even worse with a reported median income of $5,923 or 29 percent that of the U.S. general population."[10]

According to the census, approximately 30 percent of all Puerto Rican families living in the United States in 1970 were living below the poverty level established by the federal government. This was true for only 9 percent of the white population. Puerto Rican families in Puerto Rico had a 65 percent incidence of poverty in 1970. The 1980 census statistics show that Puerto Rican families living below the poverty level in the United States had risen to 34.9 percent. Sixty-six percent of all U.S. Puerto Rican families living in poverty are headed by females.[11]

Unemployment for Puerto Ricans in the United States was 15.9 percent in January of 1984. It was 9.6 percent

for all U.S. workers. The Puerto Rican unemployment
rate, according to the U.S. Bureau of Labor Statistics, was
higher than that of all other Hispanic groups. Puerto
Ricans in 1980 are still highly concentrated in low-skilled
and low paying occupations doing what is still viewed as
dirty work.[12]

The October 16 issue of Time magazine features an
article entitled, "Hispanic Americans: Soon the Biggest
Minority: or It's Your Turn in the Sun," which states that
U.S. citizens of Spanish origin, "have increased in number
by 14.3% in the last five years alone."[13] The article
highlights black and Hispanic rivalry. "Hispanics may
outnumber American Blacks within the next decade. Already the two groups are competing fiercely for jobs and
government aid."[14] The difference among Hispanics is also
emphasized.

> As blacks are united by race, Hispanic Americans
> are united by two powerful forces: their language
> and their strong adherence to Roman Catholicism.
> But many more factors divide them. They may be
> Castillian Spanish, or Caribbean Island black, or
> Spanish-Indian Mestizo. Among them are Cubans,
> who fled to the United States with money and
> middle class skills; impoverished Puerto Ricans or
> Mexican Americans looking for jobs—any job;
> aristocratic Spaniards, whose families settled in the
> Southwest before the Mayflower hove into Plymouth
> Harbor.[15]

The article continues, stressing the differences among
Hispanics.

> An estimated 1.8 million Puerto Ricans live chiefly
> in the north-central states, particularly in the
> Northeast . . . Chicanos comprising some 7.2
> million people of Mexican origin concentrated largely
> in the U.S. Southwest . . . some 700,000 Cubans,
> mostly refugees from Fidel Castro's regime, mainly
> concentrated in Florida . . . Dominicans, Ecua-
> dorians, Colombians, and natives of other Latin
> countries or Spain itself scattered all over the
> U.S. . . .
> The groups may mix, but so far they have
> failed to blend. Upwardly mobile Floridian Cubans
> have felt little in common with lowly Mexican-
> American migrant citrus pickers. Even in impov-
> erished New York ghettos, newly arrived Domin-

icans look down on native American Puerto
Ricans.[16]

Comparing black-white and Hispanic inequality, the article
states:

> Nearly 27% of Hispanic families in the U.S. earn
> under $7,000.00 a year, only 16.6% of non-Hispanic
> families fare as badly. For the second quarter of
> 1978 the Hispanic unemployment rate was 8.9% while
> the national average was 5.8%. As a group, His-
> panics are the most undereducated of Americans.
> . . . Only 40% have completed high school vs. 46%
> of U.S. blacks and 67% whites. . . . There are five
> Hispanics in the House of Representatives, com-
> pared to 16 blacks and 22 Jews. . . . Hispanics
> hold only 3.4% of the jobs in the federal bu-
> reaucracy, while blacks hold 16% and the Hispanic
> proportion of federal jobs holders has inched up
> only .7% in the past ten years. The same pattern
> holds true at state and local levels.[17]

In spite of the above statistics, the Time article also
takes note of the affluence of some of the Hispanic groups.
In Florida, for example, "forty percent of Miami and Dade
County's Hispanics (Cubans) earned more than $12,000 last
year. Nearly two-thirds own their own home."[18]

The Time article again emphasizes the resentment and
hostility of the black community, implying that it is the
greater affluence of the Hispanics that creates such conflict. "Miami's black community, which makes up 16% of the
local population, is particularly resentful. Garth Reeves,
publisher of the black Miami Times, warns of black hostility
because of competition with Hispanics."[19]

Black hostility is too often generalized to all Hispanic
groups. Blacks, like whites, seem unable to distinguish
between Puerto Ricans and affluent Hispanics, be they
European, South American, or Cuban.

As mentioned earlier, evidence indicates that, at least
in several cities in Massachusetts, non-Puerto Rican Hispanics have surpassed blacks in terms of employment
status, income, housing, and other variables indicating
relative affluence. In such places, blacks, at times,
become resentful and organize to protect themselves against
competition and what they see as the possible advancement
of another minority group at their expense. In places
where Puerto Ricans live in proximity to blacks, there is no
evidence to indicate any pattern of greater Puerto Rican

affluence relative to blacks. The _Time_ article to which I referred earlier confirms that:

> Puerto Ricans are even more hard pressed than New York's ghetto blacks. Forty-eight percent earn less than $7,000 a year compared with 42% among blacks. The proportion of Puerto Ricans on welfare is 34% vs. 32% for blacks. Among Puerto Ricans over 16 years old, only 6% have completed any job training. The rate for blacks is twice as high. With 14% of New York City's population, Puerto Ricans hold only 3.1% of police department jobs and 1.3% of those in the fire department.[20]

The pattern of black–Puerto Rican inequality in Boston and other cities and towns with both black and Puerto RIcan populations appears to be similar to the pattern discussed in Chapter 2.

A _New York Times_ story of October 14, 1976, comparing Puerto Rican poverty with that of other groups, discusses the Puerto Rican migration "that has extended itself to every state and to major cities that include Chicago, Philadelphia, Cleveland, Newark, Hartford, and Boston." The _Times_ notes that the "War on Poverty program of the Johnson Administration in the 1960s was of small benefit to Puerto Ricans," and further reports that "as of March, 1975, while 11.6% of all American families were below the low-income level, this was the case for 32.6 percent of mainland Puerto Ricans. That compared with 24 percent for Mexican-Americans and 14.3 percent for Cuban Americans . . . thus . . . the incidence of poverty and unemployment among Puerto Ricans is more severe than that of virtually any ethnic group in the United States."[21]

The _New York Times_ article just presented was followed by another that explored possible reasons for Puerto Rican poverty. The story reiterates the statistics of poverty for Puerto Ricans, Cubans, and Mexican-Americans and moves on to explain that:

> The Cubans and Mexican Americans, however, may not be comparable groups. Many who fled the Castro government were from the middle and upper classes who brought money, skills, and education with them. Mexican-Americans have been entering the United States for more than a century. Puerto Ricans primarily only for the last 30 years . . . the main problem appears to be that they are the last poor group to arrive in the nation's larger

cities . . . at a time when those cities have not
only stopped growing but are in decline and offering few opportunities to newcomers. . . .

New York City has lost thousands of jobs in
both the private sector and in the civil service.
Almost 50 percent of the Puerto Ricans who hold
civil service jobs lost them in the recent cutbacks.
In earlier years immigrant groups often moved
upward into such jobs and kept them.[22]

New England towns and cities with both black and
Puerto Rican populations witness a competition and rivalry
similar to that of New York City. Thus, the report of the
Massachusetts State Advisory Committee to the United States
(1972), entitled Issues of Concern to Puerto Ricans in
Boston and Springfield, states the following in its introduction:

There are 17 Massachusetts Community Action
Agencies working with the Spanish speaking community. Less than 8% of the 3,000 employees of
these agencies are Spanish speaking. The Model
Cities programs also suffer from the same
inadequate staffing patterns. But personnel is not
the only drawback. Most of the agencies' programs
are directed to the black community; the Puerto
Rican community's needs are seldom considered.
The Concentrated Employment Program (CEP),
administered by the Springfield Action Commission,
trains and develops basic working skills among the
economically deprived. Of the 1,450 persons CEP
has placed in the last 3 years, only 2 were Spanish
speaking. . . .

Model cities programs do not have a better
record. Puerto Ricans claim that the Spanish
speaking communities are not included in the
geographic boundaries of the model cities areas.
Only 1 percent of the 18,500 model neighborhood
residents in Springfield are Puerto Rican. . . .
The Federal Government has displayed little
leadership in securing total civil rights for Puerto
Ricans in Massachusetts. . . . Region I has a total
staff of 4,800 employees,[23] of whom only 30 are
Spanish speaking.[24]

The report goes on to state:

Thus, OEO is implicitly leaving the Puerto Rican community no option but to battle with the black-controlled poverty agencies for a better share of the already insufficient pie. . . . Translating dollars into people, we find that the model neighborhoods to receive these funds are predominantly black or white. . . . The Spanish speaking resident is experiencing alienation similar to that experienced by blacks before some effort was made to include them in decision making and planning for their community.[25]

The report concludes by stating:

The black directors and staffers should examine their position, and then open the benefits of these programs and the power to make policy to their Puerto Rican neighbors. The result may well be that all concerned will have to share an already small pie. But the alternative of no pie or a racially divided pie, would in the long run, be no boon for either blacks or Puerto Ricans.[26]

Puerto Ricans were initially brought to Massachusetts because they would work where others refused. They would accept low wages that others would not. They are, however, trapped at the very bottom of the U.S. socioeconomic order. To move from that status in today's society is almost impossible.

As emphasized in Chapter 8, the issue for the Puerto Ricans is one of relativity of power. Compared to others, they have less power. In the 1960s, the larger U.S. society reacted to misery and poverty with affirmative action projects and social programs, ostensibly for all those in need. However, those in need must scramble and fight over such jobs and services.

The civil rights experience provided blacks with some clout and political sophistication. Non-Puerto Rican Hispanics in Massachusetts have less need than Puerto Ricans, but they have greater economic and educational resources. They have also, for the most part, accepted and assimilated U.S. values and support of the established order. They want citizenship in this country.

In Massachusetts as in New York City, Puerto Ricans must compete. The competition is not so much with the country's middle or affluent classes, but with those at the crowded bottom of the socioeconomic and political ethnic ladder. Too often those are blacks and other Hispanics.

Given that Puerto Ricans competing are generally poor, rural, non-English speakers, the odds for mobility are against them. The competition is indeed imperfect.

NOTES

1. The larger cities with substantial Puerto Rican populations studied are Boston, Cambridge, Chicopee, Framingham, Holyoke, Lawrence, Lowell, Lynn, New Bedford, Springfield, Waltham, and Worcester. The cities with less than 50,000 inhabitants having a significant Puerto Rican population are Chelsea, Leominster, Taunton, and Westfield. The larger cities were contrasted with cities that have few if any Puerto Ricans. These are Arlington, Brockton, Brookline, Fall River, Malden, Medford, Newton, Pittsfield, Quincy, Somerville, and Weymouth. The cities with less than 50,000 inhabitants having few if any Puerto Ricans are Attleboro, Bilerica, Dedham, Fitchburg, and Winthrop.

2. U.S. Department of Commerce, Bureau of the Census, Characteristics of the Population: Massachusetts (Washington, D.C.: Government Printing Office, 1970).

3. Susan E. Brown, The Hispanic Population of Cambridge: A Research Report (Cambridge, MA: Cambridge Spanish Council, 1973), p. 51.

4. Ibid., p. 95.

5. Information was only available for towns having more than 10,000 inhabitants and more than 400 persons of Spanish language background.

6. U.S. Department of Commerce, Bureau of the Census, Persons of Spanish Origin in the United States: March 1975 (Washington, D.C.: Government Printing Office, 1976), p. 5.

7. Persons of Mexican origin are the largest Spanish-speaking group. Puerto Ricans are the second, Cubans third. Ibid.

8. U.S Department of Commerce, Bureau of the Census, Persons of Spanish Origin in the United States: March 1975 (Washington, D.C.: Government Printing Office, 1976), p.5.

9. Ibid.

10. The National Puerto Rican Coalition, "Puerto Ricans in the United States and on the Island, 1970–1980: A Demographic Profile," mimeographed (October 15, 1984), p. 18.

11. Ibid., pp. 20–22.

12. Ibid., p. 29.

13. "It's Your Turn in the Sun," Time, October 16,

1978, p. 48.

14. Ibid.

15. Ibid.

16. Ibid.

17. Ibid., pp. 50–52.

18. Ibid., p. 52.

19. Ibid.

20. Ibid., p. 58.

21. David Vidal, "Puerto Rican Plight in U.S. is Deplored," New York Times, October 14, 1976, p. 18.

22. "Puerto Ricans and Economics," New York Times, October 17, 1976, p. 5.

23. Please note that the report in quoting numbers of clients often says "Puerto Ricans," but when reporting providers tend to say "Spanish-speaking persons." Again, it is very likely that many, if not most, of the Spanish-speaking providers would be non-Puerto Rican Hispanics.

24. Massachusetts State Advisory Committee to the United States Commission on Civil Rights, Issues of Concern to Puerto Ricans in Boston and Springfield, Boston, 1972, pp. 4 and 5.

25. Ibid., pp. 76–79.

26. Ibid., p. 83.

10

Summary and Conclusions

Rivalry and competition among any of us weakens all of us. It will guarantee inequality and poverty for too many of our people. We must understand that we are not each others' enemies. On the contrary, we are natural allies. Strong coalitions among us can be beneficial not only to minority group members throughout the nation, but to all of American society. We must contribute to the struggle for human liberation for everyone. As long as one group is exploited, every group that does not object is the oppressor.

Julio Morales

Nationwide, Puerto Ricans account for approximately 2.2 million people in the United States. With the possible exception of the Native Americans and the undocumented workers, Puerto Ricans rank at the very bottom of the U.S. socioeconomic and political ladder. Fred Barbaro feels that is is difficult for Puerto Ricans to "interest the media, legislators and populace. After all, what does the average American know about Puerto Rico or Puerto Ricans? Puerto Rico is a vacation paradise that is somehow related politically to this country. Weren't Puerto Ricans involved in shootings directed against President Truman and members of Congress? Puerto Rican teenage groups 'rumbled' with other gangs in the 1950's. Whatever happened to them?"[1]

Barbaro's statements are generally valid. Very little is known about Puerto Ricans. Puerto Ricans are usually ignored by policy makers. Groups with greater political clout receive greater attention, even when their need is not as great.

Very little academic study has been directed toward Puerto Ricans. Recently El Centro de Estudios Puertorriqueños of the City University of New York and other Puerto Rican Studies Programs have begun to address that reality. The few migration studies available, before El Centro, tend to explain the Puerto Rican exodus in terms of job opportunities in New York. They often begin and end with the issue of overpopulation on the island. At the governmental level, the political and economic suffering of Puerto Ricans is revealed only by the impersonal, at times inaccurate, and often ignored Bureau of the Census.

This book has asserted that the U.S. economic system has historically exploited people. It has traditionally exploited people of color. It also exploited white European immigrants in northern factories. The abolition of slavery, the passage of immigration laws prohibiting further large scale immigration of European peasants, and increased automation and technology changed the makeup of the work force in the Northeast. Automation decreased the need for unskilled labor, but it did not, and has not, completely eliminated that need. Initially, blacks were recruited to replace the waning numbers of immigrants. Racism proved an effective tool in limiting black mobility, thus maintaining a supply of unskilled workers necessary to do dirty work, work that is poorly paid, often very physically demanding, demeaning, and unstable. As the United States dominated world markets and became involved in various twentieth-century wars, its economy continued to expand, and more workers were necessary. Puerto Ricans, being U.S. citizens, were not restricted by immigration laws and thus were also recruited to the United States. Furthermore, the colonial relationship existing between Puerto Rico and the United States necessitated a Puerto Rican exodus from the island as a "safety valve" to maintain this relationship. Masses of unemployed, discontented Puerto Ricans might have fought for a change from their colonial status were relief not available in the form of mainland jobs. In the U.S. industrial northeastern states, then, the blacks and Puerto Ricans replaced the Europeans in secondary-sector employment.

Although many similarities exist between the Europeans on the one hand and blacks and Puerto Ricans on the other (migration to cities, problems of poverty, discrimination, and so forth), differences are more important in explaining the socioeconomic status of New England's most oppressed groups. Understanding those differences is an important beginning in addressing the "if we did it, why can't they" syndrome to which the general U.S. public often resorts in perpetuating a victim-blaming mentality.

Unlike the immigrants from Europe who were not citizens, today's blacks and Puerto Ricans are internal migrants. Puerto Ricans were made citizens, although citizenship was never requested and was, in fact, resisted. Puerto Rico has been a colony of the United States since 1898, and Puerto Ricans on the island and in the United States have been used in the same manner colonized people in Third World countries have been used for centuries. Blacks were brutally brought to this country as slaves. Neither did they choose to be U.S. citizens.

Equally important is the issue of race. Jews, Italians, Irish, and other Europeans are white. Blacks and Puerto Ricans are not. The racism of U.S. society places Puerto Ricans and blacks at a tremendous disadvantage. European immigrants faced discrimination because they were newcomers. Blacks and Puerto Ricans are victims of both discrimination and racism.

Furthermore, it is perhaps the present economic order that makes the greatest difference between white European immigrants to the United States and U.S. citizens of color. As with past groups, Puerto Ricans and blacks initially were recruited to northern cities to work in marginal industries that guarantee poverty by paying very low wages, giving little employment security, and offering few benefits. These cities provided employment that was seen as demeaning, degrading, and dirty by the majority of U.S. society. Yesterday's immigrants, however, were able to move out of these jobs because of an expanding U.S. economy. Today's "minority groups" are trapped in these positions, positions that do not offer secure employment.

Historically, the poorest paid jobs in the United States have been relegated to the most recent poor group of immigrants. As each group replaced the previous one, it automatically pushed its predecessor up the socioeconomic ladder. As they took over the dirty work, immigrants raised on their shoulders the group that had done that work before them. In our competitive society, blacks and Puerto Ricans will lose to the better organized and more politically powerful white ethnic groups. In their turn, blacks have more political and economic clout in U.S. society than do Puerto Ricans. As a result, when the two groups compete, blacks will be the victors. Furthermore, the competion existing today is not only based on race and ethnicity. To the ethnic queuing of the past, we now add the competition of women, the elderly, lesbians and gays, the disabled, and others. Additionally, due to greater automation and the nature of our postindustrial society, the muscles and strong backs that enabled past newcomers to obtain jobs are totally insufficient today. Willingness to work is not enough. In the past, one could drop out of school and into a job, but that is no longer possible. Even so, schools are not able to hold blacks and Puerto Ricans. Their curriculums are too often aimed at the average, white, middle-class child, resulting in another support for the present system and thus greater inequality.

Until the early 1960s, such social scientists as Moynihan and Glazer theorized that Puerto Ricans, coming from a different homeland, being of lighter skin color than blacks, and not having the history of U.S. slavery, would be able to surpass blacks and more closely resemble the pattern of the previous immigrants. That theory has not been borne out. Poverty among the Puerto Rican population has not only not been alleviated, but has increased even when compared to black poverty and the poverty of other Hispanic groups.

Non-Puerto Rican Hispanics in New England are, as a group, not only much more affluent than Puerto Ricans, but more affluent than blacks and, in at least a few towns, more affluent than the general population. And yet it is they, more than Puerto Ricans, who are recruited in the affirmative action efforts of government and private enterprise. The black-Hispanic-Puerto Rican rivalry in New England is very similar to the ethnic rivalry in New York and among the poor in the country as a whole.

The condition of Puerto Rican communities in Massachusetts, New York, and other elsewheres is the continuation of a long history of U.S. exploitation that began with the genocide of Native Americans and the enslavement of Africans. It continued with the policies of Manifest Destiny, the Mexican-American War, the exploitation of the European peasants, Jim Crowism, and the extension of the United States into Hawaii, the Philippines, and the Caribbean. Puerto Ricans as a people are oppressed by a system in which individuals and groups continue to compete in a "fend for yourself" fashion, and in which discrimination and racism are used to support the status quo. This system is defended by U.S. policy makers as "the best there is." For Puerto Ricans "the best there is" continues to offer poverty and promises. Tables 10.1, 10.2, 10.3, 10.4, 10.5, 10.6, 10.7, and 10.8 clearly demonstrate present Puerto Rican poverty in Waltham, the state of Massachusetts, New York City, New York State, and Connecticut. The information was compiled from 1980 census data.

TABLE 10.1   Waltham City Comparative Inequality: 1980

Income	City	White	Black	Spanish Origin
Per capita	7,666	7,731	6,298	3,473
Median family	22,335	22,377	21,964	11,780
Mean family	24,403	24,495	22,467	12,647
Median individual	5,789	5,860	7,067	2,542
Mean individual	8,796	8,851	8,426	4,376
Below Poverty Level				
Numbers of families	679	633	12	76
Percentage of families	5.2	5.0	9.4	28.5
Numbers of persons	4,259	3,963	62	432
Percentage of persons	8.1	7.8	10.3	34.5
Education, Adults				
Less than 5 years*	1.9	1.9	--	15.6
High school graduate*	73.2	73.2	84.7	39.8
College,* 4 or more years	19.1	18.5	22.0	8.0
Median years school	12.6	12.6	13	9.7

*Figures represent percentage of population.

Note: Total Population, 58,200; white, 96.7% (56,287); black, 1.2% (691); American Indian, 0.12% (72); Asian and Pacific Islander, 1.3% (739); Spanish origin, 2.5% (1,426); Puerto Rican, 1.5% (870); Mexican, 0.04% (21); Cuban, 0.14% (79).

Source: U.S. Department of Commerce, U.S. Bureau of the Census, Detailed Population Characteristics--Massachusetts, 1980 Census of Population, Washington, DC, 1983.

It is the poverty and the promise of possible betterment that pushes and pulls Puerto Ricans elsewhere.

This study has been an effort to add to the sparse literature on Puerto Ricans. Because the area of Puerto Ricans and social policy is a pristine field, the book may raise questions and issues that spur interest in future investigations. Furthermore, this study in and of itself is important to Puerto Ricans and others interested in promoting greater equality and humanism.

Initially, my efforts were aimed at investigating the recent Puerto Rican in-migration to Massachusetts and the conditions and characteristics within the resulting commu-

TABLE 10.2 Population of the Five Largest Metropolitan Areas, Massachusetts*

City	Total Population	Puerto Ricans
Boston	2,679,378	29,082
Providence	796,706	3,762
Springfield-Chicopee	530,553	20,054
Worcester	276,124	5,422
Lawrence-Haverhill	211,457	7,177

*Includes Providence, RI.

Note: Total population 5,737,081; white, 93.4% (5,362,836); Black, 3.9% (221,279); American Indian, 0.2% (9,198); Asian and Pacific Islander, 0.9% (52,615); Spanish origin, 2.5% (141,043); Puerto Rican, 1.3% (76,450); Mexican, 0.13% (7,874); Cuban, 0.12% (7,009).

Source: U.S. Department of Commerce, U.S. Bureau of the Census, Detailed Population Characteristics--Massachusetts, 1980 Census of Population, Washington, DC, 1980.

nities. I was trying to understand the process of such migration with an emphasis on grasping the "pushes" and "pulls." I hoped to assess the outcome of those factors and the effects of their social environments on the lives of Puerto Ricans in the state. At first, I focused solely on the Puerto Rican populations in the state rather than on the overall Hispanic populations. Upon examining the census, I found a dramatic increase in the Puerto Rican population between 1950 and 1970, the largest increase occurring between 1960 and 1970, when the population quadrupled. However, it was soon clear that the census material did not explain the tremendous influx Massachusetts was experiencing. A review of the literature produced several articles pertaining to the in-migrations of Puerto Ricans to the mainland, and, although they were helpful in illustrating some of the fundamental economic factors involved in the migration, that is, economic opportunities on the mainland versus the island, as well as classical migration theories, they dealt only with the overall patterns involved and did little to clarify the situation in Massachusetts. Their major drawback was that they did not account for social factors that, according to several studies, seemed to be of increasing importance during the 1960s—a time when the peak migrations into the state were occurring. Blacks in the

TABLE 10.3 Massachusetts Comparative Inequality: 1980

Income	State	White	Black	American Indian	Asian	Spanish Origin	Puerto Rican	Mexican	Cuban
Per capita	7,458	7,632	4,982	5,233	6,372	3,866	2,679	4,640	7,185
Median family	21,166	21,554	13,249	13,956	20,348	10,518	6,967	13,905	19,740
Mean family	24,105	24,578	16,021	16,313	24,153	13,717	9,611	17,451	23,180
Median individual	6,491	6,597	5,680	5,680	3,852	4,501	4,316	4,417	4,994
Mean individual	8,871	9,001	7,360	7,730	6,940	6,150	5,442	5,772	7,994
Below poverty level									
Numbers of families	110,038	88,787	12,024	482	1,361	11,602	8,951	250	191
Percentage of families	7.6	6.5	23.8	22.3	12.7	36.4	52.9	17.6	11.3
Numbers of persons	532,458	436,794	53,458	2,143	8,105	51,490	38,975	1,383	766
Percentage of persons	9.6	8.4	25.3	24.3	16.3	37.6	53.2	18.8	11.6
Education, adults									
Less than 5 years*	2.8	2.9	3.2	2.5	8.7	14.5	19.2	3.2	4.0
High school graduate*	72.8	71.5	64.5	64.0	72.3	44.5	31.0	64.7	63.8
College, 4 or more years*	20.2	19.7	11.9	12.1	40.7	12.1	2.6	19.5	21.9
Median years school	12.6	12.6	12.4	12.4	13.9	10.9	9.2	12.5	12.5

*Figures represent percentage of population.

Source: U.S. Department of Commerce, U.S. Bureau of the Census, Detailed Population Characteristics--Massachusetts, 1980 Census of Population, Washington, DC, 1980.

TABLE 10.4 Five Largest Metropolitan Areas, New York

City	Total Population	Puerto Ricans
New York City	15,591,684	1,117,096
Buffalo	1,002,283	8,093
Rochester	605,719	11,314
Albany-Schenectady	409,029	1,741
Binghamton	161,355	407

Note: Total population, 17,558,072; white, 77.0% (14,033,644); black, 13.7% (2,405,818); American Indian, 0.25% (43,987); Asian and Pacific Islander, 1.9% (330,972); Spanish origin, 9.3% (1,660,901); Puerto Rican, 5.6% (978,616); Mexican, 0.23% (40,243); Cuban, 0.45% (79,378).

Source: U.S. Department of Commerce, U.S. Bureau of the Census, Detailed Population Characteristics--New York, 1980 Census of Population, Washington, DC, 1983.

1960s were showing signs of social and economic mobility. The 1960s also initiated the migration of Cubans and other Hispanics to Massachusetts and throughout the Northeast. Were these factors at all related to the Puerto Rican influx? Would they aid or hamper Puerto Rican mobility? Puerto Rican poverty, all studies showed, was not being ameliorated in the United States, and yet Puerto Rican communities in Massachusetts continued to grow.

A guiding assumption from the very beginning was that the Puerto Rican migration to Massachusetts found its impetus in the large scale importation of Puerto Rican migrant farm labor in the 1950s and 1960s by Massachusetts farmers and growers. Based on this assumption, it followed that Puerto Ricans who were brought in as seasonal farm laborers eventually stayed on, pulled by economic opportunities around industrial areas, as well as inexpensive and dilapidated, but available, housing in the inner cities. Due to a lack of data, I first investigated this assumption through personal interviews with a farmer who had imported Puerto Rican migrant labor, officials from the Migration Division of Puerto Rico, and officials from the Farm Labor Division of the Department of Employment Services (DES). I was fortunate in being able to speak at length with Mr. Antonio Del Rio, an individual who played a key role in representing and organizing Puerto Rican migrant workers

TABLE 10.5 New York Comparative Inequality: 1980

Income	State	White	Black	American Indian	Asian	Spanish Origin	Puerto Rican	Mexican	Cuban
Per capita	7,498	8,166	4,946	4,918	7,059	4,217	3,675	4,814	7,023
Median family	20,180	21,672	13,026	13,995	20,089	11,263	9,564	14,044	17,250
Mean family	23,683	25,504	15,898	16,450	24,911	14,023	12,173	17,824	20,102
Median individual	6,859	7,240	5,518	5,057	6,665	5,267	4,313	5,225	6,959
Mean individual	9,857	10,428	7,584	7,020	9,799	7,109	6,389	7,674	9,482
Below poverty level									
Numbers of families	483,340	253,453	145,357	2,178	8,729	128,330	93,332	1,703	2,807
Percentage of families	10.8	7.0	25.7	21.3	11.3	32.2	38.6	21.6	13.0
Numbers of persons	2,298,922	1,284,523	622,779	10,542	43,412	661,929	458,078	10,365	11,967
Percentage of persons	13.4	9.4	28.3	24.6	13.5	41.0	47.6	26.4	15.3
Education, adults									
Less than 5 years*	3.6	2.8	4.6	4.6	9.7	12.6	14.6	8.3	7.9
High school graduate*	66.3	68.7	57.6	55.7	70.3	42.0	36.9	51.1	53.5
College, 4 or more years*	17.9	19.4	8.8	8.3	38.9	6.8	4.0	11.8	15.2
Median years school	12.5	12.5	12.2	12.2	13.6	10.7	10.1	12.0	12.1

*Figures represent percentage of population.

Source: U.S. Department of Commerce, U.S. Bureau of the Census, Detailed Population Characteristics--New York, 1980 Census of Population, Washington, DC, 1983.

TABLE 10.6 New York City Greater Metropolitan Area, Including Northeastern New Jersey, Comparative Inequality: 1980

Income	City	White	Black	American Indian	Asian	Spanish Origin
Per capita	7,905	9,365	5,003	5,511	7,040	4,151
Median family	19,268	22,418	12,746	14,445	19,645	10,799
Mean family	23,774	27,473	15,647	17,910	24,096	13,490
Median individual	7,995	9,063	5,789	6,110	8,201	5,469
Mean individual	11,125	12,043	7,083	7,874	10,990	7,251
Below poverty level						
Numbers of families	327,689	127,566	120,259	1,261	7,838	122,931
Percentage of families	14.1	7.9	25.9	22.3	11.3	33.3
Numbers of persons	1,505,420	632,960	545,320	5,698	37,952	510,363
Percentage of persons	16.8	10.4	28.6	24.3	13.3	34.5
Education, adults						
Less than 5 years*	4.9	4.0	4.4	4.8	10.4	12.4
High school graduate*	63.5	66.9	58.2	60.7	69.2	42.0
College, 4 or more years*	19.2	22.2	12.4	12.0	37.7	6.8
Median years school	12.4	12.5	12.2	12.4	13.2	10.6

*Figures represent percentage of population.

Note: Total population, 15,591,684; white, 74.6% (11,631,765); black, 15.5% (2,722,724); American Indian, 0.15% (23,412); Asian and Pacific Islander, 2.4% (377,061); Spanish origin, 12.7% (1,984,101); Puerto Rican, 7.2% (1,117,096); Mexican, 0.25% (38,898); Cuban, 1.0% (156,959).

Source: U.S. Department of Commerce, U.S. Bureau of the Census, Detailed Population Characteristics--New York, 1980 Census of Population, Washington, DC, 1983.

TABLE 10.7   Population of the Five Largest Metropolitan Areas,
Connecticut*

City	Total Population	Puerto Ricans
Hartford	726,089	26,856
Springfield-Chicopee	530,553	20,054
New Haven	417,679	9,410
Bridgeport	395,455	23,481
Waterbury	228,145	3,217

*Includes Springfield-Chicopee, MA.

Note: Total population, 3,107,576; white, 89.5% (2,811,092); black, 6.5% (216,691); American Indian, 0.2% (4,822); Asian and Pacific Islander, 8.7% (21,116); Spanish origin, 4.0% (125,256); Puerto Rican, 2.8% (88,164); Mexican, 0.1% (3,926); Cuban, 0.2% (5,779).

Source: U.S. Department of Commerce, U.S. Bureau of the Census, Detailed Population Characteristics--Connecticut, 1980 Census of Population, Washington, DC, 1983.

and the newly founded Puerto Rican communities during the 1950s and 1960s. My interviews were extremely useful in confirming and supporting the assumption that many Puerto Ricans who were brought into the state as migrant workers did stay on to form the nuclei of the Puerto Rican communities in the state. Indeed, Massachusetts towns and cities, now having significant Puerto Rican populations, tend to be located in proximity to rural communities that use migrant labor. The process was found to be a gradual one, usually a series of trips back and forth to the island, settlement often occurring by default in view of the contrasting economic opportunities. Finding the right people to interview was the result of lengthy telephone searches of agencies, organizations, libraries, and academic institutions. As a result of these inquiries, I was also able to interview Dr. Michael Piore at the Massachusetts Institute of Technology, who had completed an economic study of the Puerto Rican migration into Massachusetts. An acknowledged expert in the field of labor market analysis, Dr. Piore offered invaluable insights into the dynamics of exploitation that were involved in the Puerto Rican migration. He suggested that Puerto Ricans were replacing blacks who, supported by the civil rights movement, refused certain types of dirty work. Furthermore, blacks had gained

TABLE 10.8 Connecticut Comparative Inequality: 1980

Income	State	White	Black	American Indian	Asian	Spanish Origin	Puerto Rican	Mexican	Cuban
Per capita	8,511	8,884	5,025	6,404	7,535	4,290	3,386	5,293	7,869
Median family	23,149	23,890	13,865	14,759	24,988	12,640	9,901	15,539	22,598
Mean family	27,203	28,142	16,519	18,347	29,067	15,798	12,619	20,118	25,937
Median individual	7,882	8,080	6,422	6,807	4,399	5,654	4,927	4,970	6,565
Mean individual	10,232	10,493	7,955	8,789	7,885	7,087	6,142	6,754	8,467
Below poverty level									
Numbers of families	50,809	33,288	12,009	225	501	9,170	8,385	134	117
Percentage of families	6.2	4.4	23.6	19.3	11.1	31.9	41.0	20.5	7.9
Numbers of persons	242,650	164,325	53,353	1,136	2,687	40,345	36,245	647	513
Percentage of persons	8.0	6.0	25.4	23.7	13.2	32.9	41.9	17.5	9.0
Education, adults									
Less than 5 years*	2.9	2.3	3.9	2.7	3.5	14.3	18.2	7.1	3.8
High school graduate	67.9	71.5	56.8	57.5	81.7	41.5	30.3	57.9	66.5
College, 4 or more years	18.8	21.5	8.6	8.0	54.4	8.8	4.2	15.1	21.3
Median years school	12.5	12.6	12.2	12.2	16.0	10.3	9.0	12.3	12.5

*Figures represent percentage of population.

Source: U.S. Department of Commerce, U.S. Bureau of the Census, Detailed Population Characteristics--Connecticut, 1980 Census of Population, Washington, DC, 1983.

employment and training options that were not available or even thought of as possible in the 1950s.

Other interviews were also very helpful. They often provided me with leads to further information. For example, officials at the Farm Labor Division of DES allowed me to examine unpublished annual farm labor reports that specifically documented the use of Puerto Rican farm workers in the state from 1950 to 1970 and offered information about Puerto Ricans leaving farms to enter industry. The consequences of the migration were investigated by looking at the 16 largest Hispanic communities in Massachusetts. These studies were begun by carefully analyzing the 1970 census data for the general, social, economic, and housing characteristics of those communities. Unfortunately, I was unable to examine the characteristics of the Puerto Rican population within the general Hispanic category for many of those communities. While the census did collect the data for the Puerto Rican populations for which I was looking, it only made the data available on a statewide basis. Lengthy attempts to secure such data at the local level proved fruitless. However, using what was available at the state level demonstrated dramatically the "result" of the Puerto Rican in-migration: that is, that Puerto Ricans in Massachusetts exist at the very bottom of the socioeconomic ladder. Perhaps even more significant from a policy-making perspective was the contrast between the state-level Puerto Rican data and that of the general Hispanic population, a difference that state policy makers seem not to have appreciated.

The reports generated by local communities in seeking funds from state and federal agencies were an extremely useful resource in studying the plight of Puerto Rican/Hispanic communities. These reports were a result of a requirement to document the plight of disadvantaged ethnic minorities, specifically the Hispanic population, in order to become eligible for funding. The town reports, the HUD Block Grant reports, and the DES manpower reports were found to be extremely useful. These documents allowed me to focus, in a very tangible way, on the economic and housing crises within the Hispanic/Puerto Rican communities. For example, the HUD Block Grants often pinpointed precisely the location in the community where the Hispanic population was living. Newspaper reports, individual studies on Hispanic communities in the state, and special publications of the census were also very valuable.

Because I have lived in Waltham and served as the first director of El Programa Roberto Clemente, the city's Hispanic community development project, I organized the

interviewing of close to 200 Hispanic families. I wanted to
know how and why they migrated to Waltham, the conditions
they faced, and how social services, including El Programa,
could best help in alleviating the problems that Puerto
Ricans and other Hispanics confronted.

Soon after becoming involved in Waltham's Hispanic
community, I realized that at least half of the Hispanics had
lived in Orocovis, Puerto Rico, a rural municipality located
in the middle of the island. I spent a week in Orocovis
attempting to understand how they had gotten to Waltham.
Chapter 7 is composed of interviews with many of Orocovis'
citizens who were kind enough to spend time talking with
me and sharing their views on the push and pull factors
that resulted in the exodus of thousands of that town's
people.

The more I looked at Puerto Ricans in Waltham and
elsewhere in Massachusetts, the more I was reminded of
Puerto Ricans in New York, where I grew up and worked
prior to moving to Massachusetts. Explaining the inevitable
poverty of Puerto Ricans and our apparent inability to
become upwardly mobile in New York or Massachusetts
became more important to me than the migration itself.
Puerto Rican poverty has traditionally been explained in
such terms as age distribution, lack of valued skills, difficulty with the English language, and cultural differences—factors verified in this book. The data collected
supported most of my initial assumptions. The first Puerto
Rican migrants to Waltham did initially work in nearby
farms. Almost all came seeking employment or to be with
loved ones. The majority came from rural towns in Puerto
Rico. Those of Waltham's Hispanics who work are overwhelmingly employed in menial, low-paying positions.
Waltham being a heavily industrialized city was able to
provide these kinds of entry-level, dead-end jobs in the
1960s. Poverty among Puerto Ricans in Waltham is shocking. The traditional explanations, however, are insufficient. For example, youth in U.S. society is seen as a
virtue, and the Puerto Rican population is a young one. In
addition, it does not require much education or English to
do some very well paying work (sanitation work, laying
bricks, mixing cement). And past immigrant groups have
moved out of poverty despite similar backgrounds. However, a combination of many factors in which low levels of
formal education, lack of valued skills, and poor English
are a part of a broader picture may explain Puerto Rican
poverty. It is that broader picture that I have explored.
I began the study by looking at those issues in New York
City and then moved on to Massachusetts. Table 10.9

briefly summarizes most of the factors addressed in this book. This study, then, has been an attempt to examine the extent of poverty Puerto Ricans confront and to understand it, since it is that poverty itself that best explains why and where we migrate.

Puerto Rican poverty, I am convinced, is systemic—built in—a given under the present Puerto Rican reality and the U.S. order. As a colonized people, we have always served a master. As a multiracial Hispanic population, we are often seen as black or as "different" by racist white U.S. society. To U.S. blacks, we are often seen as white or "different" and are too often met with hostility, anger, and resentment.[2] Because we are categorized under the Hispanic rubric, we are expected to be like the Cubans, Spaniards, and other nationality groups in the Northeast for whom Spanish is the native tongue. Our language does, at times, bind us. Our cultures do share similarities, but in Massachusetts and elsewhere in New England our socioeconomic class is different. Non-Puerto Rican Hispanics in the Northeast, like blacks and whites, often resent and use us.

An unusual set of circumstances, including the moment in which we migrated, the loss of entry level jobs, advanced technology, automation, and U.S. ethnic queuing, makes racially different groups natural allies but also competitors. In competing with other Hispanics, blacks, and the general population of this country, given today's realities, we as Puerto Ricans will not "make it" economically or politically. Researching this book has confirmed this sad fact for me.

Continuous Puerto Rican poverty is not a chance phenomenon. It is inevitable given the context of U.S. society—a society the economic system of which, capitalism, supports and is supported by certain social and political values.

The queuing process, so important in explaining the lot of Puerto Rican communities in the United States, offers partial insight into Puerto Rican poverty. Missing from such theory, however, is an explanation of why some groups immigrating to the United States do not enter at the bottom of the economic strata. Not all immigrant groups need another ethnic or racial group to push them up the U.S. economic ladder. The last chapter clearly demonstrates that Cubans, although coming after Puerto Ricans, entered the United States on a very different economic footing. Immigrating to the United States after the Cuban Revolution (1959), they are generally affluent, especially when compared to Puerto Ricans and blacks. The Cuban

TABLE 10.9 Factors Explaining Puerto Rican Poverty in the Present American Order

---

Profile of Puerto Rican Communities in the United States
    Low levels of formal education
    Racial mixture
    Large families
    Different language
    Cultural and value differences
    Young age
    Lack of valued skills
    Often from rural background
American values impeding Puerto Rican mobility
    "Dirty work" not valued and seen as offensive
    Rewards based on economic and political clout
    Racism
    A belief that poverty would not exist if people worked
    Racial, religious identification of groups
    An acceptance of ethnic politics
    Discrimination
    Victim-blaming ideology
    Competition among groups
    Fend-for-yourself attitude; stress on individualism
    General belief that the bottom socioeconomic strata should be
        relegated to last, large, poor immigrant group
    A belief that there are no better societies
Puerto Rico as a U.S. colony
    No control over migration or customs
    History of exploitation
    13 percent of land controlled by U.S. military
    Trade restrictions
    Import most of what it consumes; exports most of what it produces
    Economy controlled by U.S. investors
    U.S. shipping monopoly until 1975
    Agricultural decline
    Decline in labor-intensive industries
    A system-supported illusion of Puerto Rican inferiority
The U.S. economy
    Less need for unskilled work
    "Dirty work" very poorly paid
    Stress on profit making
    Less government support of programs for poor; budget cuts
    Jobs moving out of cities
    High price for housing and necessities
    Gentrification
    Competition encouraged among workers
    General inflation
    Automation
    Eroding tax base of cities

---

immigrants tended to be from the upper and upper-middle classes in Cuba, were well educated, and arrived in the United States with skills that enabled them to successfully enter the U.S. world of ethnic and interest-group competition. In general, lower-class Cubans did not immigrate. For them, the Cuban Revolution offered hope. For Cuba's affluent, the revolution meant losing much of their wealth. Furthermore, much of U.S. policy favored the Cuban refugees and facilitated their Americanization process. To a large extent, a similar explanation holds for most of the Asian refugees of the late 1970s and early 1980s.

Thus, the queuing theory must be amended to take into account issues of class. Cubans were not recruited for the farms and factories. They were allowed to enter the United States as political refugees. Those entering strongly identified with U.S. values of competition and supported the capitalist nation in which they sought asylum. The system rewarded the Cuban refugees with special programs often aimed at supporting their business ventures in both the United States (Florida has the largest concentration of Cuban businesses) and Puerto Rico (second largest concentration of Cuban businesses).

In Puerto Rican communities and in Puerto Rico, Cubans are seen as being very "pro-the American system" and as very conservative. In many ways, they are the most favored Hispanic group in this nation because of their conservative politics. They are progressive in terms of cultural issues (maintaining the Spanish language, customs, diet) but very traditional in their support of the present capitalist system. For example, in Puerto Rico, Cubans are strong advocates of statehood and protective of the present business climate.

Much of what is true about Cubans can be said about Hispanics of Central and South American heritage. Immigrants to the United States from those groups also tend to be wealthy or middle class. Immigrants from Mexico, migrants from Puerto Rico, and undocumented workers, however, tend to be persons from the lower class, recruited for dirty work. A U.S. Department of Housing and Urban Development study, entitled How Well Are We Housed?, provides several examples of the results of the ensuing differences:

Again it is clear that of the Hispanic groups in the United States, the Puerto Ricans, followed by Chicanos, have the greatest problems with adequate housing. Not only are the units they live in more flawed than those of Hispanics generally, but

Puerto Ricans, followed by Chicanos, have the most difficulty in affording adequate, uncrowded housing. Even if a Puerto Rican family were to spend half its income on housing, it would have a lower chance of obtaining good housing than all the other subgroups we are examining: 5 percent less than all Hispanic families, 5.5 percent less than Chicanos, 7 percent less than the total population, and 9 percent less than Cuban families.[3]

Note again that this study reports a pattern of Cuban affluence compared to Puerto Rican or Chicano poverty. Table 10 of the report is headed "Cubans Live in the Best Hispanic Housing, 1976." Table 11 is headed "Cuban Housing is Better than General American Housing in 1975."[4] The report clearly states that in 1976 Cuban housing matched the housing of the general population, and in 1975 it was 3 percent better.[5] Although Central and South Americans are not at the same level of affluence as Cubans in term of housing, "Central and South Americans also come close" to adequate housing.[6]

Cuban and legal immigrants from Central and South America have voluntarily migrated to the United States and have successfully avoided the bottom rung of the nation's economic ladder. The affluent Cubans and other middle-class Hispanics are at times the recognized leadership in poor Puerto Rican communities. Often, non-Puerto Rican Hispanics, along with Spanish-speaking Anglo-Americans, provide social services to Puerto Rican client systems.

I cannot overstate the need for U.S. social policy makers and service providers to understand the differences between Puerto Ricans and other Hispanics. The economic, political, and class differences are as important as are the similarities and differences of culture and language. Too often affirmative action efforts are able to further enhance the status of non-Puerto Rican Hispanics and are less successful in recruiting or improving the status of poor Puerto Ricans.

Equally important, we must know who the Puerto Ricans are—where and how they live, work, retire, and die. The ability to collect such data and use it to benefit Puerto Ricans is essential. For example, we know so little about the Puerto Rican elderly, the deaf, blind, and other physically disabled Puerto Ricans. Puerto Rican communities are barely beginning to address such issues and problems. Having data available is essential in order to initiate services for these very vulnerable populations.

According to Dr. Isaura Santiago-Santiago, Associate Professor at Columbia University's Teachers College, a research study in a New York school generalized about the strengths, needs, problems, and aspirations of Puerto Rican children. The generalizations were based on the assumption that the Hispanic youngsters in the school were of Puerto Rican heritage. They were not. The majority of children in that school had Dominican parents.

Equally confusing and spurious is information on Puerto Rican migration to and from Borinquen. Too often such data is based on who leaves and who enters the island with people assuming that the bulk of the travelers are Puerto Ricans. That is probably a safe assumption. However, in many instances, also migrating to the United States from Puerto Rico are Dominicans, Haitians, and others from the Caribbean who pass as Puerto Ricans in order to live in the United States. We do not know how many are Dominicans or white U.S. citizens as opposed to Puerto Ricans. We also lack data on sex, age, occupational skills, educational attainment, and other important characteristics related to those who enter or leave Puerto Rico. If the airline passengers returning to Puerto Rico are Puerto Ricans, we do not really know if they are people who lived a long while in the United States or simply came for a visit. Similar questions can be asked about the Puerto Ricans flying to the United States; are they people who are visiting relatives for the first time, or are they people who have tried living in Puerto Rico and are again migrating to New York, Massachusetts, or elsewhere in the United States? Such concrete, reliable data are essential in understanding Puerto Rican migrants and suggesting policy and programs for that population.

The data in Chapter 5 suggest that Puerto Ricans and other Hispanics frequently differed in their ranking of major problems. Puerto Ricans tended to perceive more discrimination than non-Puerto Rican Hispanics. Nevertheless, the majority of all Hispanics interviewed see Puerto Rican poverty as a function of their own inadequacies. Too often they believe that, if only they learn English, have more formal education, have greater skills, or work even harder, they will not be poor. Social scientists, organizers, progressive educators, and others identifying with the plight of Puerto Ricans must be aware of this phenomenon and attempt to break this cycle of self-blame. Paul Freire's teachings in The Pedagogy of the Oppressed, about using education to liberate the self, must be understood and put into practice. Puerto Ricans must begin to discover what forces really keep them oppressed as a people. Understanding that a political and economic system is oppressive is not easy. Liberating the minds of the victims is as difficult as attacking the problems they confront. Nevertheless, it is important that organizational efforts attempting to do so continue. It may be that until Puerto Ricans truly understand the nature of our oppression we will continue accepting the present system and validating its victim-blaming ideology.

Many efforts in Puerto Rican communities were and are important. For example, the Catholic Church can be a tool either supporting victim-blaming ideology or helping to liberate Puerto Ricans. The Catholic Church is an important socializing agent for Puerto Ricans. Baptisms, weddings, masses, confirmations, and other Catholic ceremonies continue to be important to Puerto Ricans. The church in Waltham has helped by recruiting such Spanish-speaking Anglo priests as Father Leon.[7] In addition to performing religious duties, Leon Bouvais sat on boards, attended hearings, and advocated for Hispanics. However, St. Mary's Church has not mobilized to any large extent to confront employers, politicians, landlords, schools, and other systems that may discriminate against or oppress Puerto Ricans.

Such social service programs as El Programa Roberto Clemente are important and must be supported. Unfortunately, such projects too often die from lack of funding. Skilled, culturally and linguistically competent social service providers can be instrumental in addressing immediate issues of poverty and despair. For example, they can support affirmative action programs in the areas of employment, housing, education, business opportunity, as well as bilingual, bicultural education, more equitable welfare benefits, stricter health and sanitary housing code enforcement, and other such programs and policies. They must nevertheless also raise questions about a system that seems to need poor people at the bottom and must consciously address long-range goals for human liberation.

The Puerto Rican family has historically been a strong unit that has extended its boundaries beyond the typical mother-father-and-children network associated with the U.S. family today. It often includes grandparents, uncles, cousins, and other blood relations, as well as godparents and very close friends. The migration to Waltham was facilitated through this network of family and friends, as demonstrated by the interviews with Doña Suncha, Señor Del Rio, and the Puerto Rican heads of households. Puerto Ricans have a deep sense of honor and respect for the family and feel great responsibility for their relatives. The

Puerto Rican family, like the Puerto Rican culture itself, offers Puerto Rican migrants a sense of strength and stability. The overwhelming majority of Puerto Rican families in the sample were not single-parent families but were composed of two parents, their children, and other relatives.

Unfortunately, poverty strikes the Puerto Rican family hard. Such poverty leads to poor housing, poor education, poor health, poor jobs, and an endless cycle of hardships that, coupled with clashing cultural values, too often ends in disintegration of this viable unit. Traditionally, the family helps buffer the hostility, alienation, and despair that Puerto Ricans living in poverty confront. Government policy on families must make it easier for members to secure employment. Day care, for example, should be a right. Policy must also support Puerto Rican cultural values that encourage self-help efforts and foster pride and dignity. Nevertheless, in and of themselves, such family policies are insufficient. United States citizens must support such basic humanistic values as cooperation, nurturing, loving, caring, and the right to self-determination for all people. All families, including those that differ from the U.S. norm, must be respected. Such policies by necessity would have to question old norms, values, and traditions. If all families are accepted and supported, Puerto Rican families will automatically benefit. Most importantly, perhaps, if dirty work continues to be necessary, social policy must address the poverty that accompanies that kind of work. Most Puerto Ricans are very poor even when they are employed. Minimum wage scales must be more realistic. Dirty work must be paid well, include social benefits, and provide security. More importantly, a guaranteed annual income and a national health insurance will definitely benefit Puerto Ricans and all other poor persons. Puerto Ricans, blacks, women, and other disenfranchised groups will instantly benefit from such meaningful comprehensive social security programs. With less inequality and greater security, the various ethnic, racial, and interest groups in this heterogeneous nation could stop struggling against each other and turn their attention to more humanitarian ideals and goals. David Gil notes:

> Human existence in this society is shaped by a selfish, competitive, and acquisitive mentality. Life is perceived as a zero-sum win-lose contest. Humans consider one another as objects or means for ends pursued by the self. They are usually ready to use, manipulate, and exploit one another

and they do not relate to others as whole beings but tend to interact as "roles" or "functions." They do not care about others and do not feel cared about by them. People are considered to be unequal in worth and they tend to think of themselves and others in comparative terms. Many are considered, and treated, as worthless. Being considered unequal in worth serves as justification for vast inequities of rights in every sphere of life, social, psychological, economic, civil, and political.[8]

In agenerally affluent society, we as Puerto Ricans too quickly accept our poverty, often seeing it as a function of our own individual characteristics. This is what we have been told and taught for centuries. It is my hope that the information contained in this study will help eliminate this notion and will be widely disseminated among several audiences.

The first audience I hope to reach is the Puerto Rican community in Massachusetts, in New York, Connecticut, and elsewhere. Our story is the same in most of the places that we now live in this nation. In those communities, we are usually victims of an ideology that places the onus of our poverty and misery on ourselves and those we love, not on societal forces and system dynamics. We must stop accepting so much blame. We have to stop internalizing the problems we confront and actively challenge the forces and systems that have historically exploited us. We must question the existing realities of the U.S. socioeconomic and political order. Perhaps this information may help some of us do that.

I also address this book to members of other racial minorities, especially U.S. black and non-Puerto Rican Hispanic communities. Our histories in this country bear many similarities. I hope that the material contained in this study helps to stimulate discussion about the reality of minority groups helping in the exploitation of others—consciously or by an automatic systemic process. Rivalry and competition among any of us weakens all of us. It will guarantee inequality and poverty for too many of our people. We must understand that we are not each others' enemies. On the contrary, we are natural allies. Strong coalitions among us can be beneficial not only to minority group members throughout the nation, but to all of U.S. society. We must contribute to the struggle for human liberation for everyone. As long as one group is exploited, every group that does not object is the oppressor.

I also hope that this book comes to the attention of, and is read by, progressive policy makers. I urge that policy be based more on the needs of peoples and less on the pluralist notion of political participation. The latter process guarantees that organized groups flexing their political clout be victors even if other, less powerful people and groups are sacrificed.

Teachers and social service providers are another audience to whom this work is directed. It is essential that they understand that the "we did it, why can't they" syndrome does not make sense in the 1980s. They must stop being neutral about the U.S. status quo. Their neutrality, by definition, supports the established values and order of society.[9] That order fosters competition, victim blaming, inequality, and poverty.

I also address this work to researchers. Hopefully, they will insist on more data on Puerto Ricans—on data leading to explorations that go beyond mere statistics on poverty. Research and scholarly efforts must study the adverse effects of our economic and political system on Puerto Ricans and other poor groups. Scholars and researchers must more assertively make such studies known and recommend needed changes. Lastly, I wish that other students and scholars, especially those of Puerto Rican, African, and Hispanic backgrounds, will utilize this book. I urge that they identify the gaps in the effort and do more than be critical. They must identify areas of further study and document societal forces that sanction inequality, destructive competition, poverty, and insecurity among many of this nation's peoples.

> There are, of course, certain economic safety mechanisms in operation in this society, e.g., public welfare, social security, unemployment compensation, etc. which are intended to assure the physical survival of victims of blind market forces. However, these mechanisms provide, at best, a marginal existence at high social and psychological costs, and their potential availability does not provide people with a sense of security. Hence, one must conclude that this society does not satisfy the most basic human needs for material goods and psychological security.[10]

That Puerto Ricans' basic human needs are not being met under this societal structure has been the thrust of this book. In the process, knowledge has been added, some patterns of migration have been identified, and some variables have been explored that may help in projecting the elsewheres to which Puerto Ricans may migrate in the future.

NOTES

1. Fred Barbaro, "Ethnic Resentment," Society 11 (March/April 1974):70.

2. See Clara E. Rodriguez, The Ethnic Queue in the U.S.: The Case of Puerto Ricans (San Francisco: R and E Research Associates, 1974), p. 81.

3. U.S. Department of Housing and Urban Development, Office of Policy Development and Research, How Well Are We Housed? (Washington, DC: Government Printing Office), p. 23.

4. Ibid., p. 12.

5. Ibid., p. 15.

6. Ibid., p. 23.

7. Father Leon is no longer in Waltham.

8. David C. Gil, "Clinical Practice and Politics of Human Liberation" (Paper presented at the Section on Clinical Child Psychology at the Annual Convention of the American Psychological Association, Washington, DC, September 6, 1976), pp. 9–10.

9. See Gil, "Clinical Practice," pp. 1–2.

10. Ibid., pp. 12–13.

Bibliography

Abrams, Charles. The Language of Cities—A Glossary of Terms. New York: The Viking Press, 1971.

Almond, Gabriel A., and Sidney Verba. The Civic Culture. Boston: Little, Brown, 1963.

Alvarado, Anthony. "Puerto Rican Children in New York Schools." New Generation 53(1972):22–25.

Anderson, Theodore, et.al. Bilingual Schooling in the U.S. (Austin, TX: Southwest Educational Development Laboratories). Washington, D.C.: Government Printing Office, 1970.

Appel, John J. The New Immigration. New York: Pitman Publishing, 1971.

Arciniegas, German. Biografía Del Caribe, 8th ed. Buenos Aires: Editorial Sud Americana, 1964.

Babin, María Teresa. Panorama de la Cultura Puertorriqueña. New York: Las Americas, 1958.

————. The Puerto Rican's Spirit: Their History, Life and Culture. New York: Macmillan, 1971.

Baggs, William C. "Puerto Rico Showcase of Development." Britannica Book of the Year. New York: Encyclopaedia Britannica, Inc., 1962.

Balian, Pereta, et. al. "Introduction of Puerto Rican Faculty in New York City Schools of Social Work." Social Work Education Reporter 19(December/January 1971):41–42.

Barbaro, Fred. "Ethnic Resentment." Society 11 (March/April 1974):67–75.

Barbaro, Fred, and Peacock, Carol. "Anti-Black Sentiments By Other Minorities: An Analysis of the Competition for Great Society Program Resources." Mimeographed. Columbia University School of Social Work. January 1972.

Barber, Bernard. Social Stratification: A Comparative Analysis of Structure and Process. New York: Harcourt, Brace, 1957.

Baron, Harold. The Demand for Black Labor. Cambridge, MA: Radical America, 1971.

Bayor, Ronald H. "Italians, Jews and Ethnic Conflict." International Migration Review. 6(Winter 1972):377–92.

Beaverbrook Guidance Center. "The Spanish Population of Waltham." Mimeographed. Belmont, MA.: Beaverbrook Guidance Center, 1974.

Becker, Gary S. "Economics of Discrimination" and "Human Capital: A Theoretical and Empirical Analysis." Readings in Labor Economics and Labor Relations. Edited by Lloyd G. Reynolds, Stanley H. Masters, and Collette Moser. Englewood Cliffs, NJ.: Prentice-Hall, 1974.

Bell, Daniel. The Coming of Post-Industrial Society. New York: Basic Books, 1973.

Benson, Lee. The Concept of Jacksonian Democracy. Princeton, NJ.: Princeton University Press, 1961.

Berg, Ivar. Education and Jobs: The Great Training Robbery. Boston: Beacon Press, 1971.

Berube, Maurice R., and Gittell, Marilyn, eds. Confrontation at Ocean Hill Brownsville. New York: Praeger Publishers, 1969.

Betances, Samuel. "The Prejudice of Having No Prejudice in Puerto Rico." The Rican 1(Winter 1972):41–45.

"The Big Mango." New York, August 7, 1972.

Billingsley, Andrew. Black Families in White America. Englewood Cliffs, NJ.: Prentice-Hall, 1968.

Binstock, Robert H. "Interest Group Liberalism and the Politics of the Aging." The Gerontologist 12(August 1972):265–80.

Blau, Francine D. "Women's Place in the Market." Readings in Labor Economics and Labor Relations. Edited by Lloyd G. Reynolds, Stanley H. Masters, and Collette Moser. Englewood Cliffs, NJ.: Prentice-Hall, 1974.

Bluestone, Barry. "The Characteristics of Marginal Industries." Problems in Political Economy: An Urban Perspective. Edited by David Gordon. Lexington, MA.: D. C. Health, 1971.

Blum, A., Miranda, M., and Meyer, M. "Goals and Means for Social Change." Neighborhood Organization for Community Action. Edited by John B. Turner. New York: NASW, 1968.

Board of Education of the City of New York, Office of Business and Administration. "Number and Proportions of Pupils by Ethnic Group Enrolled in Courses Offered by the Public High Schools of New York City in 1970–1971." Mimeographed. New York: Board of Education, 1972.

Borrero, Michael. "Impact Analysis of Federal Cutbacks on the Employment and Training Opportunities for Puerto Ricans." Mimeographed. Hartford, CT.: National Puerto Rican Coalition, Human Resource Planning Associates, 1983.

Boujouen, Norma, and Newton, James. The Puerto Rican Experience in Willimantic. Willimantic, CT.: Windham Regional Community Council, 1984.

Bowen, William G. "Assessing the Economic Contribution of Education." Readings in Labor Economics and Labor Relations. Edited by Lloyd G. Reynolds, Stanley H. Masters, and Collette Moser. Englewood Cliffs, NJ.: Prentice-Hall, 1974.

Brau, Salvador. Puerto Rico y su Historia. Valencia, Spain: Francisco Viver Mora, 1894.

Breed, Donald D. "Future of Hispanics in U.S. Looks Somber." Hartford Courant. April 14, 1985, p. C9.

Bremmer, Robert H. From the Depths, the Discovery of Poverty in the United States. New York: New York University Press, 1964.

Brooklyn College, Institute of Puerto Rican Studies. The Puerto Rican People: A Selected Bibliography for Use in Social Work Education. New York: Council on Social Work Education, 1973.

Brown, Susan E. "The Hispano Population of Cambridge: A Research Report." Mimeographed. Cambridge, MA.: Cambridge Spanish Council, 1973.

Cabranes, José A. "Puerto Rico: Out of the Colonial Closet." Foreign Policy 33(Winter 1978–79):74.

Campos, Angel P., ed. Puerto Rican Curriculum Development Workshop: A Report. New York: Council on Social Work Education, 1974.

Cardona, Luis Antonio. The Coming of the Puerto Ricans. Washington, D.C.: Unidos Publications, 1974.

Casiano, Inez, and Rodriguez, Hector E. Focus on Problems Faced by Mainland Puerto Ricans. Washington D.C.: U.S. Department of Labor, 1969.

"Census Shows Hispanic Families Rising in Income Faster Than Other Groups." New York Times, September 7, 1975, p. 30.

Center for Puerto Rican Studies, Research Foundation of the City University of New York. Labor Migration Under Capitalism. New York: Monthly Review Press, 1979.

Center for the Study of Public Policy. Education Vouchers: A Report on Financing Elementary Education by Grants to Parents. Cambridge, MA.: Center for the Study of Public Policy, December 1970.

Centro de Estudios Puertorriqueños, City University of New York. Taller de Migración. Conferencia de Historiografia: April, 1974. New York: Research Foundation of the City University of New York, 1975.

Centro Social Juan XXIII. Puerto Rico: Showcase of Oppression, Book 1. San Juan, 1970.

Chenault, Lawrence R. The Puerto Rican Migration in New York City. New York: Columbia University Press, 1938.

Chinoy, Ely. Automobile Workers and the American Dream. Garden City, NY.: Doubleday, 1955.

City University of New York. "Report of the Fall 1971 Undergraduate Ethnic Census." Mimeographed. January, 1972.

Commonwealth of Puerto Rico, Department of Labor, Migration Division, Puerto Ricans in the United States. New York City, 1975.

Community Council of Greater New York. Census Bulletin. New York: Research and Program Planning Information, nos. 14, 15, 16, August 10, 1972.

Cordasco, Francisco, and Bucchioni, Eugene. The Puerto Rican Experience, A Sociological Sourcebook. Totowa, NJ.: Littlefield, Adams, 1973.

Cowan, Paul. The Tribes of America. Garden City, NY.: Doubleday, 1979.

Cresap, McCormick and Pageant, Inc. Guidelines for New York City Community School Boards. New York: Cresap, McCormick and Pageant, May 1970.

Cromien, Florence M. "Negroes in the City of New York: Their Numbers and Proportion in Relationship to the Total Population, 1790–1960." Mimeographed. New York: Commission on Intergroup Relations, 1961.

Cruz, Enid J. "The Puerto Rican Seasonal Farm Laborer: A Victim." Revista. Vol. 2. Brooklyn College: Instituto de Estudios Puertorriqueños, Autumn 1972.

Cruz-Monclova, L. Historia de Puerto Rico, 1808–1895, Vols. 1–2. Puerto Rico: Editorial Universidad de Puerto Rico, 1958.

Cuadrado, María, and Hermandez, Carmen D. "Status of Puerto Ricans In the City University of New York." Mimeographed. New York: City University of New York.

Davis, John F. "Anti-Koch Strategy: Divide and Lose." Village Voice, February 19, 1985.

Davis, Kingsley, and Moore, Wilbert E. "Some Principles of Stratification." American Sociological Review 10(April 1945):

Delgado, Melvin. "Social Work and the Puerto Rican Community." Social Casework 55(February 1974):117–24.

Denis, Manuel Maldonado. Puerto Rico: A Socio-Historic Interpretation. New York: Random House, 1972.

"Denny Farrell Betrays the Coalition." Statement of Latinos United for Political Action, February 11, 1985. Village

Voice, February 19, 1985.
Department of Employment Service, Farm Placement. Annual
  Agricultural and Food Processing Report of the Post
  Season Report. Mimeographed. Boston, 1951.
—————. "Annual Agricultural and Food Processing
  Report." Mimeographed. Boston, 1953.
—————. "Placement Activities in Agriculture and Food
  Processing Report." Mimeographed. Boston, 1953,
  1954, 1955, 1956, and 1957.
—————. "Annual Farm Labor Report." Mimeographed.
  Boston, 1958, 1959, 1960, 1961, 1962, 1963, and 1964.
—————. "Annual Agricultural Report." Mimeographed.
  Boston, 1968, 1969, 1970, and 1971.
—————. "Rural Manpower Report." Mimeographed.
  Boston, 1975.
Díaz Soler, Luis M. Historia de la Esclavitud en Puerto
  Rico. Madrid: Ediciones de la Universidad de Puerto
  Rico, 1953.
—————. Historia de La Esclavitud Negra en Puerto Rico
  (1493–1890). Madrid: Imprenta Viuda de Galo Saez,
  1956.
Domhoff, William G. Who Rules America? Englewood Cliffs,
  NJ.: Prentice-Hall, 1967.
Douglas, Jack. Youth in Turmoil. Washington, D.C.: HEW
  Publication No. 2058, 1970.
Edel, Matthew, and Rothenberg, Jerome. Readings in
  Urban Economics. New York: Macmillan, 1972.
El Coqui. Newsletter of El Programa Roberto Clemente.
  Waltham, MA.: June 1975.
Epstein, Jason. "The Last Days of New York." New York
  Review. February 17, 1976.
Ernst, Robert. Immigrant Life in New York City,
  1825–1863. New York: King's Crown Press, 1949.
Fanon, Frantz. Black Skin, White Mask. New York: Grove
  Press, 1967.
—————. The Wretched of the Earth. New York: Grove
  Press, 1968.
Fantini, Mario, Gittell, Marilyn, and Magat, Richard.
  Community Control and the Urban School. New York:
  Praeger Publishers, 1970.
Fein, Leonard J. The Ecology of the Public Schools: An
  Inquiry Into Community Control. New York: Pegasus,
  1971.
Feldstein, Sylvan G. Brownsville Selects a School Site.
  New York: Limited advance edition published for ICP
  Subscribing Institutions, 1973.
"Feminidades: A las Puertorriqueñas pobres, Nueva York
  les ofrece el mundo . . . en una fábrica." Cynthia

Vice Acosia, De El Diario-LaPrensa El Diario-La Prensa, Jueves 3 de Marzo de 1983. (To the poor Puerto Rican Woman, New York offers the world . . . in a factory. Cynthia Vice Acosta, in El Diario-La Prensa, New York Spanish language newspaper, March 3, 1983.)

Fitzpatrick, Joseph P. "Intermarriage of Puerto Ricans in New York City." American Journal of Sociology 71:1965–1966.

——————. Puerto Rican-Americans: The Meaning of Migration to the Mainland. Englewood Cliffs, NJ.: Prentice-Hall, 1971.

"Flight from Inner Cities Goes On." U.S. News & World Report, September 11, 1978.

Franklin, John Hope. From Slavery to Freedom. New York: Alfred A. Knopf, 1956.

Friedlander, Walter A., and Apte, Robert A. Introduction to Social Welfare. Englewood Cliffs, NJ.: Prentice-Hall, 1974.

Friedman, Milton. "The Role of Government in Education." Capitalism and Freedom. Chicago: University of Chicago Press, 1962.

Friedman, Robert. "From Puerto Rico—With Skills." Daily News, January 31, 1980.

——————. "P.R. Retirees are Shifting their Sunsets to the States." San Juan Star, February 1, 1982.

——————. "Future Bleak for Migrants to New York." Daily News, December 4, 1983.

"Future of Hispanics in U.S. Looks Somber." Rhode Island Journal—Bulletin, April 14, 1985, p. C9.

Galbraith, J. K. "Economics As a System of Belief." American Economic Review 60(2), May 1970, Papers and Proceedings; p. 469–78.

Gallaway, Lowell E. Interindustry Labor Mobility in the United States. U.S. Department of Health, Education and Welfare, Social Security Administration Research Report no. 18. Washington, D.C.: Government Printing Office, 1967.

Gamson, William A. Power and Discontent. Homeward, IL.: Dorsey Press, 1968.

Gerlach, Luther P., and Hine, Virginia H. People, Power, Change: Movements of Social Transformation. New York: Bobbs-Merrill, 1970.

Gianturco, Adriana, and Aronin, Norman. Boston's Spanish Speaking Community. Boston: Action for Boston Community Development, October 1971.

Gil, David C. "Practice in the Human Services as a Political Act." Journal of Clinical Child Psychology 3(Winter-Spring 1974):15–20.

—————. "Social Policies and Social Development."
Mimeographed. Waltham, MA: Brandeis University,
June 25, 2975.

—————. The Challenge of Social Equality. Cambridge,
MA.: Schenkman Publishing, 1976.

—————. "Clinical Practice and Politics of Human Lib-
eration." Paper presented at the Section on Clinical
Child Psychology at the Annual Convention of the
American Psychological Association. Washington, D.C.,
September 6, 1976, pp. 9–10.

—————. Unraveling Social Policy. Cambridge, MA.:
Schenkman Publishing, 1976.

—————. Beyond The Jungle—Essays On Human Possibilities, Social Alternatives, and Radical Practice.
Cambridge, MA.: Schenkman Publishing, 1979.

Gitelman, Howard. Workingmen of Waltham. Baltimore:
Johns Hopkins University Press, 1974.

Gittell, Marilyn. Decentralization for Social Change, An
Experiment in Local Control. New York: Institute for
Community Studies, Queens College, 1971.

Gittell, Marilyn, and Glantz, Frederick B. "The Deter-
minants of the Interregional Migration of the Economically Disadvantaged." Mimeographed. Boston:
Federal Reserve Bank of Boston, January 1973.

Glazer, Nathan, and Moynihan, Patrick. Beyond the
Melting Pot. Cambridge, MA.: The M.I.T. Press, 1970.

Goldstein, Richard. "The Big Mango," New York, August
7, 1972, p. 24.

Gonzales, Augustin and Romero, Sally. "Inclusion of
Puerto Rican Curriculum Content in Social Work
Training." Social Work Education Reporter 19 (Decem-
ber/January 1971):42–43.

Gordon, David M. Problems in Political Economy: An Urban
Perspective. Lexington, MA.: D.C. Heath, 1971.

Gordon, Milton M. Assimilation in American Life: The Role
of Race, Religion, and National Origins. New York:
Oxford University Press, 1964.

Gorz, André. Strategy for Labor—A Radical Proposal.
Boston: Beacon Press, 1967.

Greenspan, Richard. "Analysis of Puerto Rican and Black
Employment in New York City Schools." Mimeographed.
New York: Puerto Rican Forum, May 1970.

Gruber, Ruth. Puerto Rico: Island of Promise. New York:
Hill and Wang, 1960.

Gunther, John. Inside Latin America. New York: Harper
and Brothers, 1941.

Handlin, Oscar. Immigration as a Factor in American
History. Englewood Cliffs, NJ.: Prentice-Hall, 1959.

—————. The Newcomers, Negroes and Puerto Ricans In a Changing Metropolis. New York: Doubleday, 1959 and 1973 editions.

—————. The Uprooted, 2d ed. Boston: Little, Brown, 1973.

Hardin, Blaine. "Expressing the Hunger of the World's Poor." Hartford Courant, April 16, 1985, p. B9.

Heilbroner, Robert L. Understanding Micro-Economics, 2d ed. Englewood Cliffs, NJ.: Prentice-Hall, June 1972.

Herberg, Will. Protestant, Catholic, Jew. Garden City, NY.: Doubleday, 1955.

Hernandez, José. "Puerto Rican Youth Empowerment. Discussion draft. New York: Hunter College, October 5, 1984.

Hernandez-Alvarez, José. Return Migration to Puerto Rico. Berkeley, CA.: Berkeley Institute of International Studies, Regents of the University of California, 1967.

—————. "The Post-Development Crossroads of Puerto Rican Migration." A New Look At Puerto Ricans and Their Society. (ed.) The Institute of Puerto Rican Studies. New York: Brooklyn College, 1973.

—————. "La Migración Puertorriqueña Como Factor Demográfico; Solución y Problema." Revista-Review Interamericana 4(Winter 1974–75) (The Puerto Rican Migration as a Demographic Factor; Solution and Problem).

Hofstader, Richard. Social Darwinism In American Thought. Philadelphia: University of Pennsylvania Press, 1944.

Hogg, Flora. "The People of Hartford Address the Visiting Mayors—To Represent Is to Listen and Report." Hartford Courant, April 18, 1985, p. D9.

Horn, Robert N. "Labor Market Segmentation and the Political Economy of Manpower and Job Creation Programs." Thesis. Durham, NH.: Whittemore School of Business and Economics, University of New Hampshire, 1978.

Howe, Irving. "Immigrant Jewish Families in New York: The End of the World of Our Fathers." Adapted by New York, October 13, 1975.

Hutchinson, E. P. Immigrants and Their Children. New York: John Wiley & Sons, 1956.

Hymer, Stephen. "The Multinational Corporation and the Law of Uneven Development." Economics and World Order from the 1970's to the 1990's. Edited by Jagdish N. Bhagwti. London: Macmillan 1972.

Ianni, Francis A. J. "New Mafia: Black, Hispanic and Italian Styles." Society, 11(March/April 1974):26–31.

Institute of Puerto Rican Studies. A New Look at the Puerto Ricans and Their Society. New York: Brooklyn College, 1973.

"It's Your Place in the Sun." Time, October 11, 1978.

"It's Your Turn in the Sun." Time, October 16, 1978, p. 48.

Johnson, Thomas A. "Term Minority, Shunned by Black Social Workers." New York Times, April 22, 1979.

Jones, Dorothy. "Community Control, Decentralization and the Black Community." Mimeographed. Position Paper for the National Urban League, New York, 1969.

Jones, Maldwyn Allen. American Immigration. Chicago: University of Chicago Press, 1960.

Junta de Planificacion de Puerto Rico. Informe Economico Al Governador 1982–83, Vol. 2, 2d ed. Estado Libre Asociado de Puerto Rico, Oficina Del Governador. (Puerto Rican Planning Board. Economic Report to the governor 1982–83. Vol. 2, 2d ed. Commonwealth of Puerto Rico, Office of the governor.)

Katzman, Martin T. "Discrimination, Sub-culture and the Economic Performance of Negroes, Puerto Ricans and Mexican-Americans." American Journal of Economics Sociology 27:4:(1968):371–76.

Kaufman, Jacob J., and Foran, Terry G. "Minimum Wage and Poverty." Readings in Labor Economics and Labor Relations. Edited by Lloyd G. Reynolds , Stanley H. Masters, and Collette Moser. Englewood Cliffs, NJ.: Prentice-Hall, 1974.

Kihss, Peter. "Census Shows Hispanic Families Rising in Income Faster Than Other Groups." New York Times, September 7, 1975, p. 30.

—————. "Job Study Issued on Puerto Ricans." New York Times, June 1, 1975, p. 37.

Kirchheimer, Anne L. "Lure of Jobs Attract Puerto Ricans to U.S." Boston Globe, January 16, 1978.

Kluckholm, Clyde, and Kluckholm, Florence R. "American Culture: Generalized Orientations and Class Patterns." Conflicts of Power in Modern Culture. New York: Harper, 1946.

Kreps, Juanita. "Sex In the Marketplace." Readings In Labor Economics and Labor Relations. Edited by Lloyd G. Reynolds, Stanley H. Masters, and Collette Moser. Englewood Cliffs, NJ.: Prentice-Hall, 1974.

Langlois, Margaret. "Special Census of School Population, Classification of Non-English Speaking Pupils." Mimeographed. New York: Board of Education, Educational Program, Research and Statistics Publication, no. 311, PN5394, October 31, 1967.

—————. "Number and Proportion of Pupils by Ethnic Group Enrolled in Courses Offered by the Public High Schools of New York City in 1970–71." Mimeographed. New York: Board of Education, 1972.

Lansing, John and Mueller, Eva. The Geographic Mobility of Labor. Ann Arbor, MI.: University of Michigan Survey Research Center, 1967.

LaRuffa, Anthony. San Cripriano: Life in a Puerto Rican Community. New York: Gordon and Breach Science Publishers, 1971.

Leebaw, Milton. "Puerto Ricans and Economics." New York Times, October 17, 1976, p.5.

Lehman, Edward W. "Toward a Macro-Sociology of Power." American Sociological Review 34(August 1969):453–65.

Lenski, Gerhard. The Religious Factor. Garden City, NY.: Doubleday, 1963.

Levin, Henry M., ed. Community Control of Schools. New York: Simon and Schuster, 1970.

Levitan, Sar. The Great Society's Poor Laws. Baltimore: The John Hopkins Press, 1969.

Levy, Gerald E. Ghetto School: Class Warfare in an Elementary School. New York: Pegasus, 1970.

Lewis, Gordon, K. Freedom and Power in the Caribbean. New York: Monthly Review, 1964.

Lewis, Oscar. La Vida: A Puerto Rican Family in the Culture of Poverty—San Juan and New York. New York: Random House, 1965.

Licha, Silvia. "Vuelve la emigración a EE. UU." El Nuevo Dia, lunes 7 de mayo de 1984. (Emmigration to the U.S. Returns.)

Lieberman, Myron. The Future of Public Education. Chicago: University of Chicago Press, 1960.

Liem, Ramsay G. ". . . And Others" A Report Card for the New York City Public School. New York: Aspira. 1971.

Lindorf, Dave. "The New Wave from Puerto Rico." New York, May 17, 1982.

Lipset, Martin Seymour. Political Man. Garden City, NY.: Anchor Books, 1963.

—————. "Education and Equality: Israel and the United States Compared." Society 11(March/April 1974):56–66.

Lipset, Martin Seymour and Bendix, R. Social Mobility in Industrial Society. Berkeley, CA.: University of California Press, 1959.

Longres, John. Perspectives from the Puerto Rican Faculty Training Project. New York: Council on Social Work Education, 1973.

Lopez, Alfredo. The Puerto Rican Papers, Notes on the

Re-Emergence of a Nation. New York: Bobbs-Merrill, 1973.

Lowi, Theodore J. The End of Liberalism. New York: W. W. Norton, 1969.

Lurie, Ellen. How to Change the School System. New York: Random House, 1970.

Lyle, Jerolyn, Equal Employment Opportunity Commission. Affirmative Action Program for Women, A Survey of Innovative Programs. Washington, D.C.: Government Printing Office, 1973.

Maldonado Denis, Manuel. Puerto Rico: A Socio-Historic Interpretation. New York: Random House, 1972.

Maldonado, Rita M. "Why Puerto Ricans Migrated to the United States in 1947–73." Monthly Labor Review 9(September 1976):7–18.

Mann, Evelyn S., and Salvo, Joseph J. "Characteristics of New Hispanic Immigrants to New York City. A Comparison of Puerto Ricans and non-Puerto Rican Hispanics." Mimeographed paper presented at the Annual Meeting of the Population Associates of America, Minneapolis, Minnesota, May 3, 1984.

Margolis, Richard J. "The Losers." Paper prepared for the First National Conference of Puerto Ricans, Aspira, New York: May 1968.

Marín, Rosa C. "Puerto Ricans are Not Being Attracted to United States Schools of Social Work." Social Work Education Reporter 19(December/January 1971):45.

Marqués, René. The Oxcart. New York: Scribner's Sons, 1969.

Martin, Vivian B. "From Unity, Black Mayors Draw Strength." Hartford Courant, April 14, 1985.

Mascisco, John J. "Assimilation of Puerto Ricans on the Mainland: A Socio-demographic Approach." International Migration Review 2:(Spring 1968):21–37.

Massachusetts Bicentennial Commission. "Directory of Ethnic Organizations In Massachusetts." Boston, 1976.

Massachusetts Department of Commerce and Development. Commonwealth of Massachusetts Industrial Directory, 1968. Boston, 1968.

——————. City and Town—City of Waltham Monograph. Boston, March, 1972.

Massachusetts Division of Employment Services. Annual Planning Report Fiscal Year 1978—New Bedford Labor Market Area. Mimeographed. Boston, 1978.

Massachusetts Office of State Planning, Local Growth Policy Committee. Local Growth Policy Statement. Cambridge, MA.: July 1976.

Massachusetts State Advisory Committee to the U.S. Commission on Civil Rights. Issues of Concern to Puerto Ricans in Boston and Springfield. Boston, 1972.

Mathews, Thomas. "The Question of Color in Puerto Rico." Mimeographed. Institute of Caribbean Studies, University of Puerto Rico, San Juan 1968.

Mayer, Robert R. Social Planning and Social Change. Englewood Cliffs, NJ.: Prentice-Hall, 1972.

McNeely, Roger. "In Public Education: Is Community Participation the Answer?" Paper presented to the Faculty of the Florence Heller Graduate School for Advanced Studies in Social Welfare, Brandeis University, New York, Fall 1973.

Merton, Robert K. Social Theory and Social Structure, revised ed. Glencoe, IL.: Free Press, 1957.

"Migración de Puertorriqueños es Motivo de Preocupación." Noticias del Mundo, jueves 4 de Octubre de 1984. (Puerto Rican Migration is Reason to Worry.)

"Migrant's Lot in Massachusetts, Toiling in the Fields . . . Weeping at Night." Boston Globe, October 18, 1970.

Miller Solomon, Barbara. Ancestors and Immigrants. Cambridge, MA.: Harvard University Press, 1956.

Mills, C. Wright, Clarence Senior and Rose Goldsen. Puerto Rican Journey. New York: Harper, Row Publishers, 1950.

Mills, Nicolaus. "Community Schools. Irish, Italian, and Jews." Society 11(March/April 1974):76–84

Milner, Thirman L. "Black Mayors: 'Growing in Numbers, Growing in Unity'—Host of City Symbolizes the Dream." Hartford Courant, April 17, 1985, p. B9.

Milton, Gordon M. Assimilation in American Life. New York: New York University Press, 1964.

Minz, Sidney. Worker in the Cane. New Haven, CT.: Yale University Press, 1960.

Miranda, Magdelena, Council on Social Work Education. Puerto Rican Task Force Report. New York: Council on Social Work Education, 1973.

Mizio, Emelicia. "The Conceptual Framework." Training for Service Delivery to Minority Clients. Edited by Emelicia Mizio and Anita J. Delaney. Family Service Association, New York: 1981.

————. "Puerto Rican Social Workers and Racism." Social Casework 53 (May 1972):267–73.

Monserrat, Joseph. "School Integration, A Puerto Rican View." Mimeographed. New York: Office of the Commonwealth of Puerto Rico, 1956.

Morales-Carrión, Arturo. Puerto Rico and the Non-Hispanic Caribbean: A Study in the Decline of Spanish Exclusivism. Puerto Rico: University of Puerto Rico Press, 1952.

—————. Puerto Rico and the Non Hispanic Caribbean. Barcelona: Artez Graficas Medinaceli, 1974.

Morales, Julio. "The Clinician as Advocate: A Puerto Rican Perspective." Training for Service Delivery to Minority Clients. (eds.) Emelicia Mizio and Anita Delaney, New York: F.S.S.A., 1982.

—————. "Puerto Rican Studies: An Example of Social Movements as a Force toward Social and Economic Justice." Towards Social and Economic Justice. (eds.) David Gil and Eva Gil, Cambridge, MA.: Schenkman Publishing Company, 1985.

Moses, Charles T. and Wiener, Caryn Eve. "New Wave of Immigrants Changing New York Society." Hartford Courant, October 25, 1982, p. C16.

National Commission on Civil Disorders. United States Riot Commission Report. New York: Bantam Books, March 1968.

National Migrant and Information Clearinghouse. "Migrant Programs in the Northeastern States." Mimeographed. Austin, TX.: Juarez, Lincoln Center, 1974.

National Puerto Rican Forum. The Next Step Toward Equality. New York, September 1980, p. 5.

National Puerto Rican Coalition. "Puerto Ricans in the United States and on the Island—1970–1980. A Demographic Profile." Mimeographed. New York: October 15, 1984, p. 18.

New York State Advisory Committee. The Puerto Rican and Public Employment in New York State. Report to the U.S. Commission on Civil Rights. Government Printing Office. Washington, D.C., April 1973.

New York State Department of Labor. Division of Research and Statistics, Manpower Requirements: Interim Projections, New York State, 1968–80. Publication B-185, July, 1971.

"New Wave of Immigrants Changing New York Society." Hartford Courant, October 25, 1982, p. C16.

New York Times. October 17, 1965.

—————. Sunday, June 1, 1975.

—————. January 30, 1976. "Depressed Puerto Ricans." Editorial, p. 28.

—————. October 17, 1976. "Puerto Rico and Economics." Section IV, p. 5.

Newman, Morris. "A Profile of Hispanics in the U.S. Work Force." Monthly Labor Review (December 1978):

Nieves Falcon, Luis. "Social Class and Power Structure in Puerto Rican Society." A New Look at the Puerto

Ricans and Their Society. (ed.) Institute of Puerto Rican Studies. New York: Brooklyn College, 1972.

Nortego, David. "Perspectiva: Emigración y Desempleo." El Nuevo Día, Viernes 3 de Febrero de 1984. (Perspective: Emmigration and Unemployment.)

Nyquist, Ewald B. Statement on the Puerto Rican Child in New York Before the United States Civil Rights Commission. Mimeographed. February 15, 1972.

Office of the Commonwealth of Puerto Rico. A Summary in Facts and Figures 1964–65. Office of the Commonwealth of Puerto Rico, New York, 1960.

Oyola, José Ramón. "Migration—Inhumane or Highly Profitable for P.R.?" San Juan Star, March 21, 1982.

Padilla, Elena. Up From Puerto Rico. New York: Columbia University Press, 1958.

Pantoja, Antonia. "Puerto Rican Migration." Mimeographed. Preliminary Report to the U.S. Commission on Civil Rights. New York: January 31, 1972.

Parsons, Talcott and Shils, Edward A. Toward a General Theory of Action. Cambridge, MA.: Harvard University Press, 1952.

Parsons, Talcott and Clark, Kenneth B. The Negro American. Boston: Beacon Press, 1965.

Pen, Jan. Income Distribution, Facts, Theories, Policies. New York: Praeger Publishers, 1971.

Perez, Gamalie. "A New Approach to the Puerto Rican in His Society." A New Look at the Puerto Ricans and Their Society. (ed.) Institute of Puerto Rican Studies, New York: Brooklyn College, 1972.

Piore, Michael J. "The Dual Labor Market: Theory and Implications." Problems in Political Economy. Edited by David Gordon. Lexington, MA.: Health, 1971.

————. "The Role of Immigration to Industrial Growth: A Case of Economics." Working paper No. 112, May, 1973.

————. "The Role of Immigration in Industrial Growth: A Case Study of the Origins and Character of Puerto Rican Migration to Boston." Working paper. Department of Economics, Massachusetts Institute of Technology, 1975.

————. Birds of Passage. Cambridge, MA.: Cambridge University Press, 1979.

Piven, Frances Fox and Cloward, Richard A. Regulating the Poor: The Functions of Public Welfare. New York: Pantheon Books, 1971.

————. The New Class War. Reagan's Attack on the Welfare State and Its Consequences. New York: Pantheon Books, 1982.

Pratt, Julius W. Expansionists of 1898: The Acquisition of Hawaii and the Spanish Islands. Baltimore: John Hopkins Press, 1936.

Prospero Altiery, Miguel A. "Migratory Movement Between the United States and Puerto Rico." Mimeographed. Presentation at the First Forum on the Human Rights of the Puerto Rican Migrant Families, sponsored by the Puerto Rican Family Institute, New York: November 29, 1983.

Puerto Rican Forum. The Puerto Rican Development Project: A Proposal for a Self-Help Project. New York, 1964.

"Puerto Ricans and Economics." New York Times, October 17, 1976.

"Puerto Ricans in New York: It's Still Despair." The Evening Bulletin—The Providence Journal, December 14, 1983, p. A17.

"Puerto Ricans Seen as Deprived." Hartford Courant, October 6, 1980, p. A4.

Puerto Rico Commission on the Status of Puerto Rico. Legal Constitutional Factors in Relation to the Status of Puerto Rico. Hearings Before the United States—Puerto Rico Commission on the Status of Puerto Rico, Vol. 1. San Juan, Puerto Rico, May 14—18, 1965, pp. 215—16.

Queens College of the City University of New York. Counseling the Black and Puerto Rican College Students. New York: Queens College, 1972.

Rand, Christopher. The Puerto Ricans. New York: Oxford University Press, 1958.

Ribes, Tovar F. Albizu Campos: Puerto Rican Revolutionary. New York: Plus Ultra Educational Publishers, 1971.

Ribich, Thomas I. "Education and Poverty." Readings in Labor Economices and Labor Relations. Edited by Lloyd C. Reynolds, Stanley H. Masters, and Collette Moser. Englewood Cliffs, NJ.: Prentice-Hall, 1974.

Riis, Jacob A. How the Other Half Lives: Studies Among the Tenements of New York. New York: Hill and Wang, 1957.

Rintel, David J. "Some Reasons Why Puerto Ricans Migrate to the United States." Mimeographed. Somerville, MA., 1975.

Ritterband, Paul. "Closing Down the Schools: The New York City School Strike of 1968." Mimeographed. New York, 1970.

————. "Community Control and the Black Agenda, 1971. Mimeographed. New York, 1971.

————. "Race, Resources and Achievement." Sociology

of Education 46(Spring 1973):167–171.

Rivera, Felipe. "The Puerto Rican Farm Worker." Centro Taller de Migración—Conferencia de Historiografía. Centro de Estudios Puertorriqueños, Research Foundation of the City University of New York, April, 1975.

Roberts, Steven V. "Blacks and Women Clash on Access to Jobs and Aid." New York Times, February 20, 1979, p. 10.

Rodriguez, Clara E. The Ethnic Queue in the U.S.: The Case of Puerto Ricans. San Francisco: R and E Research Associates, 1974.

—————. "Economic Factors Affecting Puerto Ricans in New York." Centro Taller de Migración—Conferencia de Histografía. New York: Research Foundation of The City University of New York, April, 1975.

Rodriguez Cruz, Juan. "Las Relaciones Raciales en Puerto Rico." Revista de Ciencias Sociales, San Juan (November 1971).

Rogers, David. 110 Livingston Street: Politics and Bureaucracy in the New York Schools. New York: Random House, 1968.

Rogler, Charles C. "The Morality of Race Mixing in Puerto Rico." Social Forces 25(October 1946):77–81.

Rogler, Lloyd H. and Hollingshead, August B. Trapped: Families and Schizophrenia. New York: John Wiley & Sons, 1965.

Romanyshyn, John M. Social Welfare: Charity to Justice. New York: Random House, 1971.

Rose, Arnold M. The Power Structure. New York: Oxford University Press, 1968.

Rosen, Bernard C. "Race, Ethnicity and the Achievement Syndrome." American Sociological Review 24(February 1959):47–60.

Rosenberg, Terry and Lake, Robert. "Toward a Revised Model of Residential Segregation and Succession: Puerto Ricans in New York, 1960–1970." American Journal of Sociology 81(March 1976):1142–50.

Salgado, Ramona. "The Puerto Rican Family: Present Realities and Future Developments." Discussion draft mimeographed. New York: Mayor's Office on Hispanic Affairs, October 5, 1984.

Salvatierra, Richard. "U.S. Must Set a Limit on Refugees." Nuestro 7(June/July 1983):19.

de Schmidt, Camacho. "The INS & Sojourners from Italy." Nuestro 7(June/July 1983):20.

Schneider, David M. and Deutsch, M. The Road Upward. New York: New York State Department of Welfare, 1938.

————. The History of Public Welfare in New York State: 1867–1940, Chicago: The University of Chicago Press, 1941.

Senior, Clarence. Strangers, Then Neighbors: From Pilgrims to Puerto Ricans. Chicago: Quadrangle Books, 1965.

Sereno, Renzo. "Cryptomelanism, A Study of Color Relations and Personal Insecurity in Puerto Rico." Psychiatry 10(August 1947):263.

Service Employees, International Union, AFL-CIO-CLC. 38 Jan, 1980. pp. 6–7.

Sexton, Patricia Cayo. Spanish Harlem: Anatomy of Poverty. New York: Harper and Row, 1966.

Sibley, Elbridge. "Some Demographic Clues to Stratification." American Sociological Review 7(1942):322–30.

Silberman, Charles E. Crisis in Black and White. New York: Vintage Books, 1964.

Silen, Juan Angel. We the Puerto Rican People. New York: Monthly Review Press, 1972.

Smelser, Neil J. Theory of Collective Behavior. New York: Free Press, 1962.

Spier, Adele. The Two Bridges Model School District: A Profile. New York: Institute for Community Studies, Queens College, 1969.

Stampp, Kenneth M. The Peculiar Institution: Slavery in the Ante-Bellum South. New York: Vintage Books, 1956.

Sterba, James. "In a Recession, Erosion of Jobs Feared for City." New York Times, November 14, 1978, p. 7.

Steward, Julian. The People of Puerto Rico. Champaign-Urbana, IL.: University of Illinois Press, 1957.

Stockton, William. "Going Home: The Puerto Ricans' New Migration." New York Times Magazine, November 12, 1978, p. 20.

"Study Shows Black Migration to Cities Has Ended." Hartford Courant, December 1, 1978.

"Study: Puerto Ricans Making Little Progress." Transcript-Telegram, Holyoke, MA., February 9, 1985.

Tabb, William K. The Political Economy of the Black Ghetto. New York: W.W. Norton, 1970.

————. "Puerto Ricans in New York City: A Study of Economic and Social Conditions." Mimeographed. Bureau of Labor Statistics, New York, 1972.

Taeber, Karl E. and Taeber, Alma F. "Recent Immigration and Studies of Ethnic Assimilation." Demography 4(1967)798–808.

Task Force on Children Out of School. The Way We Go to School: The Exclusion of Children in Boston. Boston:

Task Force on Children, 1970.

————. Suffer the Children: The Politics of Mental Health in Massachusetts. Boston: Task Force on Children, 1972.

Theodorson, George A., and Theodorson, Achilles G. A Modern Dictionary of Sociology and Related Disciplines. New York: Thomas Y. Crowell, 1969.

Thomas, Piri. Down These Mean Streets. New York: Alfred A. Knopf, 1967.

Tienda, Marta. "The Puerto Rican Worker: Current Labor Market Status and Future Prospects." Discussion draft. Department of Rural Sociology, University of Wisconsin-Madison, October 5, 1984.

Todd, Roberto H. Desfile de Gobernadores de Puerto Rico, 2d ed., Madrid: Ediciones Iberoamericanas, 1966. (A Parade of Governors of Puerto Rico.)

Tumin, Melvin M. "Some Principles of Stratification: A Critical Analysis." American Sociological Review 18 (August 1953):387-98.

Tumin, Melvin M. and Feldman, Arnold. Social Class and Social Change in Puerto Rico. Princeton, NJ.: Princeton University Press, 1961.

Tunner, Christopher, and Reed, Henry. American Skyline. New York: The New American Library, 1956.

Turner, Harry. "More P.R. Professionals Leaving Island for the U.S." San Juan Star, February 1, 1982.

U.S. Commission on Civil Rights. "Demographic, Social and Economic Characteristics of New York City and the New York Metropolitan Area." Hearings on Civil Rights of Puerto Ricans. Staff report. Washington, D.C.: February 1972.

————. Public Education for Puerto Rican Children in New York City. Staff report. Washington, D.C.: February 1972.

————. "The Puerto Rican Migration." Mimeographed. Washington, D.C.: February 1972.

————. Press Release. Washington, D.C., February 14, 1972.

————. Hearing Before the United States Commission Civil Rights. New York, February 14-15, 1972. Washington, D.C.: Government Printing Office, 1973.

————. Puerto Ricans in the Continental United States: An Uncertain Future. Washington, D.C., October 1976.

————. The Tarnished Door, Civil Rights Issues in Immigration. Washington, D.C.: Government Printing Office, September 1980.

U.S. Department of Commerce, Bureau of the Census. Characteristics of the Population: Massachusetts, Vol.

1.   Washington, D.C.: Government Printing Office, 1973, p. 23.

—————.   The Social and Economic Status of the Black Population in the United States, 1973.   Current Population Reprints, Special Studies, Series P, 23, no. 48. Washington, D.C.: Government Printing Office, 1974.

—————.   Characteristics in the Population by Ethnic Origin: March 1972 and 1971.   Current Population Reports, Series P, 20, no. 249.   Washington, D.C.: Government Printing Office, 1973.

—————.   Persons of Spanish Origin in the United States: March 1972 and 1971.   Current Population Reports, Series P, 20, no. 250.   Washington, D.C.: Government Printing Office, 1973.

—————.   Current Population Survey: Persons of Spanish Origin in the United States.   March 1974.   Washington, D.C.: Bureau of the Census, 1975.

—————.   Persons of Spanish Origin in the United States. Current Population Reports, Population Characteristics, Series P, 20, no. 396.   Washington, D.C.: Government Printing Office, March 1983.

—————.   Persons of Spanish Origin By State: 1980. Washington, D.C., 1982.

—————.   The Social and Economic Status of the Black Population in the United States, 1973.   Population Reports, Special Studies, Series P, 23, no. 48.   Washington, D.C.: Government Printing Office, 1974.

—————.   Housing Characteristics for States, Cities, and Counties, Vol. 1, Part 23.   Massachusetts.   Washington, D.C.: Government Printing Office, 1983.

—————.   Persons of Spanish Origin in the United States: October, 1969.   Series no. 213, Washington, D.C.: Government Printing Office, February 1971, p. 20.

—————.   Persons of Spanish Origin in the United States: March, 1975.   Washington, D.C.: Government Printing Office, 1976.

—————.   Characteristics of the Population: Mass.   1970. Washington, D.C.: Government Printing Office.

—————.   Persons of Spanish Origin in the United States. 1979.   Washington, D.C.: Government Printing Office.

—————.   U.S. Census of Population: 1970.   General Social and Economic Characteristics.   PC(1)-C34. Washington, D.C.: Government Printing Office.

—————.   U.S. Census of Population: 1960.   Characteristics of the Population.   New York, Vol 1, Part 34. Washington, D.C.: Government Printing Office.

—————.   U.S. Census of Population: 1960.   Subject Reports.   Puerto Ricans in the United States.   Final

Report PC(2)-1D. Washington, D.C.: Government Printing Office, 1963.

——————. Supplementary Report—Persons of Spanish Origin by State: 1980. Washington, D.C.: Government Printing Office, 1981, p. 2.

U.S. Department of Housing and Urban Development, Office of Policy Development and Research. How Well Are We Housed? Washington, D.C.: Government Printing Office, January 1979, p. 23.

U.S. Department of Labor, Bureau of Labor Statistics. Poverty Area Profiles, New York's Puerto Ricans: Pattern of Work Experience. No. 19. Washington, D.C.: Government Printing Office, May 1979.

——————. Middle Atlantic Regional Office. A Socio-Economic Profile of Puerto Rican New Yorkers. Regional Report 46. New York, July 1975.

U.S. House of Representatives, Hispanic Higher Education Coalition. "Testimony Before the Subcommittee on Postsecondary Education Committee on Education and Labor": Hearings on the Reauthorization of the Higher Education Act. Mimeographed. April 5, 1984.

U.S. Riot Commission Report. Report of the National Commission on Civil Disorders. New York: Bantam Books, March 1968.

Universidad de Puerto Rico, Servicio de Extensión Agrícola. Estudio de la Situación Agrícola en el Area de Orocovis. 1963. (A Study of the Agricultural Situation in the Area of Orocovis.)

——————. Recinto de Mayaguez, Colegio de Ciencias Agrícolas, Servicio de Extensión Agrícola. la Agricultura de Orocovis. (The Agriculture of Orocovis) 1975.

"Urban Agenda Should Include Statehouse" Hartford Courant, April 17, 1985, p. B9.

Vargas, Edwin, Jr., and La Luz, José. "The People of Hartford Address the Visiting Mayors—Join Hispanics In Tackling Shared Goals." Hartford Courant, April 18, 1985, p. D9.

Vazquez, Hector I. "Discrimination Against Puerto Rican Professionals and Puerto Rican Pupils in New York City Public Schools." Statement delivered at the Hearings on the Minority Hiring Practices of the Board of Education by the New York City Commission on Human Rights. New York, January 1971.

Vazquez de Rodriguez, Ligia. "Needs and Aspirations of the Puerto Rican People." Reprint from Social Welfare Forum, 1971. New York: Columbia University Press, 1971.

Vidal, David. "Puerto Rican Plight in U.S. is Deplored." New York Times, October 14, 1976, p. 18.

————. "Returning Migrants Find Puerto Rico Inhospitable." New York Times, October 3, 1975, p. 1.

Wagenheim, Karl. A Survey of Puerto Ricans in the United States Mainland in the 1970s. New York: Praeger Publishers, 1975.

————. "General Economy Current Fiscal Year Looks Like Major Migration Period." Caribbean Business, December 22, 1982.

Wakefield, Dan. Island in the City. Boston: Houghton Mifflin, 1959.

Weber, Max. The Protestant Ethic and the Spirit of Capitalism. New York: Charles Scribner's Sons, 1930.

Wells, Henry. The Modernization of Puerto Rico. Cambridge, MA.: Harvard University Press, 1969.

"Why More and More People Are Coming Back to Cities." U.S. News & World Report, August 8, 1977, pp. 69 71.

Wilensky, Harold L., and Lebeaux, Charles N. Industrial Society and Social Welfare. New York: Free Press, 1965.

Williams, E. "Race Relations in Puerto Rico and the Virgin Islands." Foreign Affairs 23(1945)308–17.

Willis, Robert M. "An Analysis of the Adjustment and Scholastic Achievement of 40 Puerto Rican Boys Who Attended Transitional Classes in New York City." Doctoral dissertation. New York University, New York, 1960.

Wilson, William Julius. The Declining Significant of Race—Blacks and Changing American Institutions. Chicago: University of Chicago Press, 1978.

Wood, Forrest G. Black Scare: The Racist Response to Emancipation and Reconstruction. Berkeley: University of California Press, 1970.

Wood, Robert. "Black Mayors: 'Growing in Numbers, Growing in Unity'—Urban Agenda Should Include Statehouses." Hartford Courant, April 17, 1985, p. B9.

Woodward, C. Vann. The Strange Career of Jim Crow. London: Oxford University Press, 1955.

Zorilla, Frank. "Some Remarks Regarding the Puerto Rican Migration to the United States and Recent Trends in our Labor Force Employment and Income." Mimeographed. Address to the Eleventh Social Welfare Workshop jointly sponsored by the School of Social Work of the University of Puerto Rico and the Migration Division of the Department of Labor of the Commonwealth of Puerto Rico. San Juan, Puerto Rico, June 1963.

Index

About the Author

Julio Morales, Jr., was born in Vieques, Puerto Rico, and migrated to New York City with his parents and siblings at eight years of age. He lived and attended public schools in Harlem, East Harlem, and the South Bronx. While in high school, he became involved in the activities of the Puerto Rican Association for Community Affairs (PRACA) and has remained involved in community-related issues. He was the first president of the New York City Commission on Bilingual Education, and he is the founder or cofounder of several Puerto Rican agencies and programs in New York, Massachusetts, and Connecticut.

A graduate of Hunter College, Dr. Morales obtained his MS from Columbia University School of Social Work and his Ph.D. from the Heller School, Brandeis University. From 1969 to 1973 Dr. Morales served as assistant Professor at Brooklyn College of the City University of New York and was cofounder of the Institute for Puerto Rican Studies and the Department of Puerto Rican Studies at Brooklyn College. He was on the faculty of Boston University School of Social Work before joining the faculty at the University of Connecticut School of Social Work, where he presently is a full professor and where he served as assistant dean from 1981 to 1984. At both Boston University and at the University of Connecticut, Dr. Morales began Puerto Rican Studies Programs as part of the Master's in Social Work curriculum.

Dr. Morales has served on the board of editors of both Social Work and Social Casework and has written several articles on the effects of racism and poverty. He has received numerous awards from community and student groups, grants from the National Institute of Mental Health, was a National Hispanic Leadership Fellow in 1985, and has been awarded fellowships by the John Hay Whitney and Ford foundations.

Although he views himself as an educator, a community organizer, and an activist, Dr. Morales has been a single parent for many years and has made the raising of his two children, David and Raquel, his highest priority.